Gaze into HEAVEN

NEAR-DEATH EXPERIENCES IN

Early Church History

Gaze into HEAVEN

NEAR-DEATH EXPERIENCES IN
Early Church History

MARLENE BATEMAN SULLIVAN

CFI
An Imprint of Cedar Fort, Inc.
Springville, UT

This is not an official publication of The Church of Jesus Christ of Latter-day Saints. The opinions and views expressed herein belong solely to the author and do not necessarily represent the opinions or views of Cedar Fort, Inc. Permission for the use of sources, graphics, and photos is also solely the responsibility of the author.

ISBN 13: 978-1-4621-1127-5

Published by CFI, an imprint of Cedar Fort, Inc., 2373 W. 700 S., Springville, UT 84663
Distributed by Cedar Fort, Inc., www.cedarfort.com

LIBRARY OF CONGRESS CATALOGING-IN-PUBLICATION DATA

Sullivan, Marlene Bateman, author.
  Gaze into heaven : near-death experiences in early church history / Marlene Bateman Sullivan.
    pages cm
  Includes bibliographical references and index.
  Summary: A collection of nearly fifty documented near-death experiences of early members of The Church of Jesus Christ of Latter-day Saints.
  ISBN 978-1-4621-1127-5 (alk. paper)
  1. Near-death experiences--Religious aspects--Church of Jesus Christ of Latter-day Saints. 2. Church of Jesus Christ of Latter-day Saints--Doctrines. 3. Future life--Church of Jesus Christ of Latter-day Saints. 4. Mormon Church--Doctrines. I. Title.

  BX8643.F87S85 2012
  236'.10882893--dc23

                    2012042549

Cover design by Angela D. Olsen and Rebecca J. Greenwood
Cover design © 2013 by Lyle Mortimer
Edited and typeset by Michelle Stoll

Printed in the United States of America

10 9 8 7 6 5 4 3 2 1

Acknowledgments

Many thanks to Chaleh Reed, Holly Horton, Kelly Sullivan, Rebecca Talley, and Rachael Anderson, who spent many hours reviewing the manuscript. I also want to thank Braden Bell, Connie Sokol, Donald Carey, and Duane Crowther, for their thoughtful input. A special thanks to my editor, Michelle Stoll.

Contents

Foreword

I'll never forget the day my young philosophy professor at University of California, Berkeley, said the following:

"If there's a life after death, why hasn't anyone ever come back to tell about it?"

All I could think to say was that Jesus came back to tell about it, but if I said that, the professor would want to know how I knew the Bible is true. He didn't think it was, and since it was his class he would win that argument too. I was glad he didn't call on me.

Now, more than fifty years later, I wish I could go back to that class for a second chance to answer his question. I would raise my hand, and when he called on me, I'd mention a Gallop survey in which the polling company estimated that over six million Americans have experienced near-death experiences wherein human spirits departed from bodies, had some kind of adventure in a world of spirits, and then returned to their natural bodies to tell family members, friends, and medical personnel what had happened. Millions of people have come back to tell about it.

Starting with Raymond Moody's book, *Life After Life*, published in the early 1980s, hundreds more books have been published in which thousands of people have been interviewed about their near-death experiences—what it was like leaving their bodies and then returning to share their experiences with others. My Beyond the Veil volumes, including interviews with more than a hundred subjects, are included in this body of evidence.

But near-death experiences didn't begin with Raymond Moody. He was merely the first person in modern times to write a popular book about it. Such experiences have been happening throughout human history, almost entirely unrecorded, except in the early pioneer history of the Mormons where devoted followers of Joseph Smith and Brigham Young were commanded by Church leaders to record the important events of their lives in personal journals and histories, leaving behind many hundreds of documents for historians to explore.

I have long suspected that the early Mormon history contained near-death experiences, perhaps enough for an entire book. I always figured there would be many brushes with death in the history of a pioneer people traveling on foot or in crude wagons pulled by stubborn oxen and spirited horses over thousands of miles of rough, ungraded roads, eventually settling in a rugged wilderness with hostile Indians and outlaws. Over the years, I have encouraged several writers and historians to seek out these near-death experiences so Cedar Fort could publish their work beside my *Beyond the Veil* volumes.

Marlene Bateman Sullivan accepted the challenge. She found dozens of near-death stories, more than enough to fill this volume. I shed tears reading how Phoebe Woodruff, while trying to care for her new-born infant on a wagon trek from Maine to Ohio, passed into the spirit world, where heavenly messengers gave her a choice to continue her heavenly journey or return to her new baby and husband, Wilford Woodruff. I had to laugh as Matthew Cowley tells how the Relief Society sisters scattered when a good brother in New Zealand, already prepared for burial, suddenly sat up, demanding a blessing because he didn't feel very well.

Now for the first time in the history of the Church, many near-death experiences from Mormon pioneer history are available in a single volume, *Gaze into Heaven*, by Marlene Bateman Sullivan.

—Lee Nelson

Introduction

If You Could Gaze Into Heaven

Why Learn About Near-Death Experiences?

Gaze Into Heaven contains more than fifty documented accounts of near-death experiences that occurred during the early years of the Church and tells about life beyond the veil from those who have actually been there after dying. Why should we read and study these near-death experiences? The Prophet Joseph Smith supplied the definitive answer:

> All men know that they must die. And it is important that we should understand the reasons and causes of our exposure to the vicissitudes of life and of death, and the designs and purposes of God in our coming into the world, our sufferings here, and our departure hence. What is the object of our coming into existence, then dying and falling away, to be here no more? It is but reasonable to suppose that God would reveal something in reference to the matter, and it is a subject we ought to study more than any other. We ought to study it day and night, for the world is ignorant in reference to their true condition and relation. If we have any claim on our Heavenly Father for anything, it is for knowledge on this important subject. . . . Could you gaze into heaven five minutes, you would know more than you would by reading all that ever was written on the subject.[1]

The Doctrine and Covenants also counsels us to learn more. We are to study "of things both in heaven and in the earth, and under the earth; things which have been, things which are, things which must shortly come to pass" (Doctrine and Covenants 88:79).

Studying near-death experiences can bless us with a better understanding of this life and increase our knowledge of the life to come. By reading about those who actually entered the spirit world and saw conditions there, we can benefit from the insights they gained and use that information to reevaluate our lives and use our time on earth productively. There is a wealth of information contained in these personal glimpses of life beyond the veil that can help us gain crucial insights about our life on earth and allow us to redirect our energy to what really matters—the eternity that lies before us.

Death Is Not the End

Job posed the question of the ages when he asked: "If a man die, shall he live again?" (Job 14:14). Jesus Christ answered the question, "Because I live, ye shall live also" (John 14:19).

When the Savior came to earth, died, and rose again, he laid the foundation for and opened the doors of salvation to mankind. As these accounts show, death is only a temporary separation of the body and spirit. Like birth, death is a necessary step in our eternal progression—a doorway that leads into the next life.

Learning About Near-Death Experiences Can Change Lives

Those who visit the spirit world come back changed, having expanded their knowledge of God and of their place in His kingdom. They appear newly cognizant of why they came to earth and where they will go when they leave mortality. But they are not the only ones who benefit—those who read their stories can profit as well.

Dr. Kenneth Ring, a professor at the University of Connecticut and one of the founders of the International Association for Near-Death Studies (IANDS) states in his book *Lessons from the Light—What We Can Learn from the Near-Death Experience* that not only were people who had near-death experiences profoundly changed by their experience, but those who read about such experiences were also changed—simply by learning about them.[2]

Near-Death Experiences in the Scriptures

Near-death experiences are nothing new. In the New Testament, Lazarus rose after being dead. "Then when Jesus came, he found that he [Lazarus] had lain in the grave four days already. . . . He [Jesus] cried with a loud voice, Lazarus, come forth. And he that was dead came forth, bound hand and foot with graveclothes" (John 11:17, 43–44).

Shortly before his death by stoning, Stephen "looked up stedfastly into heaven, and saw the glory of God, and Jesus standing on the right hand of God . . ." (Acts 7:55–56).

Tabitha was called back to mortality by Peter (Acts 9:36–42).

Eutychus, the boy from Troas, fell asleep while sitting in a window and died after falling to the ground. Paul restored him to life. "And they brought the young man alive, and were not a little comforted" (Acts 20:12).

In the Old Testament, Elijah brought back the son of the widow of Zarephath after the child died from a virulent illness. Elijah prayed, "O Lord my God, I pray thee, let this child's soul come into him again. And the Lord heard the voice of Elijah; and the soul of the child came into him again, and he revived. And Elijah took the child . . . and delivered him unto his mother: and Elijah said, See, thy son liveth"(1 Kings 17:17–24).

There is the account of the Shunammite boy who had a head injury and died in his mother's arms. She went to find Elisha, who returned to the house and restored her son to life. (2 Kings: 4:18–37).

In Third Nephi in the Book of Mormon, Nephi traveled to various cities, preaching the gospel. Nephi was given great power as he traveled about, and he was even able to bring people back from the dead. "And in the name of Jesus did he cast out devils and unclean spirits; and even his brother did he raise from the dead, after he had been stoned and suffered death by the people" (3 Nephi 7:19).

Common Elements of Near-Death Experiences

Careful research of near-death experiences in early Church history shows a large number of common elements, which are listed in the table of contents. In addition, the appendix lists common elements along with the near-death experiences that contain that specific element.

The similarity of these common elements is remarkable when you consider that, at that time in history, near-death experiences were not widely circulated like they are presently. Today, the widespread availability of newspapers, magazines, TV, radio, and the Internet increases the possibility that some elements in modern accounts are reported simply because those elements are the ones that people have heard the most about. Also, unlike modern near-death experiences, none of the people in this book were interviewed, which further increases the possibility that more elements could have been present but were simply not recorded.

Although near-death experiences in *Gaze Into Heaven* contain similar elements, no two are exactly alike. While a few people wrote extensively about their visit to the spirit world, most were short and succinct. Again, this raises the possibility that some elements may have been present but were not recorded. The fact that these near-death experiences contain such similar elements further substantiates that they actually occurred. Most of the accounts are written by simple, humble people who shared their experiences, not for fame or notoriety but out of love and concern for others—a desire to inform people about what lies ahead. Those who wrote these accounts had little to no contact with each other, and there was none of the media we have today to regale them with similar stories. What else, then—other than the truth—could account for so many experiences having similar elements?

Some may wonder why all near-death experiences are not alike. One thing to consider is that since the spirit world is large enough to accommodate all of God's children, it must be an immense sphere. Hence, it seems unlikely that everyone will go to the same exact place and have the same experience. Also, people are unique and notice different things. If a group of people visited the Smithsonian Air and Space Museum and were later asked what they saw, one person might mention the history of airplanes exhibit that features planes dangling from the ceilings, another might mention the original space suits worn by Neil Armstrong and Buzz Aldrin, and yet another might talk about the Voyager spacecraft that traveled to other planets.

There are a few accounts where people relate experiences that differ from one another. One example is when a woman saw a baby in the spirit world and recognized the infant as her sister, but in another experience, a man saw a woman in the spirit world and recognized her as his daughter who had died when she was a young girl. It is not known why experiences differ. Although we can learn much from these accounts, some questions are left unanswered. As mortals, our knowledge is incomplete. When Nephi was asked a question he did not know the answer to, he replied, "I know that he loveth his children; nevertheless, I do not know the meaning of all things" (1 Nephi 11:17).

I hope readers will not be disturbed by small incongruities but will look instead at the overall message of these experiences, which is to testify that life continues beyond the grave. The accounts in *Gaze Into Heaven* do not explain everything there is to know about the next life, but they do serve to increase our understanding of what lies ahead.

Questions We Might Ask about the Spirit World

If we were able to talk to someone who visited the spirit world, we would undoubtedly have many questions. All of the following questions, and many more, are addressed in *Gaze Into Heaven*:

- What happened first after you died?
- Did someone meet you?
- Did you see departed family members and friends?
- Did you have a review of your life?
- What was your spirit body like? Did it have any physical disabilities?
- How were you able to move around without a body?
- What does the spirit world look like?
- Do animals exist there?
- What were people doing there?
- How are spiritual bodies different from mortal bodies?
- Do spirits know what is happening on earth?
- What did spirits say to you while you were there?
- How did it feel when you returned to your physical body?
- What is the most important thing you learned from your experience?

The Reality of Near-Death Experiences

Some people do not believe in near-death experiences. They believe such things are the result of wishful thinking, drugs, or the brain malfunctioning at the time of death. In the 1800s, when most of the near-death experiences in *Gaze Into Heaven* occurred, there was no scientific evidence to support this type of phenomenon as actual out-of-body occurrences. But since then, there has been much significant research done. New, empirical evidence and up-to-date studies overturn common physiological explanations that people once used to explain away near-death experiences.

In 1981, IANDS was established and began rigorously and scientifically studying near-death experiences. One of the founders of IANDS, Dr. Kenneth Ring, studied various explanations for near-death experiences in his book *Lessons from the Light—What We Can Learn from the Near-Death Experience*. Dr. Ring studied experiences from three types of groups. The first group consisted of people who saw or heard things they could not possibly perceive through normal means. The second group included children who had near-death experiences, and the third group was composed of people who were congenitally blind. After thoroughly researching near-death accounts from these groups of people, Dr.

Ring concluded there was solid evidence that near-death experiences are authentic, objective, and real.[3]

Research has also found that near-death episodes cannot be considered hallucinations because hallucinations are rambling, unconnected, and often unintelligible, whereas near-death experiences tend to have similar elements linked in a clear, connected pattern. Wishful thinking can also be eliminated when one considers cross-cultural findings that show near-death experiences occur in similar forms all across the world. In addition, dreams, anesthetics, temporal lobe involvement, cerebral anoxia, and other psychological or neurological explanations do not seem to be factors in inducing a near-death event. Drugs may also be discounted, since most drugs tend to reduce rather than enhance the clarity and complexity of near-death experiences.

People from all walks of life have had near-death experiences, including Christians from all denominations as well as atheists. It is unlikely that such diverse groups of people, including atheists, would invent such stories if they did not happen.

Dr. Melvin Morse, MD, conducted a study of near-death experiences in children, which was published in the *American Journal of Diseases of Children*, the American Medical Association's pediatric journal. During this study, Dr. Morse reviewed medical records, documenting the kind of drugs given, the type of anesthesia used, the amount of oxygen in the blood, and various lab tests, as well as carefully matching the ages of control patients and those in the study group.

Dr. Morse concludes, "The reason for this matching was to see if near-death experiences are hallucinations caused by drugs or lack of oxygen in the blood as many physicians believe. The answer is that they are not. Many of the patients who had full-blown near-death experiences were not being treated with any hallucinogenic medications at all. The control group had nothing resembling near-death experiences despite being treated with such drugs as morphine, Valium, and Thorazine and such anesthetic agents as Dilantin, Phenobarbital, mannitol, and codeine."[4]

Another noted psychiatrist, Dr. Raymond Moody Jr., MD, author of the ground-breaking *Life After Life*, studied more than one hundred people who were declared clinically dead and were then revived. After twenty years of carefully researching near-death experiences, he concluded they are indisputable evidence of life after life. "What greater proof is needed that persons survive the death of their physical bodies

To my family.

May we always be together.

than many examples of individuals leaving their bodies and witnessing attempts to save it?" Dr. Moody adds, "How is it that the patients can give such elaborate and detailed accounts of resuscitations, explaining in their entirety what the doctors were doing to bring them back to life? How can so many people explain what was going on in other rooms of a hospital while their bodies were in the operating room being resuscitated?"[5]

Dr. Elisabeth Kubler-Ross, an eminent doctor, and her associates studied twenty thousand cases of people all over the world who were declared clinically dead. In one of their scientific projects, Dr. Kubler-Ross and her staff studied near-death experiences of blind people who had had no light perception for at least ten years. When these blind people were revived, they were able to tell their loved ones exactly what color clothing people around them had been wearing. They also described patterns in a relative's sweater, the color of a man's tie, and various types of jewelry loved ones had worn. Dr. Kubler-Ross said, "These statements refer to facts which one cannot invent." When asked if she tries to convince skeptics, Dr. Kubler-Ross replied, "One shouldn't try to convince other people. When they die, they will know it anyway."[6]

It is noteworthy to mention that before IANDS was even established and began researching near-death experiences, Duane S. Crowther wrote the ground-breaking and scholarly *Life Everlasting*, which gave valuable insights into post-mortal life drawn from scriptural studies, interviews, research, and discourses from LDS Church leaders. Since then, there have been a number of LDS books written about this subject. Arvin S. Gibson, founder of the Utah chapter of IANDS, wrote a number of books on near-death experiences, such as *Glimpses of Eternity, They Saw Beyond Death, Fingerprints of God*, and others. Lee Nelson also wrote an inspiring series—*Beyond the Veil*—about near-death experiences. It is beyond the scope of this book to expand further on modern-day research of near-death experiences. Skeptics who read these stories may remain doubtful, but these experiences still stand as a testimony of what lies ahead. Read them with a prayer in your hearts for discernment. "If ye shall ask with a sincere heart, with real intent, having faith in Christ, he will manifest the truth of it unto you, by the power of the Holy Ghost" (Moroni 10:4).

Are Near-Death Experiences Consistent with LDS Doctrine?

It is enlightening to see how well near-death experiences in early Church history correspond to the teachings of the Prophet Joseph Smith and doctrine of The Church of Jesus Christ of Latter-day Saints. These experiences testify that the LDS doctrine and revelation given by Joseph Smith and other modern-day prophets are in harmony with revealed scripture. These remarkably consistent accounts are especially significant when one considers that these experiences come from a widely diverse population—from unlearned men, women, and children to highly educated doctors and professors, to prophets and apostles well versed in religion.

The Spirit World Is Nearby

"Where is the spirit world?" Brigham Young asked. He then answered his own question: "It is right here. . . . If the Lord would permit it, and it was His will that it should be done, you could see the spirits that have departed from this world, as plainly as you now see bodies with your natural eyes."[7]

The Prophet Joseph Smith, when speaking of loved ones, also said the spirit world is close by, saying, "They are not far from us."[8]

A modern day prophet, President Ezra Taft Benson, also said, "The spirit world is not far away. . . . Our loved ones who have passed on are not far from us."[9]

As mortals, we cannot see the spirit world, because there is a veil over our eyes that renders that sphere invisible. Speaking of the spirit world, Parley P. Pratt said, "As to its location, it is here on the very planet where we were born; or, in other words, the earth and other planets of a like sphere, have their inward or spiritual spheres, as well as their outward, or temporal. The one is peopled by temporal tabernacles, and the other by spirits. A veil is drawn between the one sphere and the other, whereby all the objects in the spiritual sphere are rendered invisible to those in the temporal."[10]

Where Did These Accounts Come From?

The experiences in this book came from personal journals and other writings, early Church magazines and newspapers, and accounts written by family members and close friends.

The accounts of near-death experiences in *Gaze Into Heaven* are presented as they were written. Because of this, there may be (and often are) mistakes in spelling, capitalization, and grammar, and some may have unusual punctuation. I did not "modernize" the antiquated language because I felt it was important to present the material in its original form and in the writer's own words, without imposing my interpretation on their experiences.

This book is organized, as far as is possible, in chronological order of the elements that occur after a person dies. However, elements in near-death experiences do not always occur in the same order and vary from person to person.

Notes:

1. Joseph Smith, *History of the Church,* (Salt Lake City: The Church of Jesus Christ of Latter-day Saints, October 9, 1843), 6:50.

2. Kenneth Ring and Evelyn Elsaesser Valarino, *Lessons from the Light—What We Can Learn from the Near-Death Experience*, (Reading: Perseus Books, 1998), 5.

3. Kenneth Ring and Evelyn Elsaesser Valarino, *Lessons from the Light—What We Can Learn from the Near-Death Experience,* (Reading: Perseus Books, 1998).

4. Melvin Morse, MD, with Paul Perry, *Closer To The Light*, (New York: Villard Books, 1990), 41.

5. Raymond A. Moody, Jr., MD, with Paul Perry, *The Light Beyond*, (New York: Bantam Books, 1988), 197, 169–170.

6. Elisabeth Kubler-Ross, *On Life After Death*, (Berkeley: Celestial Arts, 1991), 13–14.

7. Brigham Young, *Journal of Discourses,* June 22, 1856, (Liverpool, 1854–86), 3:369.

8. Joseph Smith, *History of the Church,* October 9, 1843, (Salt Lake City: The Church of Jesus Christ of Latter-day Saints), 6:52.

9. Ezra Taft Benson, "Life is Eternal," *Ensign*, June 1971, 33.

10. Parley P. Pratt, *Key to the Science of Theology*, 10th ed., (Salt Lake City: Deseret Book, 1966), 126–27.

> "The spirits of all men, as soon as they are departed from this mortal body, yea, the spirits of all men, whether they be good or evil, are taken home to that God who gave them life." (Alma 40:11)

Chapter One

What Happens First During a Near-Death Experience

See Lifeless Mortal Body

Of all the many elements in near-death experiences, seeing one's physical body before going to the spirit world is one of the most common. People who had these experiences reported looking down at their lifeless bodies and frequently mentioned seeing weeping loved ones mourning their death.

At the moment of death, the spirit separates from the physical body. The spirit does not cease to exist but goes to the spirit world. Brigham Young said, "Our bodies are composed of visible, tangible matter. . . . What is commonly called death does not destroy the body, it only causes a separation of spirit and body, but the principle of life, inherent in the native elements, of which the body is composed, still continues."[1]

When Joseph Eldridge had a near-death experience, he said the first thing he saw was his own body. "I looked down on my body and could see myself lying there. My father and mother were leaning over each other weeping for me."[2]

Peter E. Johnson said, "Soon after that, my spirit left the body; just how I cannot tell. But I perceived myself standing some four or five feet in the air, and saw my body lying on the bed."[3]

It was much the same for Harriet Ovard Lee when she died. She said,

"I saw my husband and all the people in the room, some of them crying and wringing their hands over my lifeless body, at the sight of which I shuddered."[4]

Albert M. Boyce

Albert M. Boyce was born in 1854, in Spanish Fork, Utah. Later, Albert moved to McCammon, Idaho, where he served as a bishop for fifteen years. When Albert had his near-death experience, his spirit rose upward, and he saw his physical body lying face-down in the water. His granddaughter Jennie Boshart relates his experience:

"This is a true story about my grandfather, Albert Boyce who was a very devout man. Close to his home town of Lava Hot Springs, Idaho, nestled in the mountains was a small natural hot springs where the local people bathed during the depression years. It was in a lonely, out-of-the way place. It was close to a river that ran through town, and only a foot path lead [sic] to the pool from the river.

"One day Grandfather, aged 74 at the time, took his towel and soap to the hot springs to take a bath. No one else was there. About half an hour after getting into the pool, Grandfather began to feel faint and attempted to get out of the pool. He couldn't make it. He felt everything blacking out as he fell back into the pool.

"Coming down from the hills by following another pathway was an Indian on his way to town. He knew Grandfather quite well, and as he approached the pool he saw Grandfather's body lying face down in the water. He hastily pulled him out, turned him over on his back and felt for his pulse. There was no pulse. The Indian put his head on Grandfather's chest to listen for a heartbeat. There was none.

"At the same moment, as Grandfather testified later, he found himself standing next to his own body, watching these proceedings. He said that he knew his soul had been 'lifted' out of his body to watch the Indian attempt to get his heart to beat again. This went on for what seemed a long period of time. To the Indian, he felt it was useless, but he knew that he couldn't give up trying to revive him as long as he had the strength to try.

"But suddenly Grandfather felt himself re-entering his body, and the next thing he knew he was bringing up water from his stomach. It wasn't long before Grandfather could move and talk with the Indian whom he thanked profusely for saving his life.

"When Grandfather later manifested his testimony, he said that when he 'left' his body and stood by, it was the strangest phenomenon he had ever witnessed. The Indian later said that he was so positive that Grandfather was dead when he pulled him out of the pool.

"My Grandfather told of this experience time and time again through the years and said that he felt God had taken him, but released his soul to rejoin his body for some unknown reason. As you can imagine, he was most grateful, and lived a full life for 20 more years."[5]

Herman Stulz

Herman Stulz had two near-death experiences during his lifetime, and each time he saw his physical body after his spirit had left it. Born in Germany in 1886, Herman grew up on a farm in the Black Forest in the small town of Muehlheim, which lay at the base of a small mountain that had many waterfalls. There were frequent cloudbursts that caused flooding as swollen streams carried debris over the cascading waterfalls.

When Herman was ten, his family went to a health resort that had a large waterfall, which had swelled from recent rains. His parents, aware of the danger, gave their children strict orders to stay away. However, Herman wanted to see the waterfall so badly that he persuaded his big sister, Jda, to go watch. As they stood above the waterfall, they watched debris tumble about in the dirty brown water that rushed over the roaring falls.

Then they heard the shrill sound of a whistle. It was Herman's mother summoning them. She carried a whistle so her children could hear her when they were out in the forest. Jda turned around and started to run, but Herman became dizzy from staring at the waterfall and fell twenty feet into the swirling water. The avalanche of water spun Herman around, keeping him under water. Herman said he gulped down so much dirty water it felt like he was being strangled. Although he kept struggling to reach the surface, Herman was no match for the tremendous force of the rushing water.

Herman states, "Slowly my struggle ended, the choking ended and I felt calm and serene. It was like I was in a dream and I saw myself standing on the opposite shores, watching little Herman spinning around under the fall, once in a while the undercurrent would drag my body from under the water a few feet downstream; and then back again into the torrential avalanche of the fall.

"I felt no more pains and was only attracted by the sight of my body tumbling around under the fall. My sister said it must have been thirty minutes before she could find my big brother Hans and I saw both of them running to my rescue. I saw the expression of fear on the face of Hans when he saw his brother Herman's body spin around under the fall, as he looked down in the swirling pool."

Hans was determined to save his brother. "After a moment of hesitation he jumped down, landing on the edge and squatting down, he reached out, whenever my body impelled by the undercurrent drifted a few feet downstream where he could reach my foot. After several attempts he succeeded in getting a good grip of my foot, and slowly pulled my lifeless body to shore. All this was a frightful experience which stayed with me to this very day, now as an old man.

"Hans was already in High School and . . . had learned how to revive drowned persons. Well, I saw him try on my own watersoaked body as he rolled me over a log that had come floating down the steam as I was watching him, squeezing the water out of me, until of a sudden my spirit walking towards Hans took possession of my body again. I found [myself] pretty weak from this unusual experience and Hans and my sister Jda helped me walk home.

"My father applied a whipping for my disobedience in going to the waterfall and the hike was postponed . . .

"I had no bad after-effects after the drowning, but I was bewildered and confused that I actually saw what happened to me by standing in my spirit near this scene of drowning. I told my parents and sisters and they just laughed at me and told me I was a dreamer, like Joseph in Egypt. But this incident worried me and I asked several preachers to explain to me if this experience was what is called death, that man fears so much and yet knows very little of."

As an adult, Herman met missionaries from The Church of Jesus Christ of Latter-day Saints in England. The elders explained to Herman that mortals are dual beings, in that they have a spirit residing within a mortal body. They told Herman that man is an eternal being who lived in the premortal world before coming to earth and that he would return to the spirit world when he died.

Herman said, "After 14 years I finally found the answer to my horrible experience of drowning in a waterfall. . . . This was my first experience in an adventure with death, the second time, [related later] I was 35 years of age and had joined the Church. . . . I returned with a message to all Latter-day Saints."[6]

Pain Is Gone

Although pain may be present because of an accident, illness, or disease that causes death, near-death experiences indicate that pain ceases immediately when a person's spirit departs from its physical body. Many people who experienced pain just before death declared that it stopped immediately when their spirit left their body, causing them to feel tremendous relief and joy and a wonderful glow of health.

After death, one's spiritual body will no longer be subject to diseases and illnesses that so often afflict people on earth. Brigham Young said, "Here, we are continually troubled with ills and ailments of various kinds, and our ears are saluted with the expressions, 'My head aches,' 'My shoulders ache,' 'My back aches,' 'I am hungry, dry, or tired;' but in the spirit world we are free from all this and enjoy life, glory, and intelligence."[7]

During Walter P. Monson's near-death experience, he said, "I was now without pain, and the joy of freedom I felt and the peace of mind that came over me were the sweetest sensations I had ever experienced in all my life."[8]

When Bertha Duesnup Elder died, she realized that "the pain and discomfort of a few moments earlier was suddenly gone."[9]

George Washington Brimhall commented that when he died, "My spirit arose out of my body and was ascending from it very slowly, feeling perfectly happy and without pain."[10]

Earl Stowell

As a child, Earl Stowell lived in Utah before his family moved to California. They had little contact with the Church, until one day when his mother announced they were going to start attending church every Sunday. In time, Earl was ordained a teacher in the Aaronic Priesthood. During the summer, Earl worked at odd jobs, selling newspapers and running errands on his bicycle. When school started, he began working at a fruit stand after school and on Saturdays. It was hard work, and the long hours wore him down physically.

One night, Earl became very ill, and his spirit left his body. While in the spirit world, Earl met a man who told him he could either stay or return to mortality. The man seemed intensely interested in Earl but did not explain why. Earl decided to return to his body. Years later, Earl discovered that the man was his grandfather. Earl writes:

"It was during my last few months at the fruit stand that I had one of my most memorable spiritual experiences. . . . On this particular night, I came home from work so exhausted I told mother I was too tired to eat any supper. It was a weekday. I had pedaled my bicycle several miles to high school . . . put in a long, trying day . . . pedaled back to the fruit stand, worked until about seven o'clock, and pedaled home. I felt sick all over. . . .

"I sank down onto my bed on my back without undressing. I had more and more difficulty breathing and I was in such pain I did not know what to do. For some time I had been suffering from pain and heaviness in my chest, but had learned to give it no particular attention. It just seemed to be part of living.

"Outside, it was quite dark. The pain increased until it was unbearable. When my breathing seemed to be cut off almost entirely, I was too tired to fight it. Then, I found myself just below the ceiling looking down at a body stretched out on its back on the bed. I didn't feel as if it were my body; it was just a body. Vaguely, I wondered how someone would get through the locked door to take care of it.

"I felt well, very well. Until then I had not realized how much pain and pressure I had become accustomed to. I had blamed it on being too tired or some kind of stomach upset. Although I never saw or heard them, two beings placed themselves on each side of me, and I knew I was to go with them.

"The ceiling seemed to melt away directly above us and we went out into the sky. . . . Our speed of travel increased until it seemed we caught up with rays or beams of light and passed them as if they were standing still. How long we travelled, I do not know, but it seemed hours. At last we arrived at a garden gate, not fancy, but one that might be expected at the back of a fine garden. . . . I was set down on a sidewalk just inside the gate. About ten feet from the gate, the walk ran into another that went both ways.

"I do not know why I decided to go to the right. But I followed the long walk that way until it made a sharp turn to the left and passed between two buildings. I could see those buildings and a well kept lawn and garden; probably a couple of acres in extent. I could see that far and no further. Not that there was nothing beyond; it was simply that was what I was supposed to see and no more.

"Everything was well but not brilliantly lighted, but I saw no shadows, something I only realized when I was thinking of this experience later. The building on my left was a mansion, a bit old-fashioned by my standards at that time. The building on the right was small, a cottage, seemingly frame construction.

"The cottage was of a common style with the roof ridge running parallel to the street, or sidewalk, and with a porch made by moving about one half of the front wall of the house back under the roof possibly seven feet or so . . . I walked up onto the porch, approached the door, and reached for the doorknob.

"As I did so, a voice from behind said, 'I wouldn't do that if I were you.' The voice was gentle, but it carried authority.

"To myself, I thought, 'Who says?' and again put my hand forward toward the doorknob.

"The voice repeated what it had said before, this time, urgently.

"Over my shoulder, I asked, 'why not?'

"'Because if you open that door, you can never close it.' Was the reply.

"'That's silly,' I thought to myself, but I turned around and walked a couple of steps toward the speaker. He was a small man, about my size and build. He had the most piercing blue eyes I had ever seen. He was wearing old fashioned clothing. His jacket, or vest, has slash pockets set at an angle high on his chest. He had the fingers of one hand tucked into each of these pockets. He seemed to be relaxing, walking around the property. He took one hand out of its pocket and beckoned to me. As I came forward, I realized he had not spoken in English, but in a language immeasurably more expressive and exact. Also it required far few words.

"He did not introduce himself but stood measuring me up and down with his eyes. He spoke again. 'You will be one of relatively few who have been permitted to make a choice. You can remain here, free of the pressures and pain you have known in the past, if you so choose. This cottage will be your home. Your duties will be light—to take care of this property. You will have ample time to study, learn, and socialize. But if that is your choice, you must remain on that level, singly, and without increase. You may remain here or return to your former existence. There you will get your wives.'

"The word *wives* jarred me; I had never thought of more than one.

"'You will have children, and will have certain assignments to fill there on earth. But there will be an unavoidable penalty for going back. That is to know pain and suffering beyond anything you can imagine now. But if you go back, remain faithful and meet the tests, when you return, you will have a mansion at least as grand as this one.' He indicated the mansion behind him with one hand. 'And you can go on to any degree of development you choose.'

"'What do you think I ought to do?' I asked.

"'I cannot tell you that. It must be entirely your decision.' Although the little man seemed unruffled on the outside, I could sense he was like a teakettle at full boil inside.

"'I think it would be best for me to go back,' I told him. I felt the tension drain out of him. He stepped to one side, and with a sweeping motion of one arm, indicated I was to return to the gate where I had entered. As I neared the gate, I turned and glanced back. He stood looking after me in a way I had always hoped my father might look at me some time.

"The same two beings were waiting at the gate. I got the impression they were not quite happy at the thought of a return trip. But in an instant we were making the same trip in reverse. We hovered over the roof of our house for a moment, and I noticed a few curled shingles that should have attention soon. Then the roof and ceiling opened as before. If felt myself sinking back into my room. It was painful and took quite a bit of effort to work myself back into the cold and stiff body that lay on the bed. More than a few minutes passed before I could drive the cold out of it. The morning sun was just rising as I struggled to get back onto my feet. I was so weary, I could scarcely stay upright. The trip had taken the entire night."

Years passed. In March 9 1927, Earl married Rula Jones, and they moved to Ogden, Utah. Some time later, a dear aunt of his, Eliza Allen, died, and Earl went to Huntsville to attend her funeral.

"Her husband, Alburn Allen, was not a sentimental person. After the funeral, back at his home, he tossed the tray out of a trunk on the living room floor. It was filled with family pictures. He said anyone who wanted them could have them.

"There, right on top, was a picture of the man I could never forget. It was the one who had talked to me on the other side.

"Before I remembered where we had met, I blurted out, 'I know this man. I have talked to him.' Then I remembered where, and shut my mouth.

"A bit scornfully, uncle Alburn said, 'You have never talked to that man. He died in Mexico before you were born. This could be the only picture there is of him.' He looked at me as if savoring the chance to put this city kid down. 'That man,' he went on, 'is William Rufus Rogers Stowell, your grandfather!'

"'That can't be,' I exclaimed. 'My father always told me his father was a six-footer, a big man who towered over him. Daddy was five-feet eight inches tall. When I talked to this man, I could look him straight in the eyes. I'm only a little over five foot six.' I felt more foolish all the time, but I couldn't seem to stop.

"Uncle Alburn called a young man to him and told him to go to the farm across the road and down a bit and ask someone there to come over. In a little while, a quite elderly man came in on a cane and asked what was wanted.

"Uncle Alburn said, 'Tell this man how tall his grandfather, William Rufus Rogers, was.'

"The old man looked at me for a few seconds, gathering his thoughts.

"'Well,' he said, 'I knew him. If he was here, he would look this young feller about straight in the eye. Yep, that would be it, jist [sic] about straight in the eye.' Earl still had a hard time accepting it.

"But my father always said he was a tall man."

"Uncle Alburn spoke up, 'Your pa took off while he was nothing but a kid; didn't like farming much. Wanted to be a musician. His pa did tower over him then.'

"Since that time, I have confirmed the height of my grandfather with others who knew him. This and the fact that the predictions he made have been filled to the letter leave me no room for doubt."[11]

Met by a Spiritual Guide

In most LDS near-death experiences, the newly departed are met by an angel who guides him through the change from earth life to the spirit world. Some people said it was momentarily bewildering to leave one sphere and go to another. It is a sign of God's love and mercy that He does not leave us alone during this transition but provides a guiding angel to serve as a companion and escort. In most accounts, the guide is a relative or is identified as the person's guardian angel. Others acknowledge being met by angels who were specially appointed to guide them from mortality to the spirit world.

Mary Hyde Woolf saw her escort when she passed away. The account states, "After the spirit withdrew from the body she saw a Guide by her side who said to her, 'Come with me.'" [12]

Flora Ann Mayer's account states, "A man came from that light and acted as a guide for her." [13]

Lorenzo Dow Young was met immediately. "In a moment I was out of the body, and fully conscious that I had made the change. At once, a heavenly messenger, or guide, was by me." [14]

Eliza Ursenbach

When Eliza Ursenbach passed away, her departed husband met her and served as her guide to the spirit world. Eliza's son, O.F. Ursenbach, relates her experience:

"It was about the year 1872 that Eliza Ursenbach, widow of Octave Ursenbach, died, her spirit passing into the Spirit World, leaving two small children—my sister and the writer. Phoebe Durrant, her mother, and one of those faithful converts from England, was so distracted to a frenzy that she determined that Eliza must return. To this end she sent for two elderly brethren—Elders Goble and West of the Sixteenth Ward, Salt Lake City. Upon their arrival they said they were sorry, but that they were too late.

"Grandmother answered: 'It is not too late, for Eliza must return and raise these babies, exercise your Priesthood with our faith and God will hear our prayers.'

"Quite reluctantly, the brethren attended to the administration, when suddenly mother opened her eyes and complainingly lisped: 'Why did you bring me back?'

"But for my mother's own story of the wondrous experience, there could remain some doubt as to her actually dying. Her story in substance was as follows:

"In her passing she was fully conscious that her spirit was leaving her body—that my father, who had previously died, had come for her. They had little more than reached the beautiful Spirit World, when father suddenly stopped and turning to mother said:

"'The Priesthood is so powerfully exercised in supplication for your return, that heaven has granted that you return to your body to rear our children. But let me admonish you to speak with extreme caution of things you have seen in this Spirit World.'

"The parting was an affectionate one, with the promise that he would call for her later.

"Mother lived nearly twenty years—living an invalid, yet to see her children reared beyond adolescency [sic]. Never did she lose her knowledge of life beyond the grave, and was ever ready to testify to this wondrous experience. However, in it all she disclosed but little of what she had seen other than to testify of the beauty of the Spirit World, for thus she had been cautioned by my father.

"Her testimony, together with that of those venerable elders, Goble and West; my Grandmother Durrant and especially that of Joseph Durrant, recently deceased, have become so fixed in my life that I offer, for the first time, this account for publication. O.F. Ursenbach."[15]

Notes:

1. John A. Widstoe, comp., *Discourses of Brigham Young* (Salt Lake City: Deseret Book, 1954), 368–69.
2. Inez Robinson Preece, *Life Story of Joseph Eldridge* (courtesy of the Church History Library, The Church of Jesus Christ of Latter-day Saints).
3. Peter E. Johnson, "A Testimony," *Relief Society Magazine* 7 (1920), 450–55.
4. Harriet Ovard Lee, *A Remarkable Vision 1901* (courtesy of the Church History Library, The Church of Jesus Christ of Latter-day Saints).
5. Jennie Verna Boshart, Story about Albert M. Boyce, 1973 (courtesy of the Church History Library, The Church of Jesus Christ of Latter-day Saints).
6. Herman Stulz, *Autobiography* [ca.1971] (courtesy of the Church History Library, The Church of Jesus Christ of Latter-day Saints).
7. Brigham Young, *Journal of Discourses*, September 16, 1871 (Liverpool, 1854–86), 14:231.
8. Jeremiah Stokes, *Modern Miracles* (Salt Lake City: Bookcraft, 1945), 78–81.
9. Lee Nelson, *Beyond The Veil*, vol. 1 (Springville, Utah: Cedar Fort, Inc., 1988), 37–40. Used with permission.
10. Orson F. Whitney, *History of Utah*, vol. 4 (Salt Lake City: George Q. Cannon & Sons Co., 1904), 170.
11. *Biography of William Rufus Rogers Stowell 1893* (courtesy of the Church History Library, The Church of Jesus Christ of Latter-day Saints).
12. Zina Y. Card, "Manifestation to Mrs. Mary Hyde Woolf," *The Relief Society Magazine* 8 (August 1921), 492–93.

13. Marba Peck Hale, *Papers* [ca. 2000] Folder 6 (courtesy of the Church History Library, The Church of Jesus Christ of Latter-day Saints).

14. Lorenzo Dow Young, *Fragments of Experience, Sixth Book of the Faith-Promoting Series* (Salt Lake City: Juvenile Instructor Office, 1882), 27–30.

15. Joseph Heinerman, *Spirit World Manifestations* (Salt Lake City: Magazine Printing and Publishing, 1978), 113–14.

"Blessed are the dead which die in the Lord from henceforth: Yea, saith the Spirit, that they may rest from their labours; and their works do follow them." (Revelation 14:13)

Chapter Two

Arrival in the Spirit World

After a person dies, their spirit goes to the spirit world, where they will live until the resurrection, when their spirits will be reunited with their bodies. In the Book of Mormon, Alma taught, "And then shall it come to pass, that the spirits of those who are righteous are received into a state of happiness, which is called paradise, a state of rest, a state of peace, where they shall rest from all their troubles and from all care, and sorrow" (Alma 40:12).

Spirits in paradise are separated from those in spirit prison by a great gulf. Spirits are taken to paradise if the person died before the age of accountability or if they were baptized on earth and remained obedient to God during mortality. In paradise, spirits who have accepted the gospel live in a state of happiness, peace, and restful work.

The apostle Peter referred to the postmortal spirit world as a prison (see 1 Peter 3:18–20), and it is for those spirits who have chosen evil over good. Spirits who are taken to spirit prison appear to fall into two categories: those who have not been baptized, and those who have been willfully disobedient and have chosen not to obey the commandments. Since many people will not have the opportunity to hear and accept the gospel on earth, they can—if they desire—learn about the gospel of Jesus Christ from missionaries on the other side. If they accept the gospel, they are allowed to enter paradise after the physical ordinance of baptism is done for them on earth. Members of the Church perform proxy ordinances in temples on behalf of the dead so those who have accepted the gospel in spirit prison can progress.

There are some spirits who are in prison because they have not followed the commandments of God.

> "And then shall it come to pass, that the spirits of the wicked, yea, who are evil—for they have no part nor portion of the Spirit of the Lord; for behold, they chose evil works rather than good; therefore the spirit of the devil did enter into them, and take possession of their house. . . . Now this is the state of the souls of the wicked, yea, in darkness, and a state of awful, fearful looking for the fiery indignation of the wrath of God upon them; thus they remain in this state, as well as the righteous in paradise, until the time of their resurrection." (Alma 40:13)

It seems that there are various smaller realms within the larger areas of spirit prison and paradise. Apostle Parley P. Pratt was speaking about the spirit world when he remarked, "Yes, there are many places and degrees in that world, as in this."[1]

Life Continues, Feeling Natural and Real

"He that heareth my word, and believeth on him that sent me, hath everlasting life, and . . . is passed from death unto life" (John 5:24).

People who have had near-death experiences state that after arriving in the spirit world, life continues, feeling as natural and real as life did while they were in mortality. Many stated that nothing in the spirit world appeared strange or imaginary and that everything there appeared as real and as natural as anything they had seen or felt on earth.

Brigham Young said, "And when you are in the spirit world, everything there will appear as natural as things now do. Spirits will be familiar with spirits in the spirit world—will converse, behold, and exercise every variety of communication with one another as familiarly and naturally as while here in tabernacles. There, as here, all things will be natural, and you will understand them as you now understand natural things. . . . Here, we are continually troubled with ills and ailments of various kinds. In the spirit world we are free from all this and enjoy life, glory, and intelligence; and we have the Father to speak to us, Jesus to speak to us, and angels to speak to us, and we shall enjoy the society of the just and the pure who are in the spirit world until the resurrection."[2]

Lorena A. Wilson said about her near-death experience, "it seemed real and natural."[3]

Hannah Adeline Savage commented; "There was a guide close by my side, and he talked to me and showed me the spirits who were beings real as we are."[4]

While telling his wife about his experience, Tom Gibson said, "It was as real as . . . anything I have seen or felt on earth—even more so."[5]

Mr. Bertrand

Mr. Bertrand said he felt more alive after death than before and that his mind remained clear and functioned normally. He was climbing the Titlis Mountain in the Swiss Alps with a group of his students when he became tired. Even though the temperature was well below freezing, he decided to stay behind while the group went on. Mr. Bertrand was then struck with apoplexy (a stroke). His experience was reported in the *Juvenile Instructor* in 1892.

After realizing he was dying, Mr. Bertrand said he offered "a kind of prayer . . . to God, and then I resolved to study quietly the progress of death. My feet and hands were first frozen, and little by little death reached my knees and elbows. The sensation was not painful, and my mind felt quite easy. But when death had been all over my body my head became unbearably cold, and it seemed to me that concave pincers squeezed my heart, so as to extract my life. I never felt such an acute pain but it lasted only a second or a minute, and my life went out.

"'Well,' thought I, 'at last I am what they call a dead man. . . . How strange! I see better than ever, and I am dead—only a small space in the space without a body! Where is my last [physical] body?'

"Looking down I was astounded to recognize my own envelope [body]. 'Strange!' said I to myself. 'There is the corpse in which I lived and which I called *me*, as if the coat were the body, as if the body were the soul! What a horrid thing is that body—deadly pale, with a yellowish-blue color. . . .

"When my companions return they will look at that and exclaim, 'The professor is dead!' Poor young friends! They do not know that I never was as alive as I am, and the proof is that I see the guide going up rather by the right, when he promised me to go by the left."

Mr. Bertrand then discovered that he was rising upward. He said, "I had only two wishes: the certitude of not returning to earth and the

discovery of my next glorious body, without which I felt powerless. . . .
Suddenly a shock stopped my ascension, and I felt that somebody was
pulling [me down]. . . . My grief was measureless. The fact was that while
my young friends threw snowballs at each other our guide had discovered and administered to my body the well known remedy, rubbing with
snow; but as I was cold and stiff as ice, he dared not roll me for fear of
breaking my hands. . . . I could neither see nor hear any more, but I could
measure my way down. . . . I never felt a more violent irritation."

When he became conscious and was able to speak, Mr. Bertrand
sharply rebuked his guide for reviving him.

More than a little startled and confused, the guide replied, "You were
nearly dead."

"Dead! I was less dead than you are now, and the proof is that I saw you
going up the Titlis by the right, while you promised me to go by the left."

Wondering how Mr. Bertrand could have seen him from where he
had been sitting, the guide explained why he had taken the group up
Titlis on the right side. "Because the snow was soft and there was no
danger of slipping."

Mr. Bertrand then explained to his guide that he had died and left
his body and that was how he knew the group had gone up the mountain
on the right side.[6]

Same Person as Before Death

People who visited the spirit world and returned testified that they
were the same person after death as they had been in mortality. Alma tells
us that if we are righteous or unrighteous on earth, we will be the same
in the next life. "That same spirit which doth possess your bodies at the
time that ye go out of this life, that same spirit will have power to possess
your body in that eternal world" (Alma 34:34). Because of this, we know
our own individual personalities will remain intact, and we will have the
same feelings, attitudes, beliefs, and personality traits in the next world
as we have here.

President David O. McKay said,

> I believe with all my soul in the persistence of personality after death.
> I cannot believe otherwise. Even reason and observation demonstrate
> that to me. . . . Personality is persistent, and that is the message of
> comfort, that is the real way in which death is conquered. . . . . Death
> cannot touch the spirit of man. . . . Death may have power over the

body, for we are, in this life, open to accident and disease; and death may take advantage of these conditions, but there his power ends. Death cannot touch the spirit.[7]

The Apostle Melvin J. Ballard declared, "After death, that which existed before and independent of the body will continue, until through the resurrection of the earth body the union of spirit and matter will take place. . . . I know as well as I see you now, that I shall see you hereafter the same individuals, that as God is without the beginning of days or end, so also is the offspring of man."[8]

After he died, Peter E. Johnson said, "I turned my head, shrugged my shoulders, felt with my hands, and realized that it was I myself. I also knew that my body was lying, lifeless, on the bed. While I was in a new environment, it did not see strange, for I realized everything that was going on, and perceived that I was the same in the spirit as I had been in the body."[9]

Lorenzo Dow Young

Lorenzo Dow Young, Brigham Young's younger brother, does not explain the circumstances surrounding his visit to the spirit world, but he does mention that everything seemed quite natural. Although Lorenzo was not a member of the Church at the time of his near-death experience, it had a tremendous spiritual impact on him, and afterward, he began preaching the word of God. Then in February 1831, Brigham Young and Heber C. Kimball gave him a Book of Mormon. Lorenzo read it carefully, comparing it with the Bible. After fasting and praying to know if the book was true, Lorenzo said the Spirit seemed to say, "This is the way; walk ye in it."[10] He and his wife were baptized a few months later. Lorenzo relates his near-death experience as follows:

"In a moment I was out of the body, and fully conscious that I had made the change. At once, a heavenly messenger, or guide, was by me. I thought and acted as naturally as I had done in the body, and all my sensations seemed as complete without as with it. The personage with me was dressed in the purest white. For a short time I remained in the room where my body lay. My sister Fanny (who was living with me when I had this dream) and my wife were weeping bitterly over my death. I sympathized with them deeply in their sorrow, and desired to comfort them. I realized that I was under the control of the man who was by me. I begged of him the privilege of speaking to them, but he said he could not grant it.

"My guide, for so I will call him, said 'Now let us go.'

"Space seemed annihilated. Apparently we went up, and almost instantly were in another world. It was of such magnitude that I formed no conception of its size. It was filled with innumerable hosts of beings, who seemed as naturally human as those among whom I had lived. With some I had been acquainted in the world I had just left. My guide informed me that those I saw had not yet arrived at their final abiding place. All kinds of people seemed mixed up promiscuously [sic], as they are in this world. Their surroundings and manner indicated that they were in a state of expectation, and awaiting some event of considerable moment to them.

"As we went on from this place, my guide said, 'I will now show you the condition of the damned.' Pointing with his hand, he said, 'Look!'

"I looked down a distance which appeared incomprehensible to me. I gazed on a vast region filled with multitudes of beings. I could see everything with the most minute distinctness. The multitude of people I saw were miserable in the extreme. 'These,' said my guide, 'are they who have rejected the means of salvation, that were placed within their reach, and have brought upon themselves the condemnation you behold.'

"The expression of the countenances of these sufferers was clear and distinct. They indicated extreme remorse, sorrow and dejection. They appeared conscious that none but themselves were to blame for their forlorn condition. This scene affected me much, and I could not refrain from weeping.

"Again my guide said, 'Now let us go.'

"In a moment we were at the gate of a beautiful city. A porter opened it and we passed in. The city was grand and beautiful beyond anything that I can describe. It was clothed in the purest light, brilliant but not glaring or unpleasant.

"The people, men and women, in their employments and surroundings, seemed contented and happy. I knew those I met without being told who they were. Jesus and the ancient apostles were there. I saw and spoke with the Apostle Paul. My guide would not permit me to pause much by the way, but rather hurried me on through this place to another still higher but connected with it. It was still more beautiful and glorious than anything I had before seen. To me its extent and magnificence were incomprehensible.

"My guide pointed to a mansion which excelled everything else in perfection and beauty. It was clothed with fire and intense light. It appeared a fountain of light, throwing brilliant scintillations of glory all around it, and I could conceive of no limit to which these emanations extended. Said my guide, 'That is where God resides.' He permitted me to enter this glorious city but a short distance. Without speaking, he motioned that we would retrace our steps. We were soon in the adjoining city. There I met my mother, and a sister who died when six or seven years old. These I knew at sight without an introduction.

"After mingling with the pure and happy beings of this place a short time, my guide said again, 'Let us go.' We were soon through the gate by which we had entered the city. My guide then said, 'Now we will return.'

"I could distinctly see the world from which we had first come. It appeared to be a vast distance below us. To me, it looked cloudy, dreary and dark. I was filled with sad disappointment, I might say horror, at the idea of returning there. I supposed I had come to stay in that heavenly place, which I had so long desire to see; up to this time, the thought had not occurred to me that I would be required to return.

"I plead [sic] with my guide to let me remain. He replied that I was permitted to only visit these heavenly cities, for I had not filled my mission in yonder world; therefore I must return and take my body. If I was faithful to the grace of God which would be imparted to me, if I would bear a faithful testimony to the inhabitants of the earth of a sacrificed and risen Savior, and His atonement for man, in a little time I should be permitted to return and remain.

"These words gave me comfort and inspired my bosom with the principle of faith. To me, these things were real. I felt that a great mission had been given me, and I accepted it in my heart. The responsibility of that mission has rested on me from that time until now.

"We returned to my house. There I found my body, and it appeared to me dressed for burial. It was with great reluctance that I took possession of it to resume the ordinary avocations of life, and endeavor to fill the important mission I had received. I awoke and found myself in my bed. I lay and meditated the remainder of the night on what had been shown me. . . .

"The memory of it is clear and distinct with me to-day, after the lapse of fifty years with its many changes. From that time, although belonging to no church, the Spirit was with me to testify to the sufferings and Atonement of the Savior. As I had opportunity, I continually exhorted the people, in public and private, to exercise faith in the Lord Jesus Christ, to repent of their sins and live a life of righteousness and good works."[11]

Feel Joy, Peace, Love, and Happiness

Those who enter paradise will find it a place of joy, peace, love, and happiness. While in the spirit world, people commented that they were filled with overpowering love and that they were perfectly happy. When the apostle Francis M. Lyman spoke about dying, he remarked, "It will be all right when our time comes, when we have finished our work and accomplished what the Lord requires of us. . . . We will be full of joy and happiness, and we will enter into a place of rest, of peace, of joy, rest from every sorrow. What a blessed thing that will be!"[12]

Thomas S. Thomas testified that while in the spirit world, "Your soul is endowed with wisdom and knowledge and filled with everlasting love."[13]

"Everyone was so happy." Charles R. Woodbury commented about the spirit world after his near-death experience.[14]

Flora Ann Mayer

Flora and Everett Van Orden Peck married in 1878 and, over time, had twelve children. Flora's near-death experience occurred when she contracted diphtheria while caring for her children, who also had the disease. While Flora was in the spirit world, she felt so much peace and happiness that she wanted to stay. Her granddaughter Marba Peck Hale relates Flora's experience as it was told by her grandfather Everett.

"Grandpa said she [Flora] died. She stopped breathing and her heart stopped. They knew she was dead. Grandpa gave her a blessing and called her back from the dead. She returned and later told this story:

"She said she felt herself being drawn into a whirlpool-like tunnel. Then she saw a very bright light. A man came from that light and acted as a guide for her. She saw many people she knew who were dead, both friends and family. They greeted and welcomed her. It was a happy reunion. She said it was so beautiful and peaceful there she didn't want to leave. She was happier than she had ever been.

"Then someone, whether her guide or not, I don't remember—came and told her she should go back because her family needed her. She didn't want to go, but her guide informed her that it was not yet her time to be there. Nevertheless, she was free to decide for herself whether she would return to her family and finish raising them or stay there. Now it seems to me Grandpa said that she heard him calling her back, but I'm not really sure of that part.

"At any rate, she decided she had better return. It was a hard decision for her, but she knew her children needed her so she said she would return.

"Grandpa said returning to this life was very painful and difficult for her. For many years I thought he meant because she didn't want to come back, it was very hard to make herself do it. But when I read accounts of others experiences of returning to life, I realized he may well have meant it was physically painful for her too. Grandpa testified to me over and over again that he knew she was dead and had been dead for awhile when he, through the priesthood, was inspired to call her back."[15]

Have a Review of Life

Although having a review of one's earthly life is a common element in modern near-death experiences, it is mentioned only rarely in early Church history experiences. Latter-day Saints believe that at the time of the final judgment, everyone will have a complete review of their life (Revelation 20:12).

George Albert Smith, the eighth president of the Church, had a review of his life after he died. "Everything I had ever done passed before me as though it were a flying picture on a screen—everything I had done. Quickly the vivid retrospect came down to the very time I was standing there. My whole life had passed before me."[16]

Charles John Lambert

Charles John Lambert should have listened to his mother. Like most children, Charles intended to obey her warning, but the thrill of playing in the water with a friend overrode his good intentions. While playing, Charles was trapped underwater and drowned. Shortly afterward, Charles said that "every action, and even every thought of my life, good, bad and indifferent, was clearly before my comprehension." Charles related his near-death experience to a friend, J. N., who wrote the following:

"When I was about thirteen years old I was on the point of leaving my home to go to the vicinity of the Jordan River to bring the family cow from the pasture.

"As I was departing, my mother said, 'Charles John, you must not go into the water.'

"I fully intended to comply with this wish, but when I reached the pasture I set aside my scruples regarding disobedience to my parent and, in company with Harrison Shurtliff, entered a tributary of the Jordan, near to where it emptied into the stream, to bathe.

"We amused ourselves tumbling over a log that lay in the water. In going down I caught under this log, was there held fast, and found it impossible to reach the surface. I knew I was drowning, and as the water gurgled down my throat, a sleepy, painless sensation pervaded me, then all was blank.

"When I recovered consciousness I was no longer in the body, but my spirit was out of the water. No human power could describe my condition. Every action, and even every thought of my life, good, bad and indifferent, was clearly before my comprehension. I could not tell by what process this effect was produced, but I knew that my whole life in detail was before my view with terrible clearness.

"One idea seemed more vivid than the rest—the fact that I had lost my life by my own sinful act—disobedience to my mother.

"There were spiritual persons with me, and I understood that they also knew all about the nature of the deeds I had done in the body. They seemed to have taken charge of me in the spirit, and I seemed to be on the most familiar terms with them.

"I saw Harrison Shurtliff looking for my body in great excitement, but I had no power to communicate with him. I looked into the water and beheld my body, and wondered why he did not see it: then I observed that I saw clear through the log, under which the body was lying. I saw young Shurtliff, after looking for it in vain, run along the bank a distance of about two blocks, and tell John Harker what had taken place. The two then came rapidly to the spot where the drowning occurred.

"I discovered that I could move about without the slightest effort and with great rapidity. My spirit friends took me away from the scene of the incident and in a twinkling, as it were, I was in the city. They told me that my death was caused by disobedience to my parent. I felt keenly on this point, and informed them that if I were allowed to re-enter my body I should never be guilty of the same sin again. I was then informed that I might return to it.

"In an instant—almost as quick as thought—I was at the spot where the drowning occurred and saw my body lying on the bank. Young Shurtliff and John Harker had placed it in such a position that the head was downhill and they were working hard to get the water to flow from the mouth. It looked loathsome to me, notwithstanding I had expressed a desire to return to it.

"Suddenly I became insensible to what transpired. I began to recover sensibility in my body, to which I had returned in the interval that appeared blank. My agony while recovering was fearful. It seemed as if the suffering of an ordinary life-time had been concentrated into a few minutes duration. It appeared as if every sinew of my physical system was being violently torn out. This gradually subsided, I was raised to my feet, some boys took charge of my cow, and others helped me to go to the city.

"On arriving in town I had so far recovered as to be able to walk alone, and wended my way home. I was so thoroughly ashamed of my conduct that I carefully concealed what had happened from the knowledge of my mother. She did not learn of it for several weeks, and would not then had not John Harker visited the house.

"On seeing me he remarked: 'Is not this the boy who was drowned while down at the pasture after the cow?' Then turning to me he said: 'You are the boy, are you not?'

"I was in the act of slinking out of the house when this question was put, but I, of course, answered that I was the boy in question. This was news to mother, who felt quite exercised about it.

"The incident narrated above made an indelible impression upon my mind, and doubtless has more or less influenced my life since it occurred. Some people may think that the statements regarding my leaving the body are based upon imagination. What I have described, however, was as real as anything could be, and was not imaginary. While my spirit was separate from its earthly tenement I saw and understood all that took place, as afterwards verified by the parties whom I have named in connection with the drowning. The effect produced upon me has been to cause me to avoid ever disobeying my parents. I have never, from that time to the present, so far as I know, acted contrary to their expressed wishes, and I trust I never shall. I have therefore kept the condition upon which I appeared to be allowed to again take possession of my body.

"Thus ends the story of my experience in being drowned and coming to life again. The incident may serve to point a moral by which some young people may profit."[17]

Notes:

1. Parley P. Pratt, *Journal of Discourses*, April 7, 1853 (Liverpool, 1854–86), 1:9.
2. John A. Widstoe, comp., *Discourses of Brigham Young* (Salt Lake City: Deseret Book, 1954), 380–81.
3. Lerona A. Wilson, *An Open Vision: An Afternoon With My Deceased Parents* (courtesy of the Church History Library, The Church of Jesus Christ of Latter-day Saints).
4. Hannah Adeline Savage, *Record of Hannah Adeline Savage* (Provo, Utah: L. Tom Perry Special Collections, Harold B. Lee Library, Brigham Young University), 3–5.
5. Arvin S. Gibson, *Margaret and Marshall Gibson, An Old-fashioned Love Story: A Biography* (courtesy of the Church History Library, The Church of Jesus Christ of Latter-day Saints).
6. "How One Feels When Dying," *The Juvenile Instructor* 27 (September 15, 1892), 572–73.
7. David O McKay, *Gospel Ideals, Selections from the Discourses of David O. McKay* (Salt Lake City: Improvement Era Publication, 1953), 54–56.
8. Melvin J. Ballard, *Crusader for Righteousness* (Salt Lake City: Bookcraft, 1966), 108.
9. Peter E. Johnson, "A Testimony," *The Relief Society Magazine* 7, (1920), 450–55.
10. James Amasa Little, "Biography of Lorenzo Dow Young." *Utah Historical Quarterly*, vol. 14, (1946), 35–36.
11. Lorenzo Dow Young, *Fragments of Experience, Sixth Book of the Faith-Promoting Series* (Salt Lake City: Juvenile Instructor Office, 1882), 27–30.
12. Francis M. Lyman, Conference Report, October 1909, 19.
13. Thomas S. Thomas, "A Glimpse of the Future" (courtesy of the Church History Library, The Church of Jesus Christ of Latter-day Saints).
14. Charles R. Woodbury, *Faith Promoting Experiences of Patriarch Charles R. Woodbury* (courtesy of the Church History Library, The Church of Jesus Christ of Latter-day Saints).
15. Marba Peck Hale, Papers [ca. 2000] Folder 6 (courtesy of the Church History Library, The Church of Jesus Christ of Latter-day Saints).
16. George Albert Smith, "Your Good Name," *The Improvement Era*, March 1947, 139.
17. Charles John Lambert, as told to J. N., "A Curious Experience in Drowning," *Juvenile Instructor* 21, (December 1 1886), 359.

> "The heavens were opened upon us, and I beheld the celestial king-
> dom of God. . . . I saw Father Adam and Abraham; and my father and
> my mother; my brother Alvin, that has long since slept."
> (Joseph Smith, Doctrine and Covenants 137:1–5)

Chapter Three

Meet with Loved Ones

The most common element in near-death experiences in early Church history is meeting with departed family members and friends. Many people reported seeing their grandparents, spouse, parents, siblings, and friends in a grand and happy reunion. Brigham Young said, "We have more friends behind the vail [sic] than on this side, and they will hail us more joyfully than you were ever welcomed by your parents and friends in this world; and you will rejoice more when you meet them than you ever rejoiced to see a friend in this life."[1]

Knowing we will be reunited with loved ones can make it possible to regard going to the other side with a certain measure of anticipation. The Prophet Joseph Smith said, "I have a father, brothers, children, and friends who have gone to a world of spirits. They are only absent for a moment. They are in the spirit, and we shall soon meet again. . . . When we depart, we shall hail our mothers, fathers, friends, and all whom we love, who have fallen asleep in Jesus . . . it will be an eternity of felicity."[2]

After his near-death experience, Thomas S. Thomas said, "The grand greeting you first receive is from your closest of kin—father, mother, brother and sisters—and all that are near and dear to you who passed from earthly life and arrived in the Great Beyond [sic] before you. Your nearest and dearest friends and many others come to greet and converse with you."[3]

Flora Mayer was greeted by a number of people. "She saw many people she knew who were dead, both friends and family. They greeted and welcomed her. It was a happy reunion."[4]

Bertha Deusnup Elder said her guide "escorted her into a large room where she was greeted by many of her departed friends."[5]

Iva Langford

The doctors operated on Iva Langford in one last, desperate attempt to save her life. She survived the operation but shortly afterward had a near-death experience. While in the spirit world, Iva was reunited with her grandfather, brother, sister, and many other relatives. Iva relates her experience:

"On the eleventh of May, 1916, I was taken severely ill. Parents and kind friends did all they could and also called in the elders who, after praying, administered to me; but nothing relieved the severe pain. A physician was sent for who had operated on me six months before and he felt sure that nothing could be done for my relief except another operation. However, owing to my weak condition he did not like to undertake it and he preferred to try some other means first.

"His treatment continued for one week but I gradually grew worse and experienced no relief only when under the influence of morphine. The elders came day and night to administer to me, but apparently to no avail as I was rapidly sinking.

"Two more physicians were called for consultation and gave it as their opinion that I had but one chance in a thousand to live and that chance depended on an operation. I was then so weak that I did not care to live and suffer longer; but my parents were pleading for me to submit, and so on the eighteenth of May, I was put on the operating table in our own home, as I was too weak to be taken to the hospital.

"The physicians asked all present to exercise their faith, as they were afraid I would not be able to stand the ordeal. Special prayers were offered in the adjoining room and in several homes in our ward. I was on the table four hours and fifty minutes, when I was put back in my bed with little hope for recovery. After twenty hours the physicians left saying it was impossible for me to live.

"I was then having sinking spells and while in one, it seemed that my spirit left my body, for I was shown my grandfather, brother, and sister, and a host of relatives and friends that had passed from this life, and the beautiful place they were in. I wanted to stay with them but my grandfather told me that they had intended taking me with them, but the faith and prayers that had been exercised in my behalf had been so great my life would be spared for a time.

"When I came to myself, I told my parents where I had been, and of the beautiful experience which had been mine. From that time I started to improve. It is now eleven weeks and since the operation I am up and getting well and strong. This is not only a living testimony to me, but to all who knew of my serious condition."[6]

W. W. Merrill

W. W. Merrill, the father of apostle Joseph F. Merrill, had an extremely unusual near-death experience. When Elder Merrill visited the spirit world, he saw a young woman to whom he had recently given a priesthood blessing. At that time, she had expressed a desire to die so she could be with her mother, whom she desperately missed. This account was related by Apostle Rudger Clawson and written by J. Berkeley Larsen.

Although Elder W. W. Merrill was elderly and ill when asked to administer to the sick young woman, he did not hesitate but got up from his sickbed and went to her home.

"When he reached the young woman's bedside, she said, 'Now, Brother Merrill, I haven't anything to live for. My parents are gone, I don't have any close friends, I am alone. I don't want you to bless me to live; I want you to bless me to die.'

"Brother Merrill said, 'That is a strange request for a beautiful young woman like you to make. You are just budding into womanhood with all of your life before you. You have the prospects of a husband and home, everything a young woman could hope for. Why in the world should you want such a blessing?'

"President Clawson said, "I have forgotten the type of blessing he gave her; I'm not sure I did know, but at any rate Brother Merrill went back to his bed, and later both he and the young lady died.

"They went over to the Other Side, and as Brother Merrill was walking down a sidewalk with some brethren, he met this young lady who said, 'This is my mother; this is one of the reasons I wanted to come.'

"Well, it just so happens they both came back. They saw each other over there. They conversed together. They met other people they knew and talked to, then came back and both remembered the incidents. President

Clawson said, 'That is one of the most singular instances of this type in the history of the Church.'"[7]

See Jesus, Joseph Smith, or Other Prophets and Leaders

Many people who have had near-death experiences report seeing Jesus Christ while in the spirit world. A number of people also reported seeing the Prophet Joseph Smith, Hyrum Smith, Brigham Young, and other modern-day and ancient prophets and Apostles.

William Wallace Raymond said, "I have been to the spirit world and have seen many things, and many people that I knew, I saw Joseph and Hyrum Smith and Brigham Young and members of the twelve that are dead."[8]

Harriet Salvina Beal Millet said, "I was very pleasantly surprised to see the Prophet Joseph Smith walking up and down a very long room . . . At long tables on either side of the room and down the center also, many men sat . . . Among these men were the Prophet's brother Hyrum, also other men I had known well."[9]

Harriet Ovard Lee

After suffering serious injuries from a fall, Harriet Ovard Lee was operated on twice in two months. Still her condition worsened, and she had a near-death experience where she saw Joseph Smith and Hyrum Smith.

"About the year 1860, I, Harriet Lee, was residing with my husband in Old Lexington, Massachusetts. My husband, Brother Henry Ovard, was a butler and I had been a lady's maid at Evanson House, where we were domiciled. . . . One day myself and two girl companions, in a spirit of fun, mounted a haystack where a wagon of hay was being unloaded. I got too close to the edge of the stack, which was very high, and I overbalanced myself and fell backwards onto the hay rack of the wagon, landing on the bow over the wheel. I was picked up more dead than alive, blood streaming from my mouth, nose and ears, and was carried on a litter to the house. . . .

"After examining me the doctors decided I was seriously injured in the bowels, so they opened me while I was yet unconscious and found that the membrane of the bowels was ruptured in a number of places. They took my bowels out and laid them on a board by my side, and after sewing them where they were broken they replaced them.

"I lay in bed in great distress for thirteen weeks, with my arms tied down to my sides and my legs firmly tied together to prevent me from moving. . . . At the expiration of thirteen weeks, my condition steadily growing worse, my kind mistress sent to the city of Boston for five of the best doctors that could be secured. These doctors, putting me under an anesthetic, also opened me and discovered that the doctors in the former operation had twisted part of my bowels, and they expressed great surprise that I had not long before died from mortification.

"For eighteen months after this operation I suffered a great deal. . . . I was frequently visited by the late Elder William Paxman and Elders John Stone and John West. . . . They, with my husband, administered to me often, and it was only through the power of God . . . that my life was preserved, for the doctors said it was utterly impossible for me to recover.

"My heart and lungs kept getting worse until one afternoon . . . the doctors who were present pronounced me dead and asked my husband to allow them to dissect my body for scientific purposes. My husband would not admit that I was dead, at once sent for Elder Paxman and his two companions in the ministry. Upon the arrival of the Elders my husband led them into my room and requested all others who were present to retire. When the door was closed all of these brethren, including my husband, formed themselves into a circle and they prayed earnestly for my recovery. . . . They remained shut up in my room fasting and praying (not even taking a drink of water) and administering to me for forty-eight hours.

"At about five o'clock the next evening after my spirit departed from my body . . . my friends, led by Brother Paxman, were saying almost incessantly, 'She is not dead but only sleeping, and she will wake again tomorrow.'

"At this time my body was cold and stiff and all in the house, excepting my husband, my sister and the three Elders believed me to be dead and seemed to think my friends were fanatics to hold on to me. Prior to this, in the afternoon, my coffin was brought into the room, this, together with other funeral arrangements, having been made by the lady of the house.

"Some time after this the doctors were admitted to my room where they again renewed their request for my body, but my husband was obdurate, maintaining that I would yet be restored to life. Brother Paxman then addressed the doctors, five in all, saying, 'We are going to have prayer, and if you would like to join us, we shall be happy to have you, but if you do not feel that way, please retire.'

"The Doctors smiled but remained in the room, and everyone present knelt, and my friends engaged in silent prayer. . . . About this time I began to sense what was going on in the room, but I had no power to move or make any signs of life whatever. Elder Paxman had one hand on my forehead and held my right hand with the other, and, as near as I can remember, said: 'Father in heaven, we Thy humble children come before Thee at this time, and we ask Thee if it be Thy holy will, show these people a sign that they may believe, and cause that this sister may arise in their presence, and if it is Thy will make it manifest, etc.'

"At that instant I lifted up my right arm and in a few seconds my eyelids began to twitch and a faint flow came to my cheeks.

"Elder Paxman, continuing, said, 'Harriet, arise,' and I arose straight up in the bed, opening my eyes and looking around me in wonderment. . . . The doctors stood aghast in my presence. Three of them out of the five (all Catholics) afterwards joined the Church, being baptized by Elder Paxman and confirmed by Elder Stone.

"I will now endeavor to recount my experience during the forty-eight hours that my spirit was out of my body. . . . I heard a voice calling me by name, saying, 'Harriet,' three times, 'Come, I am waiting.' . . . I saw my husband and all the people in the room, some of them crying and wringing their hands over my lifeless body, at the sight of which I shuddered.

"The voice said, 'Come,' and I saw a personage whom I followed . . . and we passed out at the door into what appeared to be unlimited space. Again my guide called me by name, commanding me to follow him, which I did, and we kept moving forward and I felt as light as a feather and as free as a bird on the wing, all pain and uneasiness having entirely left me. . . .

"Presently we drew near to a river which looked beautiful in the distance, but when we got to it, it looked dark, dismal, misty and forbidding, and I wanted to turn back, but my guide said, 'No, you have got to cross this dark river.'

"I looked all around me wondering how I could ever obey, when some power seemed to pick me up off my feet and I crossed to the other side of the river without touching the water. I now found myself in the midst of a beautiful greensward [grassy area] and I sat down and gazed in wonderment and admiration on the grandeur and loveliness of my surroundings.

"But my guide said, 'Come,' and we traveled over this magnificent greensward until we came to another river, which shone as clear as crystal, its bed being covered with what appeared to be diamonds and other precious stones. I stooped down and bathed my face with my hands, which greatly refreshed me.

"My guide sat and looked at me, smiling so pleasantly, and he repeated the word, 'Look,' three times. I looked, and in the distance above I beheld a mighty mountain approaching us. . . .

"My guide again said, 'Look,' and the mountain kept lowering towards us, and I soon observed that it was inhabited by millions of miserable fellow-creatures. They were in great confusion, wringing their hands, holding them up, and tossing their bodies to and fro in fearful anguish.

"My guide said, 'These are the spirits in prison; they know the punishment that awaits them and they are in great distress by reason of this knowledge. They have crossed the dark river, but they have not been permitted to go near the bright and clear river which we have passed.' As he finished speaking, the mountain, with its millions of unhappy occupants, receded and gradually disappeared from our view.

"My guide again said, 'Look,' and there appeared another great mountain, not so high nor so dismal as the first; it looked brighter and more verdant. Again he said, 'Look,' three times, and I looked and beheld the mountain gradually draw nearer to us, and soon I could see that it also was inhabited. The people who lived on it looked just as happy as the inhabitants of the former mountain looked miserable. Some were reading books, some walked about and all were busy. The children played and romped around, while the grown people, especially the men, were very busy, and it seemed to be such a beautiful place.

"I said to my guide, 'Who are these?'

" 'These are the spirits in paradise,' he answered. 'Don't you see that great black gulf? These two mountains separate the righteous from the wicked.'

"And I looked and beheld. . . . My guide turned around and bade me follow onward, and after we had traveled quite a long distance, he again said, 'Look,' three times, and he beckoned with his right hand, and I looked and there I saw a beautiful crystal mountain, having the appearance of ice. It dazzled so that I could scarcely look upon it.

"While I looked on it in admiration, the mountain gradually split in twain until there was quite a wide opening between its two parts, and out of this opening came the Prophet Joseph Smith and his brother, Hyrum, followed by a great multitude walking two abreast. The faces of all except the Prophet and his brother, Hyrum, had the appearance of a light copper color.

"I said to the guide, 'That is our Prophet Joseph Smith and his brother Hyrum, but who are these who follow?'

"He answered, 'Those are the ten tribes of the house of Israel. Joseph and his brother have been preaching to them and they are gathering them home.'

"There seemed to be millions of them and when they had all passed out of the opening, the mountain immediately closed up again with a loud report.

"My guide said, 'Look, look, look,' and I looked and beheld a massive building of indescribable magnificence, its dimensions extending beyond my vision. One of its pillars seemed to be larger than our Salt Lake Temple, and the building itself was of a dazzling whiteness. I again saw Joseph and Hyrum, this time preceding the great multitude of copper-colored people into this building. We sat and looked on until the last of them had entered.

"Then my guide said, 'Come and we will follow.' We entered the building on another side. The distance there seemed very long, but we glided along with perfect ease and without touching the ground with our feet. My guide led me up to a massive door on which was a large knocker. He lifted this knocker, making a great noise, upon which the door gradually swung open.

"A voice from within said, 'Who is here?'

"My guide answered by taking from his bosom a paper and handing it to this personage inside the door. The personage unfolded it. He then read it carefully, which took him some little time, then folded it up and returned it to the guide.

"He next opened wide the door and said, 'Enter.'

"We entered and walked along a beautiful hall, I noticed for the first time that I wore a pair of fine white sandals. I also wore a white shroud and robe. . . .

"Then we entered a dark, misty room, where seven men were seated at a table writing, and all were very busy. One of them lifted up his head and said, 'What's wanted?'

My guide handed him the same paper as before, which he opened and partially read. Then he looked in a large book, evidently to see if the two records corresponded, after which he returned the paper to my guide and said, 'Enter.'

"We then proceeded along a very large, open hall until we came to a massive door which opened itself without knocking. Inside sat a tall man clothed in a long, white robe, which covered him completely from neck to feet. He wore a long, flowing beard of snowy whiteness, with an abundance of hair of the same hue.

"He said, 'Well done, enter, you are welcome.' I entered alone, my guide leaving me outside of the door. This was a very large room, and in the center was a massive fountain, bright and sparkling, and the water was so clear that I could see to the bottom of it. The water was thrown up in silvery sprays and there were steps all around which seemed to be of polished white marble. . . .

"[He said] 'You have done well so far; you have got to return back to the earth to complete the course marked out for you, for you have got a great deal of work yet to do. You will be tried and tempted in every way. Your troubles and trials will be great and your life will hang on a hair's breadth, but you will come off conqueror in the end. You have a mighty work to do both for the living and for the dead.'

"He told me the very year in which I should return, but neither the month nor the day. Many other things he told which he commanded me not to tell to a living soul.

"At the last he said: 'Now . . . go and finish your work that the Lord thy God giveth thee to do, and see to it that you do it well; go and be faithful and all will be well with you here and hereafter. Thou shalt have many, many enemies, but thou shalt triumph over them all. Now I will show you . . . a glimpse of the Celestial Kingdom of our God.'

"He went to the wall opposite . . . A massive door opened slightly and he said, 'Look.'

"I looked through the narrow opening of the door and I could see a place of surpassing grandeur, having the appearance of pure gold. At the far end there seemed to be a big throne or altar of gold. There seemed to be a silvery light in this place. Tongue cannot tell nor pen describe the grandeur and dazzling magnificence of this place.

"He said, 'This is the Celestial Kingdom of our God.'

"The door closed and the personage said . . . 'Go my child, and be faithful. I know you will. I know you will. I know you will.'

"I turned to leave and when I was about to ask him where to go to get out, I discovered that I was alone and that he had vanished. I went across the room and a door gradually opened and there stood the one who [had] admitted me. . . .

"I followed him and he took me through another beautiful place, and I heard the most beautiful singing. A door opened and I saw another large room, in which were a great number of women and children playing. They were all dressed in white, and the women were tending the children, some having babies in arms. We then went into another large room where there seemed to be millions of men who were at work. They also were happy, some singing and some preaching to crowds. They seemed to have all kinds of music which sounded as coming from the distance as well as close by.

"I have since heard some of the same tunes here; but I could not distinguish the words. While I was listening to this music, my chaperone . . . opened another door and, putting his hand in his bosom, he drew forth my paper of credentials and handed it to my first guide, who stood just outside this door and who said, 'Come,' and immediately I heard Brother William Paxman saying, 'She is not dead, but only sleeping and she will wake again tomorrow.'

"Harriet Lee, born in Maxtock, Warwickshire, England, September 6, 1836. The foregoing remarkable statement was taken stenographically from the lips of Sister Harriet Lee, at her home in the Thirteenth Ward, Salt Lake City, in June 1901, by Elder Martin S. Lindsay, in the presence of Elder William Sanders and Sister Lee's husband, Elder James Lee."

Notes:

1. Brigham Young, *Journal of Discourses*, July 31, 1859 (Liverpool, 1854–86), 6:349.
2. Joseph F. Smith and his assistants in the Historian's Office, comp., *Teachings of the Prophet Joseph Smith*, fifth printing (Salt Lake City: *Deseret News* Press, 1946), 359–60.
3. Thomas S. Thomas, "A Glimpse of the Future" (courtesy of the Church History Library, The Church of Jesus Christ of Latter-day Saints).
4. Marba Peck Hale, Papers [ca. 2000], Folder 6 (courtesy of the Church History Library, The Church of Jesus Christ of Latter-day Saints).
5. Lee Nelson, *Beyond The Veil*, vol. 1, (Springville, Utah: Cedar Fort, Inc., 1988), 37–40. Used with permission.

6. Iva Langford, "Testimonies that Prayers are Answered," *Young Woman's Journal* 28, (1917), 112–113.

7. J. Berkeley Larsen, "The Reality of Life After Death," *BYU Speeches of the Year*, October 6, 1953 (1953–1955), 4.

8. William Wallace Raymond, "Vision 1881 Aug. 12" (courtesy of the Church History Library, The Church of Jesus Christ of Latter-day Saints).

9. Cora Anna Beal Peterson, [biographical sketch of William Beal, n.d.], (Salt Lake City: LDS Church Archives).

10. Harriet Ovard Lee, "A remarkable vision 1901" (courtesy of the Church History Library, The Church of Jesus Christ of Latter-day Saints).

Chapter Four

Light in the Spirit World

*L*ight is another common element in modern-day and early Church near-death experiences. Many people struggle to describe the unusual, wondrous light. Some call it bright and dazzling—beyond anything they can describe. Others say it is soft and opal-like—a pure light. Many people said they felt peace, love, and joy from this light.

Light is an important concept in the scriptures. We gain an inkling of its significance when we find that the word *light* appears 535 times in the scriptures. Light is often equated with glory and intelligence. "The glory of God is intelligence; or, in other words, light and truth" (Doctrine and Covenants 93:36). Light is also often linked with truth. "For the word of the Lord is truth, and whatsoever is truth is light, and whatsoever is light is Spirit, even the Spirit of Jesus Christ. And the Spirit giveth light to every man that cometh into the world; and the Spirit enlighteneth every man through the world, that hearkeneth to the voice of the Spirit" (Doctrine and Covenants 84:45–46).

The light of Christ is a divine influence that allows everyone to distinguish between good and evil. "And if your eye be single to my glory, your whole bodies shall be filled with light, and there shall be no darkness in you; and that body which is filled with light comprehendeth all things" (Doctrine and Covenants 88:67). We can be partakers of that truth and light by following the Savior. "He that keepeth his commandments receiveth truth and light, until he is glorified in truth and knoweth all things" (Doctrine and Covenants 93:28).

Certain scriptures indicate that light emanates directly from the Savior's person. When talking of the New Jerusalem, John said; "And the city had no need of the sun, neither of the moon, to shine in it: for the glory of God did lighten it, and the Lamb is the light thereof" (Revelation 21:23). In the Doctrine and Covenants, Christ is said to be the source of light: "This is the light of Christ. As also he is in the sun, and the light of the sun, and the power thereof by which it was made. And the light which shineth, which giveth you light, is through him who enlighteneth your eyes, which is the same light that quickeneth your understandings; Which light proceedeth forth from the presence of God to fill the immensity of space—The light which is in all things, which giveth life to all things, which is the law by which all things are governed" (Doctrine and Covenants 88:7, 11–13).

Charles R. Woodbury said that while he was in the spirit world, "I saw a real bright light, brighter than noonday. In the light I saw people, men and women dressed in light clothing."[1]

Tom Gibson was taken by a good friend, Daniel, to the spirit world. He said, "Daniel next led me to a city. It was a city of light."[2]

Loisie M. Goates

After a difficult delivery giving birth to twins, Loisie Goates had a near-death experience where she was told to follow a light.

"I want to relate an instance of my life that I may leave with my children as a testimony when I am gone from their midst. In the year 1890 I was confined to my bed with sickness [and] later gave Birth [sic] to a pair of twins Emma and Alvin Goates, the girl born first, later the boy dies [sic].

"While on the bed of sickness my spirit left my body and by all that loving hands could do I was called gone. The Doctor was called and he said I can do nothing the woman is gone, the heart has quit beating.

"My sister Annie called an alarm and the family of Goates and [illegible writing] all that could be called with Grandpa Goates, circled my bed and prayed for me to live. William Goates being mouth. [During the] time this was going on I could see my body crampted [sic] and [illegible writing] in bed (I being above it) my sister calling or speaking to me asking me who I wanted to take my baby, when two personages came. One was made known to me to be that of my husband's mother whom I had never seen before. I was told to follow a light that looked to me to be like a star at first when it soon grew to be a Brilient [sic] Light I followed and was taken to a place heavenly to me: when I entered the building with two guides the music being lovely.

"A vail [sic] was lifted and I was told to look and oh there was a room or hall with all the Goates loved ones all [illegible writing] and seemed like a meeting was going on. On the stand was a congress chin [congregation] and there was William Goates, not yet dead in his earthly clothing showing to me he was not yet in place.

"I saw my own little ones and wanted to take my baby Louise that I recognized in a lady's, my husband's mother's, arms, when I was told no, not yet. They were praying for me below and I might return to my family for a space of time. The two boy[s] that raised the vail was told me was my husband's brother John that had dide [died] and the other one I did not recognize, they were so busy and happy I wanted to stay but could not and had to return.

"I saw many other things that I shall never forget. But this much I want to say to my children when my spirit return[ed] they were praying [illegible] all night. Bro. Goates Sen. never left my bed side and I know today if he had I should have dide [died] for the priesthood was with me and my little Bert sitting by my bed—and all working over me.

"My sister Annie never leaving me night and day and fed me with a spoon for five days and my Guide visited me several times stood by my bed and all ways talked in tongs [tongues] which I knew was a gift of God and all so another testomoney [testimony] to me that it was the power of God. Before this I had greaved [sic] so much over my little ones but after this I could not greave for my loved one was so happy and cared for that these words were a comfort to one, God giveth and God taketh and blessed be his name. A truthfull testimony. Loisie M. Goates. They were so busy and happy I wanted to stay but could not and had to return."[3]

Light Around Angelic Personages

Sometimes light is spoken of as coming from a spiritual being. Heavenly messengers who come to earth are often surrounded by light, which illuminates the room or area around them when they appear. When Jesus appeared to the Nephites after his death, angels came down from heaven surrounded by an intense, bright light. "And behold, they were encircled about as if it were by fire; and it came down from heaven, and the multitude did witness it, and did bear record; and angels did come down out of heaven and did minister unto them" (3 Nephi 19:14).

When Joseph Smith had the First Vision, he stated, "I saw a pillar of light exactly over my head, above the brightness of the sun. . . . When the light rested upon me I saw two Personages, whose brightness and glory defy all description."[4]

Joseph Smith compared the light that surrounds holy personages to a flame when he spoke about the departed. "The spirits of the just are exalted to a greater and more glorious work; hence they are blessed in their departure to the world of spirits. Enveloped in flaming fire, they are not far from us."[5]

When Tom Gibson saw Jesus Christ in the spirit world, he said of the Savior, "He was bathed in light."[6]

Just before David Brooks saw his departed wife, the room filled with light. "Immediately I saw a dim light filling the room, it was not a brilliant light but a soft light, then it began to part in the center like a curtain. As it parted, I saw in the opening the most beautiful sight in all the world, my lovely wife."[7]

Enveloped in a Brilliant White Light

It was a dangerous operation in 1920—removing a large tumor near a man's jugular vein. The patient (whose name is not given) was anxious but insisted that the doctor go ahead with the operation. However, problems arose, and during surgery, the man's spirit left his mortal body. While in the spirit world, he found himself enveloped in a brilliant light that surrounded a spiritual personage.

Frederick Babbel relates the story and explains that when the doctor made the incision in the operating room and exposed the tumor, it was perilously close to the jugular vein, just as he had feared. At this moment, the man's spirit rose above his body, and he heard the doctor tell the nurse, "I can't go on. If I do, he will die."

The nurse replied, "But you promised him you would make the effort. Even if it should cost his life. You must keep your promise."

As the doctor tried to remove the tumor, the jugular vein split open, just as the doctor had feared. The man's spirit then left the operating room.

"He found himself entering into the spirit world where he met loved ones who had departed earlier. All at once he was enveloped in a brilliant white light.

"'I have brought you back into my presence,' said the voice in the midst of the dazzling white light, 'because you have so greatly feared the transition which you call death. You now perceive that there is nothing to fear, but rather the opportunity to enjoy a boundless future much more glorious than that which you have known.'

"Then this glorious personage continued: 'You must return to the earth. Your mission in life is not yet finished. You will lose all that you have held dear and cherished. However, if you will trust me, you shall yet accomplish many great things and realize some of the sweetest blessings that are available for my Father's children upon the earth.'

"Upon returning to his body, which was now covered with a sheet, he saw the nurse preparing to leave the room. As his spirit reentered his body, the nurse noticed movement and breathing.

"She called out excitedly, 'Doctor! Come back! He's alive and breathing again!'"

The man then lapsed into unconsciousness. Later, one of the nurses said to him, "We never expected you to leave here alive. You were dead for several minutes!"

The man made a full recovery. Everything he had been told would happen did. He lost virtually everything that he had treasured when his wife divorced him and took nearly everything he owned. However, other great and wonderful blessings came his way. A short time before the infamous events at Pearl Harbor in 1941, he became a member of The Church of Jesus Christ of Latter-day Saints. Not long after that, he married a beautiful woman who had been on a mission. Sustained with their knowledge of the gospel, they lived together happily in the knowledge that God loves us and that there is indeed life after death.[8]

Notes:

1. Charles R. Woodbury, *Faith Promoting Experiences of Patriarch Charles R. Woodbury* (courtesy of the Church History Library, The Church of Jesus Christ of Latter-day Saints).

2. Arvin S. Gibson, *Margaret and Marshall Gibson, An Old-fashioned Love Story: A Biography* (courtesy of the Church History Library, The Church of Jesus Christ of Latter-day Saints).

3. Loisie M. Goates, *Faith-promoting Collection 1882–1974*, box 2, folder 13 (courtesy of the Church History Library, The Church of Jesus Christ of Latter-day Saints).

4. Joseph Smith—History 1:16–17.

5. Joseph F. Smith and assistants, comp., *Teachings of the Prophet Joseph Smith*, fifth printing (Salt Lake City: *Deseret News* Press, 1946), 326.

6. Arvin S. Gibson, *Margaret and Marshall Gibson, An Old-fashioned Love Story: A Biography* (courtesy of the Church History Library, The Church of Jesus Christ of Latter-day Saints).

7. Duane Crowther, *Life Everlasting* (Salt Lake City: Bookcraft, 1967), 59–60. Used with permission of Springville, Utah: Horizon Publishers & Distributors, Inc. (Springville, Utah).

8. Frederick and June Babble, *To Him That Believeth: Claiming Heaven's Blessings* (Springville, Utah: Cedar Fort, Inc., 1997), 25–27. Used with permission.

"The soul shall be restored to the body, and the body to the soul; yea, and every limb and joint shall be restored to its body; yea, even a hair of the head shall not be lost; but all things shall be restored to their proper and perfect frame." (Alma 40:23)

Chapter Five

Attributes of the Spirit Body

Spirits Are Composed of Pure, Refined Matter

Although the spirit looks like the physical body, it is composed of different matter. Joseph Smith taught that there is a difference in composition between the physical and spiritual body. "We shall find a very material difference between the body and the spirit; the body is supposed to be organized matter, and the spirit, by many, is thought to be immaterial, without substance. With this latter statement we should beg leave to differ, and state the spirit is a substance; that it is material, but that it is more pure, elastic and refined matter than the body; that it existed before the body, can exist in the body; and will exist separate from the body."[1]

Brigham Young explained why mortals cannot see spirits. "Spirits are composed of matter so refined as not to be tangible to this coarser organization."[2]

Once the spirit leaves the physical body, it will regain the capabilities it had in the premortal world. Orson Pratt said, "Man will be endowed, after he leaves this tabernacle, with powers and facilities which he, now, has no knowledge of, by which he may learn what is round about him."[3]

The Spirit Body Looks like the Physical Body

Members of the Church know that after death our spirits will retain their bodily form and look the same as they do now. The Savior explained

53

this to the brother of Jared when He said, "Behold, this body, which ye now behold, is the body of my spirit; and man have I created after the body of my spirit; and even as I appear unto thee to be in the spirit will I appear unto my people in the flesh" (Ether 3:16).

The Apostle Erastus Snow once asked a rhetorical question during general conference. "Now what is this spirit?" He then declared, "It is a being precisely as we are seen here to-day; and if you ask, 'How does brother Snow's spirit look when it is disembodied?' Why, you just look at me now, and you can answer the question. How does the spirit of my wife look? Why, just look at her and see. . . . We are the same beings . . . the same features exactly."[4]

The scriptures testify that the likeness of the temporal body is similar to that of the spiritual body. "That which is spiritual being in the likeness of that which is temporal; and that which is temporal in the likeness of that which is spiritual; the spirit of man in the likeness of his person, as also the spirit of the beast, and every other creature which God has created" (Doctrine and Covenants 77:2).

Orson Pratt said, "That the form of the spirit is in the likeness of the tabernacle is evident from the description of the spirit of Samuel, which appeared to Saul and conversed with him."[5]

Although the spirit body looks like the physical body, it does not have any deformities or imperfections, even if its earthly body did. Dr. Elisabeth Kubler-Ross, an expert on near-death experiences, stated that the hundreds of people she has talked with after they have come back to life had no physical limitations during their time in the spirit world. Dr. Kubler-Ross stated, "People who were blind can see again. People who couldn't hear or speak can hear and speak again."[6]

Orson Pratt explains, "We, as Latter-day Saints, believe that the spirits that occupy these tabernacles have form and likeness similar to the human tabernacle. Of course, there may be deformities existing in connection with the outward tabernacle which do not exist in connection with the spirit that inhabits it. These tabernacles become deformed by accident in various ways, sometimes at birth but this may not altogether or in any degree deform the spirits that dwell within them."[7]

Vision Is Increased

People report that when they were in the spirit world, their ability to see was vastly enhanced and they could see everything clearly and distinctly. Some were even able to see through physical objects.

When Heber C. Kimball was in England, he had a vision and explains the reason he could see so well was because he was seeing with his spiritual eyes. "All at once my vision was opened, and the walls of the building were no obstruction to my seeing, for I saw nothing but the visions that presented themselves. Why did not the walls obstruct my view? Because my spirit could look through the walls of that house, for I looked with that spirit, element, and power, with which angels look; and as God sees all things."[8]

During his near-death experience, Lorenzo Dow Young said, "I gazed on a vast region filled with multitudes of beings. I could see everything with the most minute distinctness."[9]

As a spirit, Charles John Lambert was able to look through a large piece of wood to see his own dead body. Charles said, "I looked into the water and beheld my body, and wondered why he did not see it: then I observed that I saw clear through the log, under which the body was lying."[10]

Dr. Wiltse

Dr. Wiltse was in the last stage of typhus fever when he died. The account of his near-death experience was published in the *Juvenile Instructor* in 1892.

"His voice failed, and his strength weakened, and as a last effort he stiffened his legs and lay for four hours as dead, the church bell being rung for his death. He was pulseless for a long time and for nearly half an hour he appeared absolutely dead. While his body was lying in this death-like trance, he asserts his spirit was disengaging itself from its earthly tabernacle."

Dr. Wiltse said he then "woke up out of unconsciousness into a state of conscious existence, and . . . reasoned calmly thus: 'I have died, as men term death, and yet I am as much a man as ever.'" After his spirit left his body, he said, "I turned and faced the company. As I turned, my left elbow came in contact with the arm of one of two gentlemen who were standing in the door. To my surprise, his arm passed through mine without apparent resistance, the several parts closing again without pain, as air reunites. I looked quickly up at his face to see if he had noticed the contact, but he gave me no sign. . . . I directed my gaze in the direction of his and saw my own dead body.

"I saw a number of persons sitting and standing about the body, and particularly noticed two women apparently kneeling by my left side, and I knew that they were weeping. . . . I turned and passed out at the open door, inclining my head and watching where I set my feet as I stepped down on to the porch. I crossed the porch, descended the steps, walked down the path and into the street. There I stopped and looked about me. I never saw that street more distinctly than I saw it then. I took note of the redness of the soil and of the washes the rain had made. I took a rather pathetic look about me, like one who is about to leave his home for a long time. Then I discovered that I had become larger than I was in earth life and congratulated myself thereupon. I was somewhat smaller in the body than I just liked to be, but in the next life, I thought, I am to be as I desired.

"My clothes I noticed had accommodated themselves to my increased stature, and I fell to wondering where they came from and how they got on me so quickly and without my knowledge. I examined the fabric and judged it to be of some kind of Scotch material—a good suit, I thought, but not handsome; still neat and good enough. . . . *How well I feel*, I thought. Only a few minutes ago I was horribly sick and distressed. Then came that change, called death, which I have so much dreaded. It is past now, and here am I still a man, alive and thinking—yes, thinking as clearly as ever, and how well I feel!"

"In the exuberance of his joy at the thought that he would never be sick again, Dr. Wiltse says he danced in his glee. He traveled at a swift but pleasant rate of speed upward until he saw in front of him three prodigious rocks, blocking the road, when he was told that if he should pass them he could no more return to the body. He desired to go in one of the four entrances that he saw, but he was suddenly stopped.

"He became unconscious again, and when he awoke he was laying in his bed. He did not write this narrative until eight weeks afterwards, but he told the story to those at the bedside as soon as he revived. The doctor who was at his bedside said that the breath was absolutely extinct, so far as could be observed, and every symptom of the patient being dead was present.

"This doctor said: 'I supposed that he was actually dead, as fully as I ever supposed any one to be dead.'"[11]

Able to Move Quickly and Effortlessly

One of the most commonly mentioned capabilities of the spirit body is to move quickly and easily from place to place. Many people who had near-death experiences reported that their spirit body could travel great distances at enormous speeds. People commented that they could move without effort and were able to move as quickly as they could think. Earth's gravitation seemed to have no effect. Several commented that their bodies felt so lightweight they almost felt they could fly.

Brigham Young said,

> The brightness and glory of the next apartment [world] is inexpressible. It is not encumbered so that when we advance in years we have to be stubbing along and be careful lest we fall down. We see our youth, even, frequently stubbing their toes and falling down. But yonder, how different! They move with ease and like lightning. If we went to visit Jerusalem, or this, that, or the other place—and I presume we will be permitted if we desire, there we are, looking at its streets. . . . If we wish to understand how they are living here on these western islands, or in China, we are there; in fact, we are like the light of the morning.[12]

It appears that our power to travel will only be limited by ourselves and the will of God. Brigham Young said, "As quickly as the spirit is unlocked from this house of clay it is free to travel with lightning speed to any planet, or fixed star, to the uttermost part of the earth, or to the depths of the sea, according to the will of Him who dictates."[13]

Archie J. Graham reported; "I felt differently than I had ever felt before. My body was light in weight. I could move about with the least exertion as though in thought. . . . I felt as though I could fly I was so light."[14]

While traveling through space, Walter P. Monson said, "The law of gravitation had no hold upon me."[15]

Harriet Salvina Beal Millet

Harriet was fifteen years old in 1851 when her mother, Clarissa, died after giving birth to twins, who also died the next day. A year later, Harriet's father crossed the plains with his nine children. On the way, Harriet's two-year-old brother, William Francis, died. After settling in Utah, Harriet fell ill. During her near-death experience, Harriet said she was able to move by simply floating through the air.

"Lying in my bed I was overjoyed to see my Mother there by me. I was not afraid and began telling Mother of all that had happened since Mother's death. I told her that Father had hired one of the women to make over Mother's dresses for us girls.

"Mother answered, 'Yes, I know. And the right sleeve of the black dress she is making for you is not sewed in but is only basted.'"

Harriet told her of the many things that had happened to them, and to each one, her mother replied that she already knew. Harriet then told her mother that she and her sister, Emily, frequently argued. She confessed that one time they had become so angry with one another that they had torn each other's aprons off and threw them in the fire.

Clarissa answered sadly, "Yes, I know and if you and Emily do not stop quarreling you can never come where I am. . . . Remember that."

She then told Harriet to go with her, as she had a lot to tell her.

"I followed her from the room and we then left the place and floated through the air, side by side . . . all the time Mother was talking to me, telling me things she wanted me to tell Father and I was afraid, for Father was a strict man.

"She said, 'Tell Father, if he does not stop using tobacco he can never come where I am. Tell him if he doesn't stop talking about the authorities of the Church and especially President Brigham Young, he will lose his testimony of the Gospel and will apostatize; therefore he will never come where I am, worlds without end. . . .'

"I replied, 'But Mother, I would not dare tell Father that, and if I did he would not believe me.'

"She answered me by saying, 'You tell him every word I tell you and he will believe every word you say.'

"After some time we came to a beautiful building, very large but as yet unfinished. We seemed to light very easily on the porch that was around the large building as far as I could see. All the time Mother was telling me things to tell Father. She told me of temple work she wanted done and wanted Father to do it with me to help him. She said there were sealings to be done. . . .

"Mother then led me into a most beautiful bed-room which was very large. The workmanship of the room was beautiful as was also the rest of the building what I could see, although it was as yet unfinished. The floors of the bed-room were as of gold and on the floor playing was our little darling William Francis that we buried on the plains. And with him were the twins. . . . William Francis was trying to pound golden nails into the floor. Lovely beds were in the room. . . .

"Mother then said to me, 'I must go to the kitchen for awhile and I want you to sit right there in that chair until I return.'

"I said, 'Mother what is that loud noise I hear, the roosters crowing, people yelling at one another. Such confusion. What is it?'

"She said that was hell and was a long way off but at times one could hear the confusion. She then said, 'Don't you leave this room and I want you to sit right in that chair until I return.' I asked her if she had to work in the kitchen and she said, 'Of course, I take my turn just like the rest.'

"I sat still watching the children at play. . . . I could hear mother tripping down the long hall. I so wanted to see if she tripped along like she did in life. She never seemed to touch the ground. So I got up and went to the door and looked out and sure enough, there was Mother tripping along just like she used to do.

"One of the strange things about this visit for me was that although I loved little William Francis so much and was glad to see the little twins, they did not seem to notice me at all. . . . It made me want to be with Mother and I made no attempt to speak to anyone else.

"Watching mother down the hall I turned to go back to my chair but in turning I saw the door across the hall just a short distance from where I was standing, and it was open. Well I just had to see what was in that room, so I crossed very carefully and looked in.

"All my life I have been of a very inquisitive nature. Many times it has caused me much trouble. But this time I was very pleasantly surprised to see the Prophet Joseph Smith walking up and down a very long room and he had his hands clasped behind him, his head bowed as though in thought. At long tables on either side of the room and down the center also, many men sat writing as fast as they could and once in awhile the Prophet would stop and speak to one of the men and they would answer then go right on writing as fast as before. Among these men were the Prophet's brother Hyrum, also other men I had known well.

"Fearing Mother would find me across the hall I hurried back to the room and sat in the chair, and had only a short time to wait until Mother returned. Another characteristic of myself was, I could never keep anything secret or be underhanded. It must have been in my face for anyone could find me out in no time and so there was no use in trying to hide anything.

"So as usual as soon as Mother came the first thing I did was to say, 'Mother, what is the Prophet Joseph and Brother Hyrum and all the rest of the men doing in there?'. . . .

"She answered, 'Preparing genealogy so that the work can be done on earth for those who have died without having the privilege of hearing the gospel themselves.' Then for the third time she told me everything over again and told me to tell Father and he would believe every word I said to him. . . . She came to the porch with me and I started out. . . .

"The next I knew it was morning and I was in bed. I was still very sick but better than the night before and so I dressed and went outside and sat in the chimney corner as the fire from within had melted the snow from the rocks of the chimney and armed them. All were asleep within the room. The snow was all over the ground. I crouched down, frightened and crying, for I did not dare tell Father what I had to tell him.

"My sisters found me there and Emily ran to tell Father. Emily told Father I was outside in the chimney corner crying and had said I had something to tell him but I was afraid to do so. Father came out and asked me what was the matter and I told him I had something to tell him but I was afraid he would not believe me.

"Father said, 'I will believe every word you say.'

"This startled me for those were the very words Mother said to me when I told her I was afraid to tell Father. So, sobbing, I told Father my story, frightened all the time.

"When I had finished my story, Father said, 'I believe every word you say.'

"From that time forth I never heard my Father speak ill of anyone in authority and he would not allow anyone to do so in his hearing or in his house. . . .

"We went in the house to look at the dress Mother had called my attention to the night before and sure enough the right sleeve was only basted in.

"Father took me to the Endowment House and had me tell my dream to those in authority there and they said to him, 'Brother Beal, your daughter has had a vision from above and has been permitted this visitation for the good of you and your family. . . .

"My Father let me help him do the temple work Mother had told me to tell Father to do. Emily and I stopped quarreling. I being the oldest girl, Father put me in charge of the house, but I never forgot my Mother's warning about quarreling. Again peace was in our home."[16]

Resurrected Personages

One of the crowning glories of gospel doctrine is the Atonement of Jesus Christ, which makes resurrection possible and offers hope for eternal life. "I am the resurrection and the life: he that believeth in me, though he were dead, yet shall he live" (John 11:25).

To comprehend the term *resurrection*, one must understand that death is the separation of the body and the spirit. Resurrection, then, is the reuniting of an immortal body and the eternal spirit into a perfect being. All people—just and unjust—will be resurrected. "For as in Adam all die, even so in Christ shall all be made alive" (1 Corinthians 15:22).

In the spirit world, there are two types of beings: those who are resurrected personages, having bodies of flesh and bones, and the spirits of just men made perfect who have not yet been resurrected (Doctrine and Covenants 129:1, 3). Resurrected beings have bodies of flesh and bones—tangible bodies that occupy space and look like our mortal bodies.

Most people will not be resurrected until after the final judgment, but when we are, our spirit will be reunited to a perfect physical body. President Joseph F. Smith said, "Deformity will be removed; defects will be eliminated, and men and women shall attain to that perfection of their spirits, to the perfection that God designed in the beginning."[17]

Amulek testified that our physical bodies will be perfected when he told Zeezrom, "The spirit and the body shall be reunited again in its perfect form; both limb and joint shall be restored to its proper frame . . . both the wicked and the righteous; and even there shall not so much as a hair of their heads be lost; but every thing shall be restored to its perfect frame" (Alma 11:43–44).

Peter E. Johnson

Elder Peter E. Johnson was serving a mission in Mississippi in August 1898 when he fell ill with the dreaded chills and fever of malaria. He was quarantined, but as arrangements were being made to send him home, Peter had a near-death experience. In the spirit world, Peter was told that if he stayed, he would be asked to preach the gospel under the direction of the Prophet Joseph Smith. Curious, Peter wondered if Joseph was now a resurrected being. In response, Peter was told that the Prophet Joseph had his body, as did his brother Hyrum. In writing his experience, Peter spoke first about his illness.

"I became so low that the President sent his counselor and two elders to see me in relation to being released and sent home. The yellow fever quarantine came on; I was not able to leave; and then I had the following experience:

"I was lying on a bed, burning up with the fever, and the elders who had been sent to ascertain my condition were very much alarmed. They stepped out of the room and held whispered consultations. They were so far away that under ordinary conditions I could not have heard what was said; but in some manner my hearing was made so keen that I heard their conversation as well as if they had been at my bedside. They said it was impossible to think of my recovering, and that I never would go home unless I went home in a box. They therefore decided they might just as well notify the President and make necessary arrangements.

"The following day I asked to be removed into the hall, where it was cooler. I was lying on a pallet [bed]. There was an attendant with me; the others having gone to Sunday school, which was being held about one hundred yards away. Soon after they had left I was, apparently, in a dying condition, and my attendant became so fearful of my appearance and condition that he left me. I desired a drink of water but of course was unable to get it myself. I became discouraged, and wondered why it was that I was sent to Mississippi and whether it was simply to die in the field. I felt that I would prefer death, rather than live and endure the fever and the agony through which I was passing.

"I thought of my people at home and of the conditions then surrounding me, and decided that I might just as well pass from this life. Just as I reached that conclusion this thought came to me: 'You will not die unless you choose death.'

"This was a new thought, and I hesitated to consider the question; then I made the choice that I would rather die. Soon after that, my spirit left the body; just how I cannot tell. But I perceived myself standing some four or five feet in the air, and saw my body lying on the bed. I felt perfectly natural, but as this was a new condition I began to make observations. I turned my head, shrugged my shoulders, felt with my hands, and realized that it was I myself. I also knew that my body was lying, lifeless, on the bed. While I was in a new environment, it did not seem strange, for I realized everything that was going on, and perceived that I was the same in the spirit as I had been in the body.

"While contemplating this new condition, something attracted my attention, and on turning around I beheld a personage, who said: 'You did not know that I was here.'

"I replied: 'No, but I see you are. Who are you?'

"'I am your guardian angel; I have been following you constantly while on earth.'

"I asked: 'What will you do now?'

"He replied: 'I am to report your presence, and you will remain here until I return.' He informed me, on returning, that we should wait there, as my sister desired to see me, but was busy just at that time. Presently she came. She was glad to see me and asked if I was offended because she kept me waiting. She explained that she was doing some work that she wished to finish.

"Just before my eldest sister died she asked me to enter into this agreement: That if she died first, she was to watch over me, protect me from those who might seek my downfall, and that she would be the first to meet me after death. If I happen to die first, she wished me to do the same for her. We made this agreement, and this was the reason that my sister was the first one of my relatives to meet me.

"After she arrived, my mother and other sisters and friends came to see me, and we discussed various topics, as we would do here on meeting friends. After we had spent some little time in conversation, the guide came to me with a message, that I was wanted by some of the apostles who had lived on the earth in this dispensation. As soon as I came into their presence, I was asked if I desired to remain there. This seemed strange, for it had never occurred to me that we would have any choice there in the spirit world, as to whether we should remain or return to the earth life.

"I was asked if I felt satisfied with conditions there. I informed them that I was, and had no desire to return to the fever and misery from which I had been suffering while in the body. After some little conversation this question was repeated, with the same answer.

"Then I asked: 'If I remain, what will I be asked to do?' I was informed that I would preach the Gospel to the spirits there, as I had been preaching it to the people here, and that I would do so under the immediate direction of the Prophet Joseph. This remark brought to my mind a question which has been much discussed here, as to whether or not the Prophet Joseph Smith is now a resurrected being. While I did not ask the question, they read it in my mind, and immediately said: 'You wish to know whether the prophet has his body or not?'

"I replied: 'Yes, I would like to know.' I was told that the Prophet Joseph Smith has his body, as also his brother Hyrum, and that as soon as I could do more with my body than I could do without it, my body would be resurrected. I was again asked if I still desired to remain. This bothered me considerably, for I had already expressed myself as being satisfied. I then inquired why it was that I was asked so often if I was satisfied and if I desired to remain.

"I was then informed that my progenitors had made a request that if I chose I might be granted the privilege of returning, to again take up my mortal body, in order that I might gather my father's genealogy and do the necessary work in the temple for my ancestors. As I was still undecided, one of the apostles said: 'We will now show you what will take place if you remain here in the spirit world; after which you can decide.'

"When we returned to the place where my body was lying, I was informed with emphasis that my first duty would be to watch the body until after it had been disposed of, as that was necessary knowledge for me to have in the resurrection. I then saw the elders send a message to President Rich, at Chattanooga, and in due time all preparations were made for the shipment of my body to Utah. One thing seemed peculiar to me, that I was able to read the telegram as it ran along the wires, as easily as I could read the pages of a book. I could see President Rich, when he received the telegram in Chattanooga. He walked the floor, wringing his hands, with the thought in his mind: 'How can I send a message to his father?'

"The message was finally sent, and I could follow it on the wire. I saw the station and the telegraph operator at Price, Utah. I heard the instrument click as the message was received, and saw the operator write out the message and send it by phone from Price to Huntington. I also saw clearly the Huntington office and the man who received the message. I could see clearly and distinctly the people on the street. I did not have to hear what was said, for I was able to read their thoughts from their countenances. The message was delivered to my aunt who went out with others to find my father.

"In due time he received the message. He did not seem to be overcome by the news, but began to make preparations to meet the body. I then saw my father at the railroad station in Price, waiting for my body to arrive. Apparently, he was unaffected; but when he heard the whistle of the train which was carrying my body, he went behind the depot and cried as if his heart would break. While I had been accompanying the body en route, I was still able to see what was going on at home. The distance, apparently, did not affect my vision. As the train approached the station I went to my father's side, and, seeing his great anguish, I informed my companion that I would return. He expressed his approval of my decision and said he was pleased with the choice I had made.

"By some spiritual power, all these things had been shown to me as they would occur if I did not return to the body. Immediately upon making this choice or decision, my companion said: 'Good. Your progenitors will be pleased with your decision.' I asked the question why, and I was told that it was their desire that I should return to the body, hunt up my father's genealogies and do their work in the temple. In all this time no one had offered to touch me or to shake my hand.

"Just how my spirit entered the body I cannot tell, but I saw the apostle place his hands upon the head of my prostrate body, and almost instantly I realized that the change had come and I was again in the body. The first thing that I knew, I felt a warm life-giving spot on the crown of my head, which passed through my entire body, going out to the tips of my fingers and toes. I then heard distinctly the same words that had been pronounced by Elder Grant when I was set apart for my mission: 'Go in peace, and return in safety.'

"After entering the body I saw no more of the messengers who had been accompanying me, but I had a vivid recollection of all that had taken place. The local elder, who had been left to attend me, but who became frightened at my condition and went away, had not yet returned; but I later learned that he had gone to Sunday School and, at the close of the exercises, he notified them of my death.

"The Saints, elders, and friends were gathered outside the paling, or fence, discussing matters, and trying to decide just what to do. I was still very thirsty, and arose to get a drink, but found that the water was warm. I got off the pallet, or bed, on which I had been lying, carried the bucket of water to the edge of the gallery, threw out the warm water, went to the well which was seventy-five feet deep, drew a fresh bucket of water and quenched my thirst. The Saints, elders and friends, who were out at the fence, were observing all this, but they feared to come near me. Finally, Brother Morton, at whose home I was stopping, came through the gate, up the walk toward me, but before reaching me he turned icy cold and stopped.

"I went up to him, took his hand, and invited them all to come in and handle me, telling them that a spirit did not have flesh and bones, as they saw me have. Brother Morton looked at me, felt of me, turned me around, then went and looked at the bed on which I had been lying during my sickness.

"He then came back and handled me again and said: 'I never was so scared in my life, for I thought you were a spirit.'

"I told him that I was not now a spirit, but a real, tangible person.

"'How could you carry that bucket of water,' he said, 'throw it out and draw another, when for over a month you have had to be waited upon, and finally we all thought you were dead?'

"I told him I had been made well, and had come back to stay with them. This gave me a new idea; for, while in the spirit land, I did not shake hands with anyone, neither did anyone offer to shake hands with me; but now I felt a desire to shake hands with everyone.

"I thought this over, and the spirit whispered to me: 'The spirits of the righteous do not deceive; hence, no shaking of hands.' This cleared up that mystery; for the spirits of the righteous do not deceive, although they are as pleased to meet their friends in the spirit world as they are here.

"President Thos. [sic] R. Condie of the conference was notified of my recovery, and wrote me a letter in which he stated: 'Ever since I consented to your release I have had no peace on that matter. Before you came to our conference the Superintendent of the Sunday school of the conference was to be released. We had no one to take his place and so I called a special fast of three days, with the elders, and prayed to the Lord to send someone who could take the place of Elder Dye, who was soon to return home. In answer to our fasting and prayer you were sent to this conference. We become weak in the faith and asked for your release, even after we had fasted and prayed and asked the Lord to send someone here for that purpose. If agreeable, Brother Johnson, while you have been released honorably and can go home, if you choose, we would like very much for you to remain here and accept the call for which the Lord has sent you into this conference. . . .'

"While I was in the spirit world I observed that the people there were busy, and that they were perfectly organized for the work they were doing. It seemed to me a continuation of the work we are doing here,—something like going from one stake to another. There was nothing there that seemed particularly strange to me; everything being natural. I have often been asked how long I was in the spirit world. The last I remember of hearing was the singing when Sunday school commenced, and when I got up and draw the water, Sunday school had closed. The local elder did not notify them until just as they were closing. Sunday schools were held one and one-half hours." [18]

Notes:

1. Joseph F. Smith and assistants, comp., *Teachings of the Prophet Joseph Smith*, fifth printing (Salt Lake City: *Deseret News* Press, 1946), 207.

2. Brigham Young, *Journal of Discourses* (June 22, 1856), 3:371–372.

3. Orson Pratt, *Journal of Discourses* (October 15, 1854), 2:244.

4. Erastus Snow, *Journal of Discourses* (March 3, 1878), 19:273.

5. Orson Pratt, "Figure and Magnitude of Spirits," *The Seer*, March 1853, 34–35. (Also see 1 Samuel 28:12–14).

6. Elisabeth Kubler-Ross, *On Life After Death* (Berkeley, CA: Celestial Arts, 1991), 13.

7. Orson Pratt, *Journal of Discourses* (December 15, 1872), 15:242–43.

8. Heber C. Kimball, *Journal of Discourses* (June 29, 1856), 4:2.

9. Lorenzo Dow Young, *Fragments of Experience; Sixth Book of the Faith-Promoting Series*, (Salt Lake City: Juvenile Instructor Office, 1882), 27–30.

10. Charles John Lambert, as told to J. N., "A Curious Experience in Drowning," *Juvenile Instructor* 21, (December 1,1886), 359.

11. "How One Feels When Dying," *Juvenile Instructor* 27, (September 15, 1892), 570–72.

12. Brigham Young, *Journal of Discourses* (September 16, 1871), 4:231.

13. Brigham Young, *Journal of Discourses* (December 10, 1868), 13:77.

14. Archie J. Graham, "A Visit Beyond the Veil" [n. d.] (courtesy of the Church History Library, The Church of Jesus Christ of Latter-day Saints).

15. Jeremiah Stokes, *Modern Miracles* (Salt Lake City: Bookcraft, 1945), 78–81.

16. Cora Anna Beal Peterson, [biographical sketch of William Beal, n. d.], (courtesy of the Church History Library, The Church of Jesus Christ of Latter-day Saints).

17. Joseph F. Smith, "Our Indestructible, Immortal Identity," *Improvement Era* 12 (June 1902), 592.

18. Peter E. Johnson, "A Testimony," *The Relief Society Magazine* 7 (1920), 450–55.

"There is no such thing as immaterial matter. All spirit is matter, but it is more fine or pure, and can only be discerned by purer eyes; We cannot see it; but when our bodies are purified we shall see that it is all matter." (Doctrine and Covenants 131:7–8)

Chapter Six

Mental Characteristics of the Spirit Body

Mental Faculties Are Quickened

The apostle Orson Pratt explained that it is the physical body that hinders the vast capabilities of the spirit. "It is this tabernacle, in its present condition, that prevents us from a more enlarged understanding. . . .There is a faculty mentioned in the word of God, which we are not in possession of here, but we shall possess it hereafter; . . . Here . . . we can hardly think of two things at a time; if we do, our minds are distracted, and we cannot think distinctly. . . . I believe we shall be freed, in the next world, in a great measure, from these narrow, contracted methods of thinking." He adds that our mental processes will be quickened. "Instead of thinking in one channel, and following up one certain course of reasoning to find a certain truth, knowledge will rush in from all quarters; it will come in like the light which flows from the sun, penetrating every part, informing the spirit, and giving understanding concerning ten thousand things at the same time; and the mind will be capable of receiving and retaining all."[1]

Dr. Kubler-Ross also stated that the spirit's intellect will be expanded after death. "As soon as your soul leaves the body, you will immediately realize that you can perceive everything happening at the place of dying, be it in a hospital room, at the site of an accident or wherever you left your body."[2] Some people who had near-death experiences confirmed this by saying their mental faculties were brighter in the spirit world than when they had been in mortality.

Victoria Clayton McCune

During her near-death experience, Victoria Clayton McCune discovered that she possessed a new, keen intelligence. She also discovered that the fear she'd always had of dying and leaving her young children when they still needed her was unwarranted.

Victoria began relating her experience by talking about this fear. "I dreaded death for their sakes. It became a haunting fear with me that I should die while they were small and needed a mother's care. While this fear was strong upon me, the tragic and sudden death of a brother brought a very serious illness upon myself, resulting in hemorrhage peculiar to my sex. It came on without warning and the results were so rapid that within six hours my physician said life was extinct. Though the doctor remained constantly with me he did not seem to sense my danger. Nothing he did seemed to give relief.

"The trouble began about ten o'clock in the morning and continued incessantly until three p.m. I had no pain but great weakness resulted. Things in the room became indistinct to my vision. I could scarcely see the flowers on the paper which covered the wall. Towards three o' clock in the afternoon I was in a very serious condition. The doctor's face was grave. A great foreboding seemed to possess me, of what I did not know but all seemed to portend evil and I was afraid, dreadfully afraid.

"Then a feeling of nausea came over me and my feet and legs were cold and I began to chill. The doctor was intensely alarmed and tried to avert that chill because it but aggravated the other trouble. Then it seemed like a cold metal sheet was enveloping me, first upon my feet and coming slowly over my limbs and body. It was icy cold and heavy. When it had covered my chest, I threw up my hands and ceased to breathe.

"It seemed then that the thing which gave me power to think, see, hear and understand was still alive, but not of the body, but seemed to be at the side of and just above the bed. It senses no fear as before, neither was it sensible to cold or any inconvenience, but was agreeable and comfortable, and could see the body upon the bed to all appearances dead. A sense of ownership seemed there. I knew that body belonged to me. It was very pale, the eyes were closed and the features set in death—even the hands so used to toil seemed claimed by death.

"I saw the doctor standing at the foot of the bed as if stunned. My husband came in just then and asked, 'How is she?' and the doctor said, 'dead.'

"My husband said, 'What?'

"And the doctor said, "Mr.—your wife is dead.'

"The peculiar thing about it to me since is the ability which my intelligence had to tell what they were doing. It could read their thoughts and know every process of artificial restoration which they used, though in life I had never seen any thing of the kind. In life I never possessed the keen intelligence which I had then. Words were not necessary. Thinking was enough. I seemed to understand even when they only thought, though I heard, saw and understood also when they spoke.

"My husband walked over to the doctor, his face white as that of the body upon the bed, and said, 'For heaven's sake, man, don't stand there like that. Do something and do it now.' Then he walked over to the bed, lifted the body in his arms and kissed it, calling it by name.

"The tears were running down his face as he said, 'Dearest, don't give up. Fight. You know what will power has done before. Use it now. Fight and we shall win yet. For the children's sake don't give up.'

"He knew if any thing would awaken me that plea for the children would. He again kissed the lips and laid the body down. Then he again urged the doctor to do something and 'do it quickly.' Then he ran to summon another doctor—a specialist.

"In the mean time the part of me by the bed watched the doctor, who seemed to be getting control of himself and preparing something to inject into the body. Then I looked at the body. A feeling of peace was upon me, it seemed that a greater happiness was mine free from that body. An intense desire came over me to forever be free . . . and I wanted to remain as I was free from the cares and worries which I knew would continue if I entered that body and my whole intelligence longed for the new experience and sweet release and even since the skill of two physicians triumphed I have felt the same sensation and an intense longing to again feel that undefinable [sic] anticipation, a sweet reward, especially when things go wrong.

"These sensations were suddenly called to a conclusion by the doctor who began to work. When he injected some thing into my body, it seemed that I knew no more. All was a blank. When I again knew anything two doctors were bending over me, my relatives had all been summoned expecting the end. Great sighs seemed to come from the body, slow, irregular, but the lungs had begun to function. The pulse was very feeble but the heart was beating. The artificial restoratives had done their work and I was alive.

"Life is strange. We build fears out of nothing. The fear that brought the greatest shadow to my life was leaving my children. Yet in this experience the cries of my children had no effect upon me. All four of them were in an adjoining room. Their convulsive sobs could be heard plainly.

"I heard the eldest girls say 'Mother is dead,' and sob as if her heart would break while others tried to comfort her, yet it moved me not at all. Their sobs did not dampen that strong desire to remain free from the body and realize that strange, sweet anticipation.

"There are those who do not believe in spirits, but what was that great intelligence if not my spirit. It was my spirit that heard, saw, felt, knew when my body was pronounced dead by two doctors. The mysterious shade of death was upon the body but the thing we call death is misnamed and misunderstood. It opened to me a clearer vision and I know there are better joys awaiting and I shall never fear death again.

"Though the sensation just before breathing ceased was very unpleasant, yet after that, all was release and anticipation of some thing greater and better yet to be.

"The strongest tie of earth is that between a mother and her little children. Yet their sobs had no effect upon me, which convinces me that we do not take the cares of this life with us. The experience was worth the price, though it took a year for complete restoration. It taught me that death does not end our existence but opens a new era in our lives, where a bigger adventure may be ours. To that doctor I am still a curiosity for he said I was as dead as a person could be."[3]

Able to Read Thoughts

Occasionally, people reported that while they were in the spirit world, the spirits there were able to discern their thoughts. Others, while describing this same phenomena, said that while it was commonplace to converse without speaking, they could also communicate verbally.

While Peter E. Johnson was in the spirit world, he did not have to communicate verbally. Speaking about the spirits who were with him, Peter said, "While I did not ask the question, they read it in my mind."[4]

Mary Hyde Woolf

In 1914, Mary Hyde Woolf traveled to Salt Lake City, Utah, from Canada to have surgery at the Latter-day Saints Hospital. After the operation, Mary was in critical condition and then rallied unexpectedly. One day later, without warning, Mary's spirit left her body. When Mary went to the spirit world, she discovered that her guide could read her thoughts. Zina Y. Card relates Mary's experience.

"One night, after a sweet sleep, she [Mary] became very restless and knew that her spirit was passing away from her body. After the spirit withdrew from the body, she saw a Guide by her side who said to her, 'Come with me.'

"They traveled into far places and . . . through the semi-twilight she could see groups of people, many of whom bowed to her as she passed with glad reverence and respect. All were busy, but the people in the different places would bow to her as she passed by. Sometimes they were so engaged that they took no notice of her. As they rose upward from sphere to sphere, which grew lighter and more beautiful, they passed glorious mansions and spacious grounds, at length they came to a broad road bordered with trees.

"Through the openings of these trees came groups of people mostly women who stood respectfully some distance away with hands folded on their breasts as they bowed to her in passing. After she and her guide drew near what seemed to be the end of the road a larger group of women awaited her coming. These hastened toward her and met her with open arms and smiling faces. In an ecstasy of joy they held her as their friend and Savior. She felt she could never depart from them so great was her happiness.

"The guide read her thoughts and said, 'You must return for a brief season.'

"Reluctantly, she turned away to obey the messenger. As they took their departure she turned to the guide and asked him, who were the beings that met her and did not approach her?

"He replied, 'These are your kindred still in prison.'

"'And who were those,' she asked, 'who came close to me and bowed reverently but still did not offer to speak or reach out their hands?'

"'These are they,' he replied, 'whose names you have recorded in your book and they rejoice at the prospects of their deliverance but their work in the temple has not been done.'

"'And those who embraced me?' she asked.

"'They are those,' he replied, 'who have received at your hands all of the ordinances in the house of the Lord, and you beheld their joy.'

"She returned to the earth with her guide and took up her work for a little season, but passed away a little while ago, and one wonders if her kindred will remember the work which she charged them to do."[5]

Memory Is Restored

On earth, people often have trouble remembering names, places, dates, and a host of other things. Orson Pratt stated that part of this is due to limitations placed on us by our physical bodies. He said, "We read or learn a thing by observation yesterday, and to-day or tomorrow it is gone . . . common information and knowledge are constantly coming into our minds, and as constantly being forgotten . . . because of the imperfection of the tabernacle in which the spirit dwells."[6]

Speaking in general conference, Elder Glenn L. Pace said, "We have come to the earth with a veil of forgetfulness."[7] Everyone born on earth has had a veil put over their mind that takes away their memory of the premortal world, and this veil is taken off after we leave mortality. At that time, we will have perfect recall and remember everything regarding not only this life but also our life in the premortal world. All our memories of the past will be intact.

We will also remember taking part in that grand council when Heavenly Father laid out the plan of salvation, remember agreeing to it, and recall accepting Jesus Christ as our Savior and Redeemer. George Q. Cannon said, "Memory will be quickened to a wonderful extent. Every deed that we have done will be brought to our recollection. Every acquaintance made will be remembered. There will be no scenes or incidents in our lives that will be forgotten by us in the world to come."[8]

When Thomas S. Thomas returned from his visit to the spirit world, he said, "The fond memories of the past returned in all their splendor. After the reunion of all your faculties are intact, memories of your past are all made plain . . ."[9]

Herman Stulz

When World War I ended, Herman Stulz and four hundred other German prisoners of war were taken from concentration camps and sent back to Germany. With food scarce and sickness rampant, there was an outbreak of an unnamed disease, which turned into an epidemic that eventually killed more than 750,000 people. Herman contracted this disease and underwent five major operations. During his fourth surgery, Herman had his second near-death experience. When he was ten, he had a near-death experience when he fell over a waterfall. When Herman had his second experience, he remembered promising to accept the gospel when he came to earth and to do temple work for his ancestors. Herman writes:

"One night I noticed my abdomen puffed up like a balloon. The belly had been punctured already by three operations and I had great difficulties in breathing and I felt that my intestines would explode. I rang the emergency bell and the nurse came, looked at my condition and disappeared, but she came back with Doctor Nestle, and Doctor Bernstein."

The doctors told Herman that if they were going to save him, it was essential to operate at once. When the doctor asked for his consent, Herman replied, "I was in such terrible pain and told him he could cut my throat with my permission and get me out of my tortures I had endured for many weeks."

Herman was rushed to the operating room at midnight. "When my almost lifeless body was brought back and laid upon the bed where I had endured those torturing pains; and the ether from the anesthetic had gradually evaporated I began to recognize the nurse who was calling me by my name, and frantically shaking me, evidently to awaken me from the stupor after such an operation, I finally became fully conscious where I was and what had happened, I began to breathe normal again, when I saw a strange man who was clothed in a robe, standing at the foot of my bed. He greeted me with a smile and invited me to come along with him.

"Instantly my spirit came out of my tortured body and stood before my bed; and I saw the nurse taking a pair of steel tweezers, reach down my throat and pull up my tongue which had slipped into the windpipe, causing the infamous death rattle.

"I was released from all pains and the soreness and burning sensation one feels after such an abdominal operation. I felt like I was never sick at all and filled with a glow of health I never felt before in my life. But I wanted to make sure whether this was only a dream and to make sure I began to move my legs, my arms and fingers, I grabbed my hair, pulled my ears and began to walk around the room, and everything functioned like it did in mortality.

"I thought, this must be death feared by all men, it was a feeling of ecstasy I felt so light like a newborn man all my limbs worked with ease almost to perfection. I was really dead, like after I drowned under that waterfall in the black forest.

"The strange personage watched me doing all the capers and he smiled. I was a dual personality, on the bed lay my dead body of flesh and bones absolutely lifeless and dead, but my spirit in the same image stood before that bed; freed from all pains filled with new life and ambition and new hope to live. Now I understood that it is the spirit that gives the power to the mortal body of flesh, blood and bones to function and keep alive. . . . So this is what is called death, but I was more full of life than I was heretofore in my mortal life, why should we fear death, I was freed from all suffering, death was a welcome visitor, to get my spirit out of that sick body lying on the bed which was only a torture chamber for me and I had no more use for it and I wanted to get away from it."

Herman testified that what the LDS faith taught as doctrine was true. Wryly, he said, "These foolish Mormons are right, I had read in the book [sic] of Mormon what takes place after the spirit departs from the mortal body in the 40th chapter of Alma. I had taught it in Sunday School for many years and during my sickness in the Mannheimer Hospital I had actually prayed to our heavenly Father to let me go to Paradise, and now I was on my way; how wonderful.

"Here I stood in the sickroom of some 40 patients with this person-age confronting me, but I did not know where to find Paradise; I looked at him again and he asked me again to follow him, which I did. I cannot remember how long it took us, for it seems that the time element did not matter. I gladly followed him with great expectancy and filled with ambi-tion of what would happen next. My prayers were answered and I was on my way to Paradise or the world of departed spirits.

"I am everlastingly grateful to my Maker who gave me life and also let me pass through this adventure we call death. And it proved to me my former experience I had when I drowned in the Klembach [river] in that waterfall. I know without a shadow of doubt that there is life after death. Also there exists a perfect organization with rules and laws no spirit can ignore as was further shown to me. What a comfort to anyone who has a righteous cause to mourn, who loved one dearly to know we shall meet again.

"We should rejoice that we are born to live, to die, and live again. We should thank God for this intelligence. It gives us joy and peace that the world cannot give, neither can the world take it away from us. God has revealed this to us through his prophets in the restored gospel of Jesus Christ.

"Therefore I know it to be true for I passed through this transition twice and was declared to be dead. I have nothing to fear or be sad over, nothing to make me sorrowful. I had to bury my father, my darling wife and my two sons who have preceded me, for I know as sure as I live

I shall again hold them in my arms and rejoice with them together in the Lord. . . . It is the divinely inspired 'Book of Mormon' that gives us enlightenment about the great mystery of life about this most important mystery, the world knows very little about, through which all mortals have to pass through; so let us be prepared when the call comes we can meet the challenge with joy."

Herman then continues his narrative. "We approached a beautiful ornamental gate, similar in design to the Salt Lake Temple gate, but my guardian angel ushered me into a waiting room, like the room before one enters the holy temple, and asked me to wait until he had reported my arrival and obtained permission for me to enter Paradise.

"I entered a well lighted room, it had windows all around, small square windows. The light came from the outside it seemed. The only furniture was a long table but no chair to sit down. While I stood there the first thought that entered my mind was I wonder what kind of employment I will have and what kind of work it would be?

"I thought, inasmuch as I had the trade of a scientific Instrument maker I would possibly engage in the manufacture of 'Urim and Thummims, or perhaps Liahona, or Movie Cameras which I had done while I lived on this earth? But I was greatly disappointed when I heard a strong and penetrating voice, like it came from a present day loud speaker. This happened in the year 1921 and we had not yet invented the loud speaker, or radio, nor Television.

"It said, 'Go back and finish the work that you promised you would do before your spirit left here.'

"My memory of my pre-mortal life came back to me and I remembered that I had given the promise that after I was born into this mother earth, when I hear the everlasting gospel preached I would accept it and do the Temple work for my kin. And to my disappointment I was ordered to return to my lifeless body, which was very painful. . . ."

His doctors were surprised when Herman returned to his body. "Before leaving that hospital the two Doctors who saw me die told me that they never thought I would leave the hospital alive, also the nurse who damaged my tongue by trying to prolong my breathing. My recovery from that sickness was very slow and I was permitted to go to beautiful Switzerland to obtain food to nourish my weak body.

"It was there in the city of Berne where I had the privilege to be the interpreter to then Apostle George Albert Smith during his sermon to the people. . . . While interpreting his speech I stood on his right side. When he quoted a passage of the Bible from the King James translation I was not able to translate it into German.

"As I stood there with some 300 pairs of piercing eyes staring at me, a voice whispered the passage in the most perfect German into my ear, and I repeated it word for word, and the sermon proceeded to the end without any delay. I did not see anyone but I sure heard it and needed it as the chosen interpreter.

"I marveled at this miracle as such it was to me and I knew that George Albert Smith was a true servant of God, an Apostle and a special witness. Later, he married me [to my wife] in the Salt Lake Temple; also he became the prophet of God's Kingdom. In the city of Frankfurt I served as interpreter to Apostle Orson F. Whitney." In March of 1922, Herman received permission to immigrate to the United States and arrived in Salt Lake City in April. [10]

Notes:

1. Orson Pratt, *Journal of Discourses* (October 15, 1854), 2:246.
2. Elisabeth Kubler-Ross, *On Life After Death* (Berkeley, CA: Celestial Arts, 1991), 11.
3. Victoria Clayton McCune, *Collection 1891–1967*, Folder 8 (courtesy of the Church History Library, The Church of Jesus Christ of Latter-day Saints), 1–8.
4. Peter E. Johnson, "A Testimony," *The Relief Society Magazine* 7 (1920), 450–55.
5. Zina Y. Card, "Manifestation to Mrs. Mary Hyde Woolf," *The Relief Society Magazine* 8 (August 1921), 492–93.
6. Orson Pratt, *Journal of Discourses* (October 15, 1854), 2:239.
7. Glenn L. Pace, "Do You Know?" *Ensign*, May 2007, 79.
8. Jerreld L. Newquist, comp., *Gospel Truth, Discourses and Writings of President George Q. Cannon*, vol. 1 (Salt Lake City: Zion's Book Store, 1957), 77.
9. Thomas S. Thomas, *A Glimpse of the Future* (courtesy of the Church History Library, The Church of Jesus Christ of Latter-day Saints).
10. Herman Stulz, *Autobiography* [ca.1971] (courtesy of the Church History Library, The Church of Jesus Christ of Latter-day Saints).

> "But as it is written, Eye hath not seen, nor ear heard, neither have entered into the heart of man, the things which God hath prepared for them that love him." (1 Corinthians 2:9)

Chapter Seven

General Appearance of the Spirit World

*M*any near-death experiences mention the unparalleled beauty and exquisite splendor of paradise. The environment is somewhat similar to our physical world and everyone who sees it expresses a desire to stay. People state that even the lowest sphere was more beautiful and glorious than anything on earth. Brigham Young confirmed this when he spoke of the spirit world. "I have been near enough to understand eternity so that I have had to exercise a great deal more faith to desire to live than I ever exercised in my whole life to live. The brightness and glory of the next apartment is inexpressible."[1]

Martha Jane Boice told her loved ones about the loveliness of the spirit world when she was allowed to return briefly to mortality. "She remained the two hours allotted to her, bearing testimony to the Gospel and praising God for the beauties which she had seen in the Spirit world."[2]

When eleven-year old Mitchell Dalton returned back to his body, he was unhappy at having to leave the spirit world. "He opened his eyes and said, 'Oh, Papa and Mama, why did you call me back. I have been to such a beautiful place.'"[3]

Mary Hales said, "We started walking together through a place that was much like earth, but much more beautiful."[4]

79

Jennie Schnakenberg

Jennie Schnakenberg was born March 5, 1896, in Woodbury Co., Iowa, and had a near-death experience as she was giving birth. After arriving in the spirit world, Jennie passed through a strange and terrible darkness before coming to a world so beautiful she began to dance and sing praises to God.

"Twice within a year, while being very ill, I heard a voice speak to me. The first was while going through premature childbirth. I was put to sleep through anesthetic. I prayed to the Lord for to spare my life, for my little children, and I did cry unto the Lord with all my soul.

"After I had gone to sleep, I wandered in to a very beautiful place. While I stood and marveled at the beauty of place [sic], I noticed quite far from where I stood was a great gulf. . . ."

Jennie then saw an angel. "He was very beautiful, his feet did not touch the ground, and he descend[ed] backwards, and I followed until I had reached the edge of the gulf. Soon the angel passed away from my sight. Soon I heard a voice say, 'It is my will that you live,'" and he explained that she had not yet finished her mission.

Upset at this, Jennie said, "I cried, 'Oh God, let me understand what is not finished yet. Let me stay here a little while longer and let me suffer more if it need be, but let me understand what is not yet finished.'

"And the Vision of Christ on the cross came up before me close at my feet and stood high over my head. . . . While I was festing [sic] my eyes upon my blessed savior the voice said, 'As Christ paid the price so must you.'

"After the vision faded away from my sight, great darkness came upon me. I was wrapped in, and smothered with darkness. I lifted my hands to find an opening But was in vain. . . . At last I cried with despair, 'Oh God, must it be thus Through all eternity?'

"And the voice said, 'Are you willing?'

"And I said, 'Yes,' and the terrible darkness was lifted, and I beheld beauty everywhere. Green, green hills, birds, flowers and every thing I beheld, smiled on me. But when I felt an unseen presces [presence], who also smiled on me, I grew so happy that I began to dance, cry and sing, and while I was dancing and praising God, I cried, 'Oh God, I thank you for giving me this opportunity, I, a sinful, ignorant woman heard the voice of God.'

"'Oh God I thank you.' And while I was rejoyicing [sic], I began to float upward, and soon I heard the Doctors and nurse about me. And I heard a weak wail from my new born baby daughter. As God is my witness this is true. Amen."[5]

J. R. Williams

J. R. Williams was a bishop in the Blackfoot, Idaho, stake at the time of his near-death experience. J. R. told his experience to Elder J. Berkeley Larsen, who related it during a speech given at Brigham Young University. J. R.'s experience follows.

"A number of years ago I became very ill. The doctor told me that if I had anything to put in order I'd better do it, if I had anything to say to my family I'd better say it, because I had only a few hours to live.

"Of course it set off a lot of weeping in our family, but I did call my family together and apparently died. At last the doctor pronounced me dead. My spirit left my body; a messenger came and took me by the hand, and we went on a long journey.

"Finally we approached a beautiful place where there was a lovely little chapel, and out by the chapel was a grove. In this grove were twelve men kneeling. As we approached them one of the men arose and came toward us.

"When he came to me he said, 'Brother Williams, your prayers and the prayers of your family and brethren have come up to us; and we have just been discussing them, and we've decided to let you go back for a season.'

"My messenger took me by the hand and brought me back. When I came to, I was told that my body had lain out on the porch with a cloth over my face three days and nights."[6]

Trees, Flowers, Rivers, and Lakes

A number of people said the spirit world has a wide variety of flowers and vegetation, with gardens, meadows, and woodlands far superior to and lovelier than anything on earth. Many visitors report seeing gardens that were so magnificent that they could not compare with anything on earth, as well as beautiful shrubs, trees, flowers, lakes, and rivers. Some mention the striking colors of the flowers, many of which have unusual and glorious colors not seen on earth and some flowers that contain all the colors of the rainbow.

Jedediah M. Grant declared, "I have seen good gardens on this earth, but I never saw any to compare with those that were there. I saw flowers of numerous kinds and some with from fifty to a hundred different colored flowers growing upon one stalk."[7]

Archie Graham wrote extensively about plant and animal life. When he and his escort first entered paradise, Archie said; "To the right and left of us were beautiful fields of waving grain. . . . [then] we came to a beautiful forest with lawn grass covering the ground; with trees and shrubs of many sizes and kinds and of many different colorings, from a pale green to the deep green of the spruce and pine, several shades of silver and gold, reds, browns, blues and lavenders fading into a light pink. All were planted to harmonize with each other in size, color and kind, and by looking in a certain direction, one could see all colors of the rainbow.

"As we were passing through the forest, I thought nothing could compare to its beauty—it was glorious. . . . we came into the most exquisite flower gardens, wherein were small shrubs and all manner of plant life, beyond human understanding. . . . There were flowers of all sizes and colors, placed in different artistic designs . . . The flowers varied in size from no larger than a pinhead to those as large as the crown in a man's hat. The shrubs were gorgeous, all sizes and colors—many of them were pruned and kept trimmed to represent birds and animals."[8]

George Albert Smith

While serving as an apostle, George Albert Smith began suffering from ill health. Finally, he went to St. George, Utah, hoping that a change of climate would be beneficial to his health. Unfortunately, his condition worsened. During his near-death experience, George Albert Smith, who later became the prophet of the Church in 1945, saw a lake, grass, and a forest.

President Smith wrote, "I became so weak as to be scarcely able to move. It was a slow and exhausting effort for me even to turn over in bed. One day, under these conditions, I lost consciousness of my surroundings and thought I had passed to the Other Side. I found myself standing with my back to a large and beautiful lake, facing a great forest of trees. . . .

"I began to explore, and soon I found a trail through the woods which seemed to have been used very little, and which was almost obscured by grass. I followed this trail, and after I had walked for some time and had traveled a considerable distance through the forest, I saw a man coming towards me. I became aware that he was a very large man, and I hurried my steps to reach him, because I recognized him as my grandfather. . . . I remember how happy I was to see him coming. I had been given his name and had always been proud of it. When Grandfather came within a few feet of me, he stopped. His stopping was an invitation for me to stop.

"Then . . . he looked at me very earnestly and said: 'I would like to know what you have done with my name.'

"Everything I had ever done passed before me as though it were a flying picture on a screen—everything I had done. Quickly the vivid retrospect came down to the very time I was standing there. My whole life had passed before me. I smiled and looked at my grandfather and said: 'I have never done anything with your name of which you need be ashamed.'

"He stepped forward and took me in his arms, and as he did so, I became conscious again of my earthly surroundings. My pillow was as wet as though water had been poured on it—wet with tears of gratitude that I could answer unashamed.

"I have thought of this many times, and . . . I want to say to . . . all the world: Honor your fathers and your mothers. Honor the names that you bear, because some day you will have the privilege and the obligation of reporting to them and to your Father in heaven what you have done with their name."[9]

Animals, Fish, and Birds

LDS doctrine confirms that every animal contains a living spirit and possesses intelligence. Orson Pratt said, "The spirits of fish, birds, beasts, insects, and of man, are in the image and likeness of their natural bodies of flesh." He adds, "The whole [of] animal creation . . . are eternal and will exist forever, capable of joy and happiness."[10]

Some people who visited the spirit world reported seeing animals, birds, and fish. A few saw animals that were pets, and they also saw wildlife. One man commented that the souls of animals are more intelligent than people suppose.

"Animals do have spirits and that through the redemption made by our Savior they will come forth in the resurrection, to enjoy the blessing of immortal life."[11]

While in the spirit world, Archie Graham saw birds and pet animals. Later, he said, "There were many birds and animals such as deer, sheep, and antelope."[12]

William Wallace Raymond

William W. Raymond was living in Plain City, Utah, when he fell ill. His health continued to deteriorate until, on August 12, 1881, William had a near-death experience. When he returned to mortality, William was temporarily healed and gave a clear and concise description of the next world. Among other things, he mentioned that the parks abounded with all kinds of animals. One of his friends, John Carver, wrote down William's experience as it was told to him.

"I have been to the spirit world and have seen many things, and many people that I knew, I saw Joseph and Hyrum Smith and Brigham Young and members of the twelve that are dead. I also saw my parents, children and many of our neighbors. One sister from this place with whom I was personally acquainted and had charge of a number of children similar to a Sunday school, but did not see any that did not belong to the Church, but I was informed that they could come and visit friends, but could not stay. They live in beautiful cities with fine streets, paved as it were with fine copper but it was rock.

"The inhabitants numerous and are natural so much that I could distinguish them by their nationality They all look young and beautiful and dress quite natural and the material looks like white silk.

"They eat and drink, and hold meetings like we do, and I ate with them. They all live in perfect order such as I have never seen on earth and move quite natural from place to place. I did not see any one riding but was informed there were conveyances whenever they desire to go a distance.

"Brother Joseph Smith presides over the Latter-day Saints. Brother Hyrum Smith has the marks of the bullets and will wear them as Jesus to show that he fell as a martyr for the truth. Outside of the cities are lovely parks, abounding with all kind of animals.

"The people are acquainted with our doings on earth, but they said it was not wisdom for us to know much about them. Society is graded something as we are. But money and this world's plenty does not constitute the grade. But it is governed by ability and position in the holy priesthood. Should any doubt my veracity let them ask any question and I will answer to the satisfaction of any reasonable person, and with all I have seen I am still mortal and subject to imperfections and I did not have the promise of getting well or that I should tarry long on earth.

"After reciting the vision he arose from his bed dressed himself, declared himself a well man, put on his hat, walked out into the orchard, came back, went to bed and died a week later."[13]

Notes:

1. Brigham Young, *Journal of Discourses* (September 16, 1871), 14:231.
2. Samantha T. Brimhall, *Boice Family History* [ca. 1930] (courtesy of the Church History Library, The Church of Jesus Christ of Latter-day Saints).
3. Joseph Heinerman, *Spirit World Manifestations* (Salt Lake City: Magazine Printing and Publishing, 1978), 117–118.
4. Lee Nelson, *Beyond the Veil*, vol. 3, (Springville, Utah: Cedar Fort, Inc., 1990), 95–100. Used with permission.
5. Jennie Schnakenberg, letter, Mar. 25, 1993 (courtesy of the Church History Library, The Church of Jesus Christ of Latter-day Saints).
6. J. Berkeley Larsen, "The Reality of Life After Death," *BYU Speeches of the Year*, October 6, 1953, 3-4.
7. Heber C. Kimball, *Journal of Discourses* (December 4, 1856), 4:135–37.
8. Archie J. Graham, "A Visit Beyond the Veil" [n. d.].
9. George Albert Smith, "Your Good Name," *The Improvement Era* (March 1947), 139.
10. Orson Pratt, "Figure and Magnitude of Spirits," *The Seer*, (March 1853), 33–34.
11. Joseph Fielding Smith, *Answers to Gospel Questions*, vol. 2, (Salt Lake City: Deseret Book, 1976), 48.
12. Archie J. Graham, "A Visit Beyond the Veil" [n. d.].
13. William Wallace Raymond, "Vision 1881 Aug 12" (courtesy of the Church History Library, The Church of Jesus Christ of Latter-day Saints).

"And then shall it come to pass, that the spirits of those who are righteous are received into a state of happiness, which is called paradise, a state of rest, a state of peace, where they shall rest from all their troubles and from all care, and sorrow." (Alma 40:12)

Chapter Eight

Cities in the Spirit World

ased on those who have had near-death experiences, the spirit world appears to be divided into different cities and communities, much like earth. Although people will be assigned to certain spheres, we will apparently be free to choose which community we want to live in within that sphere. That decision will be based on individual tastes, our own level of development, and family relationships. When speaking of people in the spirit world, Brigham Young said, "Yes brethren, they are there together, and if they associate together, and collect together in clans and in societies as they do here, it is their privilege."[1]

The apostle Orson Pratt taught the same principle. "Beings that enter the spirit world find there classes and distinctions, and every variety of sentiment and feeling; there is just as much variety in the spirit world as in this."[2]

As people learn and progress, it appears that at some point in time, they will be allowed to move into higher areas. Brigham Young said, "And when we have passed into the sphere where Joseph is, there is still another department, and then another, and another, and so on to an eternal progression in exaltation and eternal lives."[3]

Lorenzo Dow Young saw various cities during his visit to the spirit world. "In a moment we were at the gate of a beautiful city. A porter opened it and we passed in. The city was grand and beautiful beyond anything that I can describe."[4]

Heroine Randall was with her guide when "they came without the walls of a beautiful city, one that shone in splendor. The gates were open, and she looked within and saw its glory, and the throng of bright ones, a company of life, activity, and intelligence."[5]

Thomas S. Thomas said; "Cities are most beautiful with all colors and shadings."[6]

Tom Gibson

After Tom Gibson had a heart attack, the doctor prescribed a medicine to be taken every three hours. One night, his wife, Margaret, slept through and missed giving Tom his medicine at three a.m. When she woke, Margaret discovered Tom had suffered a second heart attack. It was at this time that Tom had his near-death experience. When he came to, Tom was too weak to talk, but the next day, he had regained enough of his strength to tell his wife what had happened. One of the things he mentioned was seeing a city of light.

"Margaret, I must tell you of the experience I had—I feel well enough now." Tom then told her that he vaguely remembered Margaret waking him in the night and giving him his medicine. He went on. "The next thing I was aware of was . . . a funny sensation. It's hard to describe. Anyway, I found myself standing in a room and looking at a bed. Wondering why I was standing there, I noticed two people in the bed. I was about to take a closer look at them, when . . . when I saw another person standing in the room. Looking closer at the person standing near me, I saw, to my surprise that it was Daniel. You remember . . . the Indian boy I told you about who was my friend when we were kids. He died when we were about eighteen, and it devastated me at the time."

Margaret replied, "Yes, I remember you talking about Daniel. But where were you Tom, and who were the two people in bed?

"I was still in the bedroom with you. Daniel let me know that I had left my body, and the two people in the bed were you and I—except my spirit was standing looking at my body. . . . It was the strangest feeling— to know that I was outside my body and still alive. We only stayed in the room a short while, and I knew somehow that I was to follow him.

"Next, I found myself walking with Daniel in a completely different sphere. It was beautiful beyond description, and we were walking on a path. As we walked along, I saw—

"'What do you mean a different sphere, Tom,' Margaret asked, 'and how did you get there?'

"The world was different from this one. I'm not sure how I got there, it was . . . I don't know, I think I just followed Daniel. It seems as if all I had to do was think of where I wanted to be, and I could go there at any speed I wished. I somehow knew that I was to stay with Daniel, and I sort of wished myself to stay with him; suddenly we arrived in this new world.

"Anyway, as we walked along the path, I noticed a profusion of flowers and trees. They were of a wider variety and . . . had many more colors than on earth. Or maybe it was that I could see more colors than on earth—I'm not sure. We continued walking for a while and I noticed someone on the path ahead of us.

"'But I thought you said you wished yourself wherever you wanted to go,' interrupted Margaret, 'why were you walking?'

"I knew I must stay with Daniel, and he was now walking, so I walked too. As we got closer to the individual on the path, I could see and feel that he was a magnificent person, and it was . . . I felt overwhelmed as I looked at him. He was bathed in light. Daniel asked if I knew who that was, and I answered, yes; it was Jesus Christ.

"When we got close to the Savior, I felt a tremendous love emanating from him. It's hard to describe, but you could feel it all around him, and I felt a similar enormous love for him. I fell at his feet—not because I thought about it, but because I couldn't stand. Having this overpowering urge to fall at his feet and worship him. I stayed there for some moments with this wonderful feeling, when I saw . . ."

Tom stopped for a few moments. Puzzled, Margaret said, "Go on Tom, why did you stop?"

"I was trying to remember what happened next. I think . . . yes, all of a sudden, I became conscious of my past life being reviewed for me. It seemed to occur in a short period, and I felt the Savior's love during the entire process. That love was . . . well, it was everywhere. And, it was as if we could communicate with each other without speaking. After a period the Savior reached down and touched my shoulder, and I knew I should stand. As I did, he left.

"Daniel next led me to a city. It was a city of light—similar to cities on earth in that there were buildings and paths; but the buildings and paths appeared to be built of materials which we consider precious on earth. They looked like . . . that is they resembled marble, and gold, and silver, and other bright materials, only they were different—the buildings and streets seemed to have a sheen, or to glow. The entire scene was one of indescribable beauty.

"How did you feel as you followed Daniel? Was it like a dream or a vision?

"No, Margaret. It was as real as . . . as anything I have seen or felt on earth—even more so. There was another feeling that went with it. On earth there always seems to be something . . . you know how things bother you here. There is always some problem troubling you. Either its health, or money, or people, or war, or something. That was missing there. I felt completely at peace, as if there were no problems which were of concern. It wasn't that there were no challenges—its just that everything seemed to be under control. It was such a wonderful feeling that I never wanted to lose it.

"Daniel then brought me to a building and we met another person. Daniel introduced him as Peter, the Apostle. It seems surprising to me now that I saw both Jesus and Peter, but at the time it didn't seem unusual. Anyway, Peter asked me some questions about the Church on earth. . . . I got the idea that I should bear my testimony, so I did. I also told him how I came to join the Church.

"Entering the building with Peter and Daniel, I found myself in a large auditorium. Seated in the auditorium were many men listening to instruction from someone at the pulpit. They were dressed in clothes that looked . . . they were similar to what we wear in the temple."

"Do you mean the people were wearing temple clothes?"

"Yes, I think so."

"Peter then brought me to the front, and I was asked to describe conditions on the earth as I saw them . . . no, that's not it. I was supposed to tell them about what I knew of the Church. I'm not sure why, because I imagine they already knew more than I did, but since I was asked I responded. Responding briefly, I told them what I knew of the Church, and I explained that most members were trying hard to live the gospel. I bore my testimony of the importance of the work.

"'I got the impression, while I was in the auditorium, that there are many people involved in a lot of work expanding the gospel in their sphere . . . or world, or whatever it is, as well as ours. The two spheres are linked, though, and people there are interested in the progress in ours. . . . At least I think that's why they asked me to explain what I knew of the church. Although, it could have been a test for me—I'm not sure of the real reasons."

"How long did you stay in the auditorium, Tom?"

"I don't know. Time doesn't seem to work the same as here. I don't think it was long, though. When we left, Peter and Daniel took me along a path. For some reason, about this time, I could see you in our bedroom crying. I was concerned, and I expressed this concern to Peter.

"He told me not to worry, that everything would be all right. He said that I was to return to you.

"In a way, I wanted to return to you, and in a way I didn't. Seeing you grieving made me feel bad, and I wanted to relieve you, but I didn't want to leave the tremendous feeling of love and peace that was . . . well, as I said, it was everywhere, and I didn't want to lose it. I knew by then, though, that I must return, and that I would still feel sick when I came back.

"Was that the end of your experience?"

"Yes. The next thing I knew, I was looking at you and I felt terribly weak."[7]

Buildings

Many people who visit the spirit world mention seeing homes, chapels, schools, temples, and other buildings that ranged from small and simple to large and ornate. Most of the time, buildings are described as having magnificent exteriors and interiors, with richness and grandeur that defy description. Some commented on the impressive workmanship of the buildings.

Before His death, Jesus said, "In my Father's house are many mansions . . . I go to prepare a place for you" (John 14:2). It may be that when we go to the spirit world, we will receive a home commensurate with how valiant we were in mortality. "For they shall be judged according to their works, and every man shall receive according to his own works, his own dominion, in the mansions which are prepared" (Doctrine and Covenants 76:111).

Archie Graham described many of the buildings he saw. "Wonderful chapels and public boweries and comfortable seats and beautiful pulpits were to be seen here, being used as places for preaching the Gospel and other subjects of importance. . . The business houses were large and well constructed, close together and of an average height of six or eight stories." Later he said, "I was gazing upon some of the most beautiful homes or palaces—for no castle of any earthly king could surpass them in beauty.

The houses were all large and quite uniform in size and structure, some of stone and some of other materials."[8]

When May Neville went to the spirit world and met her recently departed brother, he told her that their grandparents had met him when he arrived. May related that he said, "They [his grandparents] had a beautiful home, and were preparing a beautiful home for his mother and her family."[9]

Harriet Salvina Beal Millet saw an unfinished building. "After some time we came to a beautiful building, very large but as yet unfinished."[10]

Mary Hales

While in the spirit world, Mary Hales saw homes of various sizes. Wondering at this, she asked her departed brother why some were so large, while others were so small. Her brother said, "That was all the material they sent up."

The beginning of Mary's story goes back to a Friday night in May of 1925. The hour was late as Mary Hales and three others drove south on Highway 89. Mary had just completed her first year of teaching in Idaho and was anxious to get home, especially because her fiancé, Vic Frandsen, was in charge of a Gold and Green Ball the next night. Mary's cousin, Lynn, was driving, and they had just passed Draper, a small town south of Salt Lake City, when Mary saw a car coming from the opposite direction swerving all over the road. Suddenly, the car cut across the road and hit their car, striking the side where Mary was sitting.

No one was seriously injured except for Mary. Her hip had been ripped from its socket, she had a crushed pelvis, and her tongue had been bitten off. During the next five years, Mary would have pieces of glass work their way to the surface, coming out of her ear, leg, and other parts of her body. The driver—a drunk, thirty-seven-year-old man—was not seriously injured.

When her family was contacted, they were relieved that Mary had survived, especially in light of the fact that they were still grieving over the loss of Mary's brother, Howard, who had died seven years earlier during World War I.

Mary was hospitalized, but the doctors were unsure what to do about her crushed pelvis. Dr. Baldwin told Mary she would not be able to have a normal married life or bear children. In that day and age, traction was in its experimental stage, but the doctors decided to try it. They placed Mary on a plank bed and started applying weights to her legs. As they did, the pain steadily increased.

Mary says, "The next thing I remember I was on top of a tall hill at the edge of a huge amphitheater filled with rows and rows of soldiers in uniform. They were listening to a speech by a man who was standing down in front of them.

"I don't remember leaving my body, passing through a tunnel or anything like that. Like Paul said in the New Testament, I don't know if I was in or out of my body. All I know is that as clearly as I remember anything in my life, I was standing at the top of that amphitheater looking at all those soldiers.

"I recognized the man speaking to them. It was my brother, Howard, who had been lost in action. He indicated that he recognized me too by smiling at me, but he continued his speech until he was finished. After he delivered his sermon, he walked up to see me.

"'What are you doing here?' he asked.

"'I don't know,' was my honest reply.

"'It isn't your time yet,' he said. We visited for a few minutes, then he said, 'You haven't seen your little sister.'

"He was referring to a sister who had been born several years before me, but had died of pneumonia when nine months old.

"'Would you like to see her?' he asked. I said I would.

"We started walking together through a place that was much like earth, but much more beautiful. It was a garden setting with many beautiful flowers of many colors and many green plants.

"When we reached my sister, to my surprise, she still looked like a baby, but she seemed much more intelligent that a normal baby her size would be. She was with other children in a little clearing in a pine forest. The children were sitting on logs while women instructed them.

"To my amazement I recognized the teachers. They were women I had known who had died. There was my mother's sister-in-law, Elenor Brockbank, who died at age 20, a Sister Prior who used to live in our neighborhood, one of Mother's cousins, and another sister-in-law named Zoe Brockbank.

"The children were seated on sawed-off logs while the older women taught them. The children seemed happy, and the forest setting for their school was one of the most beautiful places I have ever seen.

"'You might as well look around as long as you are here,' my brother said, as we continued our walk through this beautiful place. We saw many beautiful homes. He pointed out one as the one Joseph Smith lived in. I was surprised to see that while many of the homes were spacious, others were very small. Some were barely larger than a small kitchen, or large bathroom. I couldn't imagine why anyone would want to live in a house so small. I asked my brother about this.

"'That was all the material they sent up,' was his strange reply.

"'What do you mean?' I asked.

"'That was all the good works they sent up,' he replied, meaning that the size of house one gets in paradise or heaven is determined by the quantity and quality of the good deeds performed. I thought that was very interesting.

"Finally Howard said, 'Don't you think it's time you went back?'

"It was after that that I heard the doctors telling my parents that they thought they could save my life, but that I would never walk again and wouldn't be able to have children. Two or three weeks later my great uncle, Heber Jex came in to see me. He asked if I wanted a blessing. I had already received a blessing from my father and brother, but didn't see where another could do any harm. I told him I would like that very much.

"He laid his hands on my head and promised me that because of my faith, and the love I had for my Heavenly Father, I would walk without a limp.

"Within an hour of the blessing a feeling like being stuck with pins came into my little toes. Within three days that feeling went all the way to my hips. I knew then I would walk again, and soon I was. I had a limp for about a year, but have never limped since that time.

"The marriage to Vic was postponed. The doctor said we shouldn't marry for three years, so we waited. In the meantime I had to go through some very painful treatments to get my body as nearly back to normal as possible.

"Before our marriage, the doctor said I should not attempt to have children, but if I insisted on trying, I should have them three years apart, and not have any more than three. And that's exactly what we did.

"Our first child was a son. We named him Glen. Three years and three months later we had Lee, then three years and ten months later we had Ann. After that I had to stop.

"While I was in the hospital after the accident, I told my parents about my experience with Howard, and how he had been preaching the gospel to all those soldiers. After that they felt much better about losing him, knowing he had a mission on the other side of the veil."[11]

Notes:

1. Brigham Young, *Journal of Discourses* (December 3, 1854), 2:137.
2. Orson Pratt, *Journal of Discourses* (June 30, 1855), 2:370.
3. Brigham Young, *Journal of Discourses* (June 22, 1856), 3:375.
4. Lorenzo Dow Young, *Fragments of Experience: Sixth Book of the Faith-Promoting Series* (Salt Lake City: Juvenile Instructor Office, 1882), 27–30.
5. Alvin Knisley, comp., *Infallible Proofs, A Collection of Spiritual Communications and Remarkable Experiences* (courtesy of the Church History Library, The Church of Jesus Christ of Latter-day Saints).
6. Thomas S. Thomas, *A Glimpse of the Future* (courtesy of the Church History Library, The Church of Jesus Christ of Latter-day Saints).
7. Arvin S. Gibson, *Margaret and Marshall Gibson, An Old-fashioned Love Story: A Biography* (courtesy of the Church History Library, The Church of Jesus Christ of Latter-day Saints).
8. Archie J. Graham, "A Visit Beyond the Veil" [n. d.].
9. *Manifestations About Temple Work* [ca. 1918] (courtesy of the Church History Library, The Church of Jesus Christ of Latter-day Saints).
10. Cora Anna Beal Peterson, Biographical sketch of William Beal [n. d.] (courtesy of the Church History Library, The Church of Jesus Christ of Latter-day Saints).
11. Lee Nelson, *Beyond the Veil*, vol. 3 (Springville, Utah: Cedar Fort, Inc., 1990), 95–100. Used with permission.

> "But behold, the resurrection of Christ redeemeth mankind, yea, even all mankind, and bringeth them back into the presence of the Lord."
> (Helaman 14:17)

Chapter Nine

Other Aspects of the Spirit World

Time Is Different

Another feature of the spirit world—time and space—is reported to be different from how we know it here on earth. Near-death experiences suggest that time works differently in the spirit world. Neal A. Maxwell said that time is a temporary earth fixture. "When the veil which now encloses us is no more, time will also be no more (see Doctrine and Covenants 84:100). Even now, time is clearly not our natural dimension. . . . If time were natural to us, why is it that we have so many clocks and wear wristwatches?"[1]

When Joseph Smith asked the Lord about time, he received this answer. "In answer to the question—Is not the reckoning of God's time, angel's time, prophet's time and man's time, according to the planet on which they reside? I answer, Yes. . . . But they [angels] reside in the presence of God, on a globe like a sea of glass and fire, where all things for their glory are manifest, past, present, and future, and are continually before the Lord" (Doctrine and Covenants 130:4–5, 7).

In talking about how long it took his guide to take him to the spirit world, Herman Stulz said, "I cannot remember how long it took us, for it seems that the time element did not matter."[2]

When Tom Gibson's wife asked him how long he spent telling people in the spirit world about current conditions on earth, Tom replied, "I don't know. Time doesn't seem to work the same as here."[3]

Thomas S. Thomas

Thomas S. Thomas wrote extensively about his near-death experience and in it mentions that time there is different from how we experience it on earth.

In 1869, Thomas moved to a little town called St. John, four miles west of Malad City, Idaho. It was an isolated area, and even in 1888, it had no railroads, telegraph, or telephones. In January 1894, Thomas caught a severe chill while tending sheep and had to be helped to his two-room house by a farm hand. His wife, Emma, put Thomas to bed, but in a few hours, his bones started to ache and he developed a high fever. Emma called for a doctor, but nothing could be done, and after seven days, Thomas died. He writes:

"The doctor, finding no pulse or heart beats, gave me up for dead. . . . At this time my wife, mother and the nurse came in, bringing the babies. My wife hugged and kissed me and then helped the children in doing so. . . ."

While the family was making arrangements to send telegrams to his sister and uncle, Thomas watched. "I saw my brother write the telegrams and I read them. I was able to follow the messages along the wires, because my position was such that my mode of travel was much faster than the movement of telegraphy. . . . In my position, as before stated, my mode of travel was as fast as thought. I was able to see all my friends who came to see me, and those who came as far as the gate, who went away without coming inside. . . . I could discern the actual feeling of everybody with whom I came in contact, and I found in this experience that I possessed some real friends, and I must say I had no enemies.

"I could see that wealth, because it was improperly used, was turning to an implement of power of plunder on the masses, and that we should try to educate the next generation on their obligation toward mankind. Then their surplus could be used for its intended purpose and by the proper use they have manifested of the elements that have been placed here for them they would create a lasting benefit for the uplift of all good. If you were aware of the relation this life bears to our future life, you would soon have a different world to live in.

"I saw the many unhappy things which greed causes in this life. By shunning greed, we could avoid a great part of our troubles. As I wanted to thoroughly understand things about my own country and the elements surrounding it, my curiosity led me to travel about it. I visited the national capital and moved from one place to another about the United States. . . . Liberty was mine to go where I chose about this earth. . . .

"I visited the great oceans and explored their wonders. . . . I passed on around the globe, viewing all things and conditions. . . . I could see the thousands of different forms of worship. . . .

"My soul grieved for those I was leaving behind on earth, and I was very anxious about my mortal body, hoping that it might not be disturbed or molested, so I could reoccupy it if I found such a condition possible. . . .

"The soul's movements through space was natural, but differed very much from any earthly movements I had heretofore experienced. There is something very exciting and inviting in this, as your actions are quick and your movements as quick as thought in early life. As I was nearing my goal, or place of departure before coming to this earth I became more reconciled. I was commencing to regain some of my past and pre-existing recollections. . . . At last I arrived on the orb or planet where my soul was to reoccupy my eternal body."

When Thomas arrived in the spirit world, he declared, "All mental powers were restored. The fond memories of the past returned in all their splendor. After the reunion of all your faculties are intact, memories of your past are all made plain, your soul is endowed with wisdom and knowledge and filled with everlasting love. . . ."

"Distance is no barrier to transmit thought without instruments, or to travel under your own power. Your vision is magnified there; your future view is plain; desire for knowledge is inexhaustible; you are master of yourself; intelligence is the key to all realms which makes an endless trail to all advancement and is a place of satisfaction and joy to the soul. . . . Time is figured on a different basis than in earthly life.

While in the spirit world, Thomas discovered that he was acquainted with everyone there. "I realized that I met no strangers in the meeting and greeting of the millions of souls there. . . . There were two groups of souls I met there. One group had been to earth and departed before me from there, and the other group was waiting their chance to go to earth. None of either of these were strangers to me; I had always known them. The souls in the group who had been to earth inquired concerning

99

friends they had left there and I told them of all I could. To the other group the narration of my experience on earth was as strange to them as the experience I am relating of in this writing is to you . . . they realized that the only way they could understand earthly things was to experience them.

"The grand greeting you first receive is from your closest of kin—father, mother, brother and sisters—and all that are near and dear to you who passed from earthly life and arrived in the Great Beyond before you. Your nearest and dearest friends and many others come to greet and converse with you. They ask about the conditions of their kin, those whom you were acquainted with on earth, and are anxious to learn of their kin's surroundings and conditions. You will find this a great meeting place of all souls, where information is eagerly sought, concerning earth's conditions, by those who have passed from earthly life and are in this stage of existence. These souls are now busy, in the future existence, working in different habitations. Many are from different spheres. All souls are fully enjoying their positions and surroundings. You read from their cheerful countenances a condition of contentment. This gives you a picture of satisfaction. . . .

"The millions of souls waiting to come to earth cannot comprehend things told them concerning it because they have not experienced anything earthly. They are eagerly waiting to make the earthly trip. This is because they know the trip is in the plan of creation to gain knowledge. It is clear to them that, while they suffer on earth, the soul is immune from any powers of destruction. They are eager to gain this knowledge because they know these things and will benefit themselves thereby. . . . The little babe, that gets life and is called back instantly after life begins, possesses a soul that learns all of the missions or its purpose here just as much as the soul who lives on earth any number of years. . . .

"Time and knowledge is what counts for your advancement. Time is endless and so is the existence of the soul. You can advance just as fast as your efforts are made use of. It is simply up to each individual concerning his advancement . . . what each soul gains is its own.

"In the hereafter there is no color-line draw to the soul. Every human soul is deserving of all he had attainted to before taking this earthly trip. . . . It makes no difference to that soul whether it occupied a mortal body of black or white. . . .

"Rivers were most beautiful . . . they were bedecked with the grandest foliage containing all the colors of the rainbow. The ground was a carpet of green, with bushes here and there . . . there were trees where birds perched and sang their sweet songs . . . there I saw beautiful homes . . . they were most artistic and of different architectural cut than earthly homes. Cities are most beautiful with all colors and shadings . . . the homes were all in connection with each other, while separate entrances to each home was available. . . .

"Music, instrumental and vocal, was beyond the hope of humanity to ever attain to on earth. . . . You will find there is a busy place for the musician. . . .

"There are no activities for destructive purposes, which is one of the major activities on earth. . . . I saw the true condition of man on earth as I traveled about viewing conditions. I could see his littleness. . . . It was here I could see the real condition of humanity on earth, and I am lead [sic] to give a word of advice: Be lenient in your judgment: let mercy guide your soul; we know not our true position, less of the powers that control; so be mild in admonition; learn nature's laws; live for the best that is in you; your reward is a righteous cause. . . .

"Animal life everywhere there has the same purpose in view as man's life. They have to learn by the same experience to know what creation and destruction means. . . . Creation has a purpose and a place for each and every kind before they are created. . . . Animal life holds a place in the great fields of construction. . . . There is not a living creature that has not some part to fill in the great program of universal advancement. Animal souls are indestructible and similar in material to man. . . . Souls of animal life are much more intelligent than man on earth supposes."

While he was in heaven, Thomas said, "There, my visionary powers were more than they are on earth, and my mental faculties were much brighter."

Thomas then declared, "Until man pursues the course of love for his fellowman, he will suffer the folly for his actions. What you sow you reap. . . . So be it, you are not in a true position on earth to render a fair judgment. . . . Man should bestow mercy. . . . The essentials of earthly life are to know right from wrong. . . .

"After viewing these things I became anxious to return to my mortal body, because of the promise I had made to my soul at the time of my departing the mortal life. I had learned by this time that I was privileged to return if I desired. My preparations were completed for the departure. . . .

Upon leaving, there were millions of souls to wish me well on my second earthly trip of existence. I bade them farewell . . . it was only a short time before I came in view of the earth. . . . As I neared the earth I . . . made straightway for my mortal body. . . I found my mortal body in a condition to re-enter.

"I felt that I could regain its use, providing I could receive the help of those that were living. I could realize it would be an impossible task without the assistance of the friends with my body, and at this instant of realization, I made my first effort to make known to them that life existed. Life was noticeable to them through my efforts to move. All the efforts of man were put forth to bring me to life. My soul had again arrived in that state where misery haunts it. . . . I could realize the condition the body was in, and realized it would take some time to show much improvement. This uncertain feeling, in connection with the pain and agony I had to endure, was the greatest suffering my soul ever had and ever will have. By careful nursing I was soon in a condition to speak, but only in a very feeble tone of voice."

When he had regained some of his strength, Thomas told his family about the things he had heard them discuss after he died and about the telegrams they had sent and which had been received by his sister and uncle.

Then, wanting to impart some of the lessons he had learned during his experience, Thomas said, "I can assure you that this life is a mere shadow of your past and future. . . . I feel it is a duty, which has involved itself upon me, to give to the world a clear and concise description of what I have seen. I never made any promises nor was I sent back . . . to deliver this message of good cheer. . . . I have acquired this knowledge by the same method that all knowledge is obtained. I acquired it by actual experience."

In regards to the physical condition of his mortal body, Thomas said, "There was not any change granted to me by my return to earth. I was only privileged to return to earth as I had gone from it. . . . I have acquired knowledge of the past and future existence of mankind. I am the proudest man on earth today, as far as the future is concerned, and I know whether I am going and where you are going to return to for the eternal body."[4]

Music

Many near-death accounts mention music, which seems to play a vital part in the spirit world. Music, whether instrumental or vocal, was said to be more beautiful than any heard on earth. Just as choirs regularly perform at church meetings on earth, it appears they will do the same in the spirit world.

In Joseph F. Smith's vision of the redemption of the dead, he spoke of the spirits in paradise. "Their countenances shone, and the radiance from the presence of the Lord rested upon them, and they sang praises unto his holy name" (Doctrine and Covenants 138:24).

Even on earth, people have heard heavenly choirs during temple dedications. Eliza R. Snow said that during the dedication of the Kirtland Temple, "the singing of heavenly choirs was heard."[5] And at the Manti temple, "a number of the Saints in the body of the hall and some of the brethren in the west stand heard most heavenly voices singing. It sounded to them as angelic, and appeared to be behind and above them."[6]

After his near-death experience, Thomas S. Thomas spoke about the music he had heard in the spirit world. "Music, instrumental and vocal, was beyond the hope of humanity to ever attain to on earth . . . You will find there is a busy place for the musician."[7]

When Loise M. Goates was taken to the spirit world, she said, "I was taken to a place heavenly to me: when I entered the building with two guides the music being lovely."[8]

David P. Kimball

David Patten Kimball, fourth son of President Heber C. Kimball, fell ill while returning home from a trip to Prescott, Arizona, in November of 1881. At this time, he had a series of spiritual experiences. In some of them, David was visited by departed loved ones, including his father, mother, and wife. During the first experience, David heard a heavenly choir and was able to pick out the voice of his departed wife, Julia, who in life had been a wonderful singer. He later had a near-death experience. David wrote about his experiences in the following letter to his sister, Helen:

"On the 4th of November, I took a very severe cold in a snow storm at Prescott, being clad in light clothing, which brought on pneumonia or lung fever. I resorted to Jamaica ginger and pepper tea to obtain relief and keep up my strength till I could reach home and receive proper care. On the 13th I camped in a canyon ten miles west of Prescott, my son Patten being with me. We had a team of eight horses and two wagons. That night I suffered more than death . . . On the 16th we drove to Black's ranch, twenty-eight miles nearer home, and were very comfortably located in Mr. Black's house.

"About 11 p.m., I awoke and to my surprise saw some six or eight men standing around my bed. I had no dread of them but felt that they were my friends. . . . At this point I heard the most beautiful singing I ever listened to in all my life. These were the words, repeated three times by a choir: 'God bless Brother David Kimball.' I at once distinguished among them the voice of my second wife, Julia Merrill, who in life was a good singer. This, of course, astonished me. Just then my father commenced talking to me, the voice seeming to come from a long distance. He commenced by telling me of his associations with President Young, the Prophet Joseph, and others in the spirit world, then inquired about his children, and seemed to regret that his family were so scattered, and said there would be a great reformation in his family inside of two years. He also told me where I should live, also yourself and others, and a great many other things. I conversed freely with father, and my words were repeated three times by as many different persons, exactly as I spoke them, until they reached him, and then his words to me were handed down in a like manner.

"After all this I gave way to doubt, thinking it might be only a dream, and to convince myself that I was awake, I got up and walked out-doors into the open air. I returned and still the spirit of doubt was upon me. To test it further I asked my wife Julia to sing me a verse of one of her old songs. At that, the choir, which had continued singing, stopped and she sang the song through, every word being distinct and beautiful. The name of the song was, 'Does He Ever Think of Me.'

"My eyes were now turned toward the south, and there, as in a large parquette, I beheld hundreds, even thousands, of friends and relatives. I was then given the privilege of asking questions and did so. This lasted for some time, after which the singing commenced again, directly above me. I now wrapped myself in a pair of blankets and went out-doors, determined to see the singers, but could see nothing, though I could hear the voices just the same. I returned to my couch and the singing, which was all communicative and instructive, [and] continued until the day dawned."

When his vision ended the next morning, David felt better physically and decided to continue his journey. That afternoon, David and his son, Patton, stopped to water the horses. Suddenly, a vision opened and for a brief time, David saw a number of fallen spirits but said he was protected by heavenly personages that surrounded him. They traveled on, and that night he and Patton arrived at Wickenburg and rented a room at Peeples Hotel.

Shortly after David went to bed, he said, "A glorious vision burst upon me. There were thousands of the Saints presented to me, many who had died at Nauvoo, in Winter Quarters, on the plains and in Utah. I saw Brother Pugmire and many others whom I did not know were dead. When my mother came to me it was so real and I was so overjoyed that I exclaimed aloud." David told his sister that he had also seen his father. "My father sat in a chair with his legs crossed and his hands clasped together, as we have often seen him."

David continued. "This scene vanished and I was then taken in the vision into a vast building, which was built on the plan of the Order of Zion. I entered through a south door and found myself in a part of the building which was unfinished, though a great many workmen were busy upon it. My guide showed me all through this half of the house, and then took me through the other half, which was finished. The richness, grandeur and beauty of it defied description. There were many apartments in the house, which was very spacious, and they differed in size and the fineness of the workmanship, according to the merits on earth of those who were to occupy them. I felt most at home in the unfinished part, among the workmen. The upper part of the house was filled with Saints, but I could not see them, though some of them conversed with me, my father and mother, Uncle Joseph Young and others.

"My father told me many things, and I received many reproofs for my wrong-doings. Yet he was loth [sic] to have me leave, and seemed to feel very badly when the time came for me to go. He told me I could remain there if I chose to do so, but I plead [sic] with him that I might stay with my family long enough to make them comfortable, to repent of my sins, and more fully prepare myself for the change. Had it not been for this, I never should have returned home, except as a corpse.

"Father finally told me I could remain two years, and to do all the good I could during that time, after which he would come for me; he mentioned four others that he would come for also, though he did not say it would be at the same time."

On November 18, David and his son left Wickenburg. Although he was exhausted and ill, David felt sure he would be able to reach his home alive because of what his father had said. Still, his illness had weakened him and he worried about Patton, who had to care not only for him, but take care of two wagons and eight horses as well. David and his son drove twenty miles that afternoon and that night, camped on the Salt River Desert.

It was there that David faced the greatest trial of his life.

Shortly after dark, there was a commotion among the horses. Since Patton was asleep, David got up to quiet them. Unfortunately, fever and illness left him confused and disoriented, and he wandered out into the desert. When David finally regained his senses, he was hopelessly lost.

"When my mind was restored, and the fever which had raged within me had abated, I found myself lying on a bleak hill-top, lost in the desert, chilled, hungered, thirsty and feeble. I had scarcely any clothing on, was barefooted, and my body full of cactus from head to foot. My hands were a perfect mat of thorns and briars. This, with the knowledge that no one was near me, made me realize the awful condition I was in. I could not walk. . . . The wolves and ravens were hovering around me, anxiously awaiting my death. I had a long stick and I thought I would dig a deep hole and cover myself up the best I could, so the wolves would not devour my body until I could be found by my friends.

"On the night of the 21st, I could see a fire about twenty-five miles to the south, and felt satisfied that it was my friends coming after me. I knew the country where I was; I was about eight miles from houses where I could have got plenty of water and something to eat, but my strength was gone and my feet were so sore I could not stand up. Another long and dreary day passed, but I could see nothing but wolves and ravens and a barren desert covered with cactus, and had about made up my mind that the promise of two years life, made by my father, was not to be realized.

"While in this terrible plight, and when I had just about given up all hope, my father and mother appeared to me and gave me a drink of water and comforted me, telling me I would be found by my friends who were out searching for me, and that I should live two years longer as I had been promised.

"When night came I saw another fire a few hundred yards from me and could see my friends around it, but I was so hoarse I could not make them hear. By this time my body was almost lifeless and I could hardly move, but my mind was in a perfect condition and I could realize everything that happened around me.

"On the morning of the 23rd, at daylight, here they came, about twenty in all, two of my own sons, my nephew William, Bishop E. Pomeroy, John Lewis, John Blackburn, Wiley Jones and others, all friends and relatives from the Mesa, who had tracked me between seventy–five and one hundred miles. I shook hands with them, and they were all overjoyed to see me alive, although in such a pitiable plight. . . . They rolled me up in some blankets and put me on a buck-board and appointed John Lewis to look after me as doctor and nurse. After I had taken a few swallows of water, I was almost frantic for more, but they wisely refused to let me have it except in small doses every half hour.

"I had about seventy-five miles to ride home. We arrived at my place in Jonesville on the afternoon of the 24th of November, when my wife and family took charge of me and I was tenderly and carefully nourished."

David concluded his letter by saying, "Now, Sister Helen, during the last twelve years I have had doubts about the truth of 'Mormonism,' because I did not take a course to keep my testimony alive within me. And the letter I wrote you last August, and I suppose caused you to feel sorrowful, and you prayed for me and God heard your prayers. And our father and mother plead with the Lord in my behalf, to whom I will give the credit of this terrible but useful ordeal though which I have passed and only in part described, an ordeal which but few men have ever been able to endure and relate what I have seen and heard.

"Now, my dear sister, you have a little of your brother David's experience. . . . I know these things were shown to me for my own good, and it was no dream but a glorious and awful reality. . . . I know for myself that 'Mormonism' is true. With God's help, while I live, I shall strive to do good, and I will see you before long and tell you all, as it never will be blotted out of my memory."

Two years later, almost to the very day he had nearly died in the desert, David P. Kimball passed away. His nephew, Charles S. Whitney, was with David at the time of his death and wrote the following to his relatives:

"Uncle David died this morning at half-past six, easily, and apparently without a bit of pain. Shortly before he died, he looked up and called, 'Father, father.' To-day is just two years from the day his father and mother came to him and gave him a drink of water, and told him that his friends would find him and he should live two years longer. He knew that he was going to die, and bade Aunt Caroline good-by day before yesterday."[9]

Clothing

Most people reported seeing white, robe-like clothing in the spirit world, but a few commented on seeing dark clothing. Some said they saw people dressed in clothing of the period from when they died, such as Scottish outfits. Several mentioned seeing soldiers in uniforms, and one even saw an uncle dressed in clothes suitable for fishing. Some people described the clothing as silken, while another remarked that the texture of the fabric varied from person to person.

The scriptures also mention white robes. John the Revelator said, "I saw under the altar the souls of them that were slain for the word of God, and for the testimony which they held: And white robes were given unto every one of them; and it was said unto them, that they should rest yet for a little season" (Revelation 6:9, 11). The Savior appeared to the Nephites in a white robe. "And it came to pass, as they understood they cast their eyes up again towards heaven; and behold, they saw a Man descending out of heaven; and he was clothed in a white robe."(3 Nephi 11:8).

Joseph Smith gave a detailed description of the clothes the angel Moroni wore. "He had on a loose robe of most exquisite whiteness. It was a whiteness beyond anything earthly I had ever seen; nor do I believe that any earthly thing could be made to appear so exceedingly white and brilliant."[10]

After his near-death experience, William W. Raymond said, "The inhabitants [are] numerous and are natural so much that I could distinguish them by their nationality. They all look young and beautiful and dress quite natural and the material looks like white silk."[11]

Harriet Ovard Lee said, "A door opened and I saw another large room, in which were a great number of women and children playing. They were all dressed in white . . ."[12]

Charles Woodbury saw people in both light and dark clothing. "In the light I saw people, men and women dressed in light clothing. Everyone was so happy, but all busy. A voice said to me, 'This is the Celestial Kingdom, the highest degree of glory. . . . When this scene closed, the curtain dropped and what I saw before me was heart rending. I saw men and women, all dressed in dark clothing . . ."[13]

Joseph Eldridge

Joseph Eldridge was born in England on November 14, 1825. Joseph was just eight years old when he had a near-death experience and was taken to the spirit world, where he was dressed in white clothing. His granddaughter, Inez Robinson Preece, relates Joseph's experience.

"When about eight years old I had a serious illness, and [was] thought by my friends to be dead. An old nurse [illegible writing] was there to prepare me for my burial and about two hours after my supposed death discovered that I was still living. I suffered severely in this illness. Amongst other things I had this experience.

"I thought I died. I looked down on my body and could see myself lying there. My father and mother were leaning over each other weeping for me. I seemed to pass thru the case ment [sic] window which was open. . . .

"[An] Angel took me and carried me toward a beautiful white mountain of marble . . . he took me onto a large white rock where was a beautiful font of white marble filled with water clear as Crystal.

"Here the Angel stript me of the clothes I had on which seemed to be the same clothes that I wore before death, then he thoroughly washed me and pronounced blessings on me. Then he clothed me with beautiful white garments and robes. Then I heard very beautiful singing and beautiful music but could not see the musicians. I joined in the singing most heartily.

"Then I seemed to become unconscious and when I regained consciousness I was lying in bed and for a while I felt supremely happy. I was extremely weak. I hid these things in my heart for I was greatly impressed and was always a very religious lad." [14]

Notes:

1. Neal A. Maxwell, "Patience," *Ensign*, October 1980, 31.

2. Herman Stulz, *Autobiography* [ca.1971] (courtesy of the Church History Library, The Church of Jesus Christ of Latter-day Saints).

3. Arvin S. Gibson, *Margaret and Marshall Gibson, An Old-fashioned Love Story: A Biography* (courtesy of the Church History Library, The Church of Jesus Christ of Latter-day Saints).

4. Thomas S. Thomas, *A Glimpse of the Future*, (Courtesy of the Church History Library, The Church of Jesus Christ of Latter-day Saints).

5. N. B. Lundwall, comp., *Temples of the Most High* (Salt Lake City: Bookcraft, 1968), 20.

6. Ibid., 115.

7. Thomas S. Thomas, *A Glimpse of the Future*.

8. Loisie M. Goates, *Faith-promoting Collection 1882–1974*, box 2, folder 13 (courtesy of the Church History Library, The Church of Jesus Christ of Latter-day Saints).

9. Orson F. Whitney, *Helpful Visions, The 14th Book of the Faith-Promoting Series* (Salt Lake City: Juvenile Instructor Office, 1887), 10–11, 13–17, 22.

10. Joseph Smith—History 1:31.

11. William Wallace Raymond, "Vision 1881 Aug 12" (courtesy of the Church History Library, The Church of Jesus Christ of Latter-day Saints).

12. Harriet Ovard Lee, "A remarkable vision 1901" (courtesy of the Church History Library, The Church of Jesus Christ of Latter-day Saints).

13. Charles R. Woodbury, *Faith Promoting Experiences of Patriarch Charles R. Woodbury* (courtesy of the Church History Library, The Church of Jesus Christ of Latter-day Saints).

14. Inez Robinson Preece, *Life Story of Joseph Eldridge* (courtesy of the Church History Library, The Church of Jesus Christ of Latter-day Saints).

> "Sometimes people ask the question . . . 'What do the dead do?'. . . If I should make answer I would say that in my opinion they are doing over there just exactly what we are doing here. . . . The work that we are expected to do here, I am sure we will be expected to do over there, and we will have the means to do it. . . . We lose nothing by dying, except the body which must go back to the earth that gave it." —Apostle Rudger J. Clawson[1]

Chapter Ten

People in the Spirit World Are Active and Busy

*M*any people who have had near-death experiences said people in the spirit world were happy, busy, and engaged in meaningful work and various activities. George Q. Cannon said, "Heaven is a place of activity, a place of progress."[2]

Brigham Young talked about what activities people do in the spirit world. "They walk, converse, and have their meetings; and the spirits of good men like Joseph and the Elders, who have left this Church on earth for a season to operate in another sphere, are rallying all their powers and going from place to place preaching the Gospel, and Joseph is directing them."[3] He added that there is much work being done in the spirit world and that righteous spirits were busy preaching and "preparing the way for us to hasten our work. . . . They are hurrying to get ready by the time we are ready."[4]

The scriptures make it plain that we will continue doing good works in the spirit world, although we will rest from the trials we face in mortality. "If they die let them die unto me; for they shall rest from all their labors here, and shall continue their works" (Doctrine and Covenants 124:86).

Apostle Francis M. Lyman said that in the spirit world "we will never be tired any more. We will not get tired, for we will be in a condition that we can endure and enjoy our work; for we shall be occupied and employed on the other side as we are on this side; we shall have plenty to occupy our attention right along."[5]

Another Apostle, Rudger J. Clawson, said,

> When our loved ones sicken and die they are carefully laid away in their graves . . . we say that they have gone to their rest in the paradise of God, there to await the resurrection. . . . All that is very true. But what does this rest consist of? I rather think it means that they will rest from their worldly anxieties, from pain suffered in this life, from sickness and disease. All those things will pass away. Freed from the anxieties and troubles of mortality I apprehend that they will be very active. I know some people who have claimed that they saw Joseph Smith, the Prophet, in vision or in dreams, but in all such instances he appeared to be exceedingly busy, busier than ever he was in life, in order, apparently, that he might accomplish some important work he had in hand. He seemed to be in a great hurry. I think very likely that is the case with others who die. Whatever activity there is with us in this life, it is due to the spirit, or life, within us—not to the body. It is the spirit that gives action, and the spirit, when it leaves the body, undoubtedly is very much alive.[6]

President Young added that past church leaders and "every other good saint, are just as busy in the spirit world as you and I are here."[7]

When Peter E. Johnson died, he said, "While I was in the spirit world I observed that the people there were busy, and that they were perfectly organized for the work they were doing."[8]

During Mary Woolf's near-death experience, people in the spirit world were so busy they hardly noticed her. The account states; "All were busy, but the people in the different places would bow to her as she passed by. Sometimes they were so engaged that they took no notice of her."[9]

Hannah Adeline Savage

After being bedridden four years, Hannah Adeline Savage finally agreed to undergo surgery, hoping to relieve the pain she had suffered for so long. Her husband stayed home with their younger children while Hannah and her oldest daughter traveled to Utah in the fall of 1900. There, Hannah underwent two serious and lengthy operations. During the first, Hannah had a near-death experience where she saw that people in the spirit world were very busy.

Hannah wrote: "And in September 9, 1901, while passing through my first opperation [sic] the Lord touched the spiritual eyes of my understanding and I beheld many things in the spirit world of which I will here make mention. There was a guide close by my side, and he talked to me and showed me the spirits who were beings real as we are and I saw they were very busy and my guide said to me 'you know what the Prophet Joseph said concerning all spirit' and I replied, 'yes I know, he said all spirit was matter. . . .'"

"And now I behold these spirits are real and they were composed of so fine a matter that our earthely [sic] eyes could not behold them unless the Lord touched the eyes of our understanding. I was extreamly [sic] happy while in the spirit world and asked my guide that I might remain but my guide told me my family and friends were praying for my return and I must come back that I should have to make struggles in order for life to come back in to the body. . . .

"I also saw as it were a sea of glass and an exceeding straight road and a very narrow place where none could pass and only those who had been valiant for the testimony of Jesus, only those who had proven themselves faithfull [sic] through the trials and sacrifices which they were called upon to pass through while in the flesh this was the last I saw while in the spirit at this time."

Hannah continued, "I was exceeding sick for four weeks then got so as I could get up from my bed some, when again my physician decided and friends decided it would be for my best to have a nother [sic] operation which I passed through the 12 of November of the same year. My bowels was opened my right overa [sic] was so decayed that it was also removed with all tumors. I suffered great pain. But was blessed very greately [sic] of the Lord.

"While very sick there was a personage [who] stood by the side of my bed and told me my recovery was made shure [sic]."

This angelic prophecy came to pass. Hannah said, "In 11 days I could sit in my chair a few minutes. Continued to improve and the next year was better than I had been for 16 years."[10]

Earthly Activities in the Spirit World

Many activities will be familiar, as a number of those who visited the spirit world said they observed people reading, studying, attending or teaching classes, gardening, tending children, doing construction work, socializing, and engaging in other activities that are common to mortality. A number of near-death experiences mention other earthly activities, such as preaching, missionary work, and genealogical work.

Since learning and education are keys to progression, adults as well as children will be encouraged in the spirit world to continue to study and gain knowledge. Brigham Young said, "If we are striving with all the powers and faculties God has given us to improve upon our talents, to prepare ourselves to dwell in eternal life, and the grave receives our bodies while we are thus engaged, with what disposition will our spirits enter their next state? They will be still striving to do the things of God, only in a much greater degree—learning, increasing, growing in grace and in the knowledge of the truth."[11]

It will comfort many to know that learning will be easier in the next life. Brigham Young said, "I shall not cease learning while I live, nor when I arrive in the spirit-world; but there I shall learn with greater facility; and when I again receive my body, I shall learn a thousand times more in a thousand times less time; and then I do not mean to cease learning, but shall still continue my researches."[12]

Orson Pratt commented that in the spirit world, we will be able to learn in more and different ways than we can in mortality. "We shall learn many more things there; we need not suppose our five senses connect us with all the things of heaven, and earth, and eternity, and space."[13]

In addition, people will also have opportunities to socialize and enjoy one another's company. "And that same sociality which exists among us here will exist among us there, only it will be coupled with eternal glory" (Doctrine and Covenants 130:2).

Speaking generally, William Wallace Raymond said of people in the spirit world; "They eat and drink, and hold meetings like we do, and I ate with them."[14]

Harriet Ovard Lee said of people in the spirit world, "Some were reading books."[15]

After being shown the home he would live in if he decided to stay in the spirit world, Earl Stowell's guide told him, "Your duties will be light—to take care of this property. You will [also] have ample time to study, learn, and socialize."[16]

Apparently, there will be construction workers, according to David P. Kimball. "I was then taken in the vision into a vast building, which was built on the plan of the Order of Zion. I entered through a south door and found myself in a part of the building which was unfinished, though a great many workmen were busy upon it."[17]

Archie J. Graham

Archie J. Graham's near-death experience[18] is one of the most extensive in early LDS history. He said people appeared busy in the spirit world and mentions gardening, pruning, horticulture, classes, preaching, and missionary work. Archie relates his experience as follows:

"In December 1918, I contracted influenza which was raging over the country. . . . One night . . . I was surprised to hear someone speak my name. I paid no attention. Then again I heard it. The third time it was so clear and distinct that I turned over to see what was wanted. A messenger, a man in white, stood before me. He was about five feet nine inches tall and had a most penetrating smile. His presence seemed to illuminate the room. His voice was kind and gentle, yet commanding.

"'Come with me,' he said. . . . I arose from my bed and followed him, leaving my body behind. We had not gone far, when he asked if I knew where I was. I told him I felt as if I were in heaven because his influence seemed so heavenly.

"'Come then,' he said. 'We will follow this path and I will show you some of the things you have longed to know and to see.'

"The path we took seemed to be of small marble-like pebbles, snow white in color. It was about eight feet wide and continued straight and glistening as far as the eye could see. To the right and left of us were beautiful fields of waving grain. We walked through these for a long distance when we came to a beautiful forest with lawn grass covering the ground; with trees and shrubs of many sizes and kinds and of many different colorings, from a pale green to the deep green of the spruce and pine, several shades of silver and gold, reds, browns, blues and lavenders fading into a light pink. All were planted to harmonize with each other in size, color and kind, and by looking in a certain direction, one could see all colors of the rainbow.

"As we were passing through the forest, I thought nothing could compare to its beauty—it was glorious. But as we left it behind and walked along the same white path, we came into the most exquisite flower gardens, wherein were small shrubs and all manner of plant life, beyond human understanding. The ground was all covered with many varieties of lawn grass. . . . There were flowers of all sizes and colors, placed in different artistic designs, such as diamonds, crescents, ovals, oblongs, squares, and other odd shapes to add beauty and splendor to their surroundings. The flowers varied in size from no larger than a pinhead to those as large as the crown in a man's hat. The shrubs were gorgeous, all sizes and colors—many of them were pruned and kept trimmed to represent birds and animals. . . .

"While we were viewing these sights, the caretakers were busily engaged in pruning and trimming trees and shrubs, and cultivating the flowers and lawns."

Archie explains that the caretakers then put aside their tools and went to a small arbor to attend a class, which they had twice a day. Curious to see the book the instructor was using, Archie moved closer. "I was anxious to know what he was reading and was watching the book rather than him. We came opposite him, but I could not make out what it was. Just as we were about to pass through the gates, our eyes met. It was one of the happiest moments of my life, for this radiant young instructor was my dead brother. I called his name and stepped toward him. He had been watching me, but had made no advance toward me, and his smile will always remain fresh in my mind. My guide took hold of my arm [and] as I turned to him the scene changed.

"I asked my guide if that were not my dear brother. He put his finger to his lips, and said, 'That is not part of my program. I am only to show you what you have wanted to know. He is very busy teaching the art of horticulture, and preaching the Gospel. Now be content, for all is well with him.'"

They then went to a city that was so dirty and run-down that Archie asked if the people were poor. The guide said they were "benighted, ignorant, full of lust, greed and selfishness, just the same as they lived while on the earth, steeped in the iniquities of sin. They have procrastinated their day of repentance unto death, for the bad habits formed in the flesh are much harder to overcome in the spirit, as the spirit steeped in sin without the flesh is weak, indeed, and they have a hard time to master sin here."

In describing the city, Archie said, "Contention was raging in every form. The houses seemed very dilapidated. . . . The streets were disorderly and dirty . . . there was not a sign of a tree, a flower, or a blade of grass. Everything was barren as a desert. I asked my guide if people would not surely do better on earth if they knew what was waiting for them.

"'That would never do,' he said, 'as it would rob them of their full right to choose good or evil. Now they choose the thing they like most and the reward is waiting for them. . . . They choose for themselves while on the earth, which is the school of experience to test the character of the soul in the flesh, and this is their reward." When asked further, the guide said, "They always have instructors teaching better ways of living and different kinds of industries. Therefore, the Lord extends His mercy forever unto His children."

As they walked on, the homes and people gradually began to show improvement. "As we went further . . . the homes were nicer, some of them having been painted. There were now more signs of industry. Some parts were cultivated, some trees and lawns came into sight and some of the people looked happy." The people here were more interested in religion and there were more missionaries preaching the first principles of the gospel. "All kinds of characters were to be observed among the throngs of people. By their countenances, homes, groups and communities, you could tell the difference. Each individual finds his level.

"As we continued talking, the scene was suddenly changed to one of beauty. There were trees, shrubs, lawns and flowers, beautiful painted and stone houses, gardens, parks and playgrounds, and many things to keep the people busy. . . . Most of the people were happy and busy at something and seemed to be more united and showed more cooperation in their communities and groups. There was now an even greater number of missionaries, more encouraged in their work, as this class enjoyed the Gospel and was more eager to learn. . . . We began to see large chapels for worship and many public places erected after the manner of our stadiums, in the open air, for people to sit and hear the Gospel taught, most of these being filled with large crowds.

"'Nearly all these people are interested in religion,' my guide explained, 'but it takes a long time to prepare them for the Gospel. It is so much harder for the spirit to overcome the weaknesses of the flesh without the flesh, even for these good people. . . .'

"The streets were paved and wide, the houses were lovely, and the further we went, the more beautiful everything became. . . . I was informed, however, there were no children under the age of eight years, as the atoning blood of Jesus Christ has paid for all children under that age, as they are sealed Christ's regardless of creed, or nationality."

Archie's guide then explained that the people in spirit prison had to remain there until they accepted the gospel, repented of their sins, and received the ordinances of the gospel.

"Even though they may repent, progress in wisdom and knowledge," the guide said, "they are still held in prison . . . and they remain in that same station until they are released."

The guide led Archie on, and the scene changed again. Archie said, "I was gazing upon some of the most beautiful homes or palaces—for no castle of any earthly king could surpass them in beauty . . . children and all kinds of animal life . . . added real life to its beauty. There were numerous parks and playgrounds, filled with happy and intelligent children. They were kind and generous in their play. Everything seemed to be love and smiles. The houses were all large and quite uniform in size and structure, some of stone and some of other materials. The walks and streets were paved with different colors of cement to harmonize with the different shades of green of the lawns and shrubs. They were indeed beyond description. The homes and gardens each covered from five to ten acres of land on which trees, flowers and shrubs [grew] in great profusion. . . . Wonderful chapels and public boweries and comfortable seats and beautiful pulpits were to be seen here, being used as places for preaching the Gospel and other subjects of importance. . . .

"My guide explained, 'Before they can receive either baptism or laying on of hands here, the work must be done for them on earth, by proxy. It is the same in receiving the Priesthood and all other ordinances. . . . As soon as this work is done on earth, they may receive the same over here, by the authority of the Holy Priesthood. It is very important that the people on earth should turn their hearts more to this work, and have the work ready for them; but in nearly all cases, these poor people are ready and waiting long before their work is recorded there. Many have waited for hundreds of years. . . .'

"We now came into the center of this massive city with throngs of people. . . . The business houses were large and well constructed, close together and of an average height of six or eight stories. . . . Everyone had a place to go, something definite to do, but each had a smile and a pleasant word for a friend."

Archie and his guide went to a side street and saw more beautiful homes, similar to what they had seen before entering the middle of the city. They saw more missionaries preaching the gospel and completing genealogy so temple work could be done on earth. Archie asked his guide if all the missionaries did was teach the gospel.

The guide replied, "Think of the countless millions and millions of people who have been born in the flesh. The Gospel has been on the earth but a few times and then only short periods. . . . Most of them . . . are here to be taught the true Gospel by a very few who have the right and authority to teach it. . . . This is shown unto you to impress upon your mind the magnitude of the work there is to be done, both here and on earth, and to impress upon your mind your responsibility, as you were chosen to help this work along in the last days."

Next, they came to a large white building, grand in design and architecture. Archie declared, "It was glorious, but it is beyond my powers to describe it in full." He said it resembled the Salt Lake Tabernacle, only it was much larger. "There was a wonderful pipe organ the music of which sounded like that of angels. My guide informed me that we were invited to a meeting where the twelve apostles and the Presiding Presidency met weekly to give instruction to their officers."

Soon the building was filled with nearly twenty thousand people. When the authorities came in, everyone rose respectfully, standing until they were all seated. Archie saw the Prophet Joseph Smith, Hyrum Smith, Brigham Young, Lorenzo Snow, and a few others he did not recognize. The guide informed him that although Joseph was presiding there, he only did so at special meetings and conferences, as he had so many things to do. The meeting then started with prayer, followed by talks and music from the choir. Afterwards, the guide took Archie to meet a vast throng of relatives.

His guide introduced him. "This is Elder Archie J. Graham, your kindred from the earth." Many in the group asked if Archie could come to the spirit world—that they needed him. But one large man, seemingly a leader, said that Archie should go back to earth, that they needed him more there so he could do temple work for them. The crowd seemed to agree, but the guide said that the decision had not been made yet.

As Archie and his guide continued on, Archie commented that being out of his physical body was an unusual sensation. "I felt differently than I had ever felt before. My body was light in weight. I could move about with the least exertion. . . . I felt as though I could fly I was so light."

Archie commented about his surroundings. "There were many varieties of trees and shrubs, and flowers; lakes, ponds, fish, birds and pet animals and every thing that would make a home and surroundings beautiful and peaceful."

They came upon a particular home that was so magnificent that Archie stopped to look at it in awe. The home was nestled among trees, vines, and flowers, and had a rolling, terraced lawn with beautiful fish-ponds. The water in the ponds was clear as crystal and came bubbling up out of the ground. There were many birds and animals, such as deer, sheep, and antelope. The house itself was made of fine white marble, with huge white pillars on each side of the veranda. The doors and windows were of the finest crystal. When Archie asked his guide whose home it was, the angel said the owner hadn't come yet.

"What must a man do to inherit a place like that?" Archie asked.

"He must live his religion in all things as he understands it," the guide replied. "If much is given much is expected. Keep all the laws of God, and pay all his tithes and offerings. To be a servant of God, you must be a servant of your fellowmen. Remain true and faithful to your covenants, always fearing and trusting in the Lord and you will inherit a mansion like unto this, for one of the eternal laws to man is that he shall receive according to his faith or according to his faithfulness to the degrees of knowledge he has acquired through obedience to eternal law."

They walked on for a time and then his guide turned to Archie. "Now you have had a wonderful privilege to see for yourself what is being done beyond the veil. The many things you have seen and heard are all for your benefit and you should make sense of them. You have seen the great mis-sionary work awaiting you, also how they need your testimony and influ-ence. You have seen your own people and how they wanted to hear from you. They showed you that they knew you and asked for your help. . . . You have seen the mansion which is prepared for you—the mansion and the grounds you examined are yours."

Archie said, "My soul leaped with joy at his words, then my heart melted within me as I thought of my weaknesses and imperfections. How could I be worthy, what had I done to deserve this? This was sacred and I was not prepared.

"My guide continued with the kindness of a loving father. 'The Lord, our Master, has given me charge concerning you, that you may choose for yourself, after knowing the things that are in store for you over there. You may come and enjoy these things in the Spirit World, or you may remain upon the earth.' . . . He said no more, but waited for my answer."

Archie thought about his ancestors and how they had asked him to go back. He then thought of his shortcomings and how he might better himself if he returned. He turned to his guide. "If that be the case, I prefer to remain upon the earth."

The angel smiled. "May I ask why?"

Archie explained that he wanted to work in the Church and devote his life to saving the souls of men and that he also wanted to work in the temple for his deceased loved ones. In addition, Archie said he hoped to raise an honorable family and send them into the mission field. At that moment, the guide underwent a change.

"A shining glory radiated from his countenance," Archie said. "His clothing was already white, but now the glory of the Lord radiated from him . . . he looked through me and saw the innermost thoughts of my heart . . . he said with a most thrilling, vibrating voice, yet gentle and kind, 'The Lord, your Master, loves you for your integrity. Have faith and trust in the Lord, and He will bless you and strengthen your back for every burden if you will trust Him. . . . You have only 14 years to make your preparations, for after your forty fifth anniversary, the Lord wants your heart, your time and your talents to be devoted to a special charge. . . . Now be content for all shall be well with you, for first, the devil will seek to destroy you and block your way. But if your faith is strong enough, you will be able to overcome the weaknesses of the flesh. . . . Now, go thy way in peace, trusting in these things and depending upon the Lord for guidance. . . . Come, let us return to your body.'

"In a flash we were in my bedroom. I saw my wife and children in their beds as I had left them. I saw my own body lying by the side of my wife. . . . I looked at the clock. It was just seven a.m. 'We have been gone five whole hours as it was two o'clock when we left,' I said to my guide.

"We stopped [sic] over to the bed. My body was lying on its back. It really looked to me to be dead. I said to my guide, 'It looks hard to have to go back into that cold lifeless body after seeing all I have seen.'

"'It doesn't only look hard, but it is hard,' he said. 'You don't have to go back, but if you want those blessings in the flesh, you must go back.'

"'Yes, yes, I do want those blessings in the flesh and I do want to go back at any cost.' I turned back to the body again to take it up. I touched it and shuddered. 'Oh,' I said, 'how can I, it's cold and clammy.'

"I tried again to take it up, then cried out, 'I can't do it!' Being filled with the horror of the coldness of death, I cried out again, 'I can't do it, I can't do it.'"

Still, Archie knew that this was something he had to do and so "with positive determination, I forced myself back into my cold, lifeless body. . . . I was cold and stiff and could not move. . . . I could not even open my mouth or move my lips or utter a word. . . . I began to offer a silent prayer, trusting my Heavenly Father to hear it, and He did hear it. My body began to warm up. I moved my arms, my legs and head. I opened my eyes and there stood my faithful guide smiling at me.

"I could not speak, but he said, 'You have done it fine. You are all right now, I must go. Peace be unto you and farewell.' While he was departing he waved his hand and . . . slowly faded from my mortal view.

"It is beyond my vocabulary to describe the sense of feeling of coming back to my earthly body. But suffice it to say, my guide must have known it to have been an ordeal as he stayed with me until he was sure I was all right. But I can truthfully say, it was a terrible feeling. . . .

"I lay upon my bed, meditating upon the singularity of the experiences I had been privileged to enjoy. In humbleness I poured out the gratitude of my heart to my Heavenly Father for these marvelous gifts and blessings. . . .

A week later, Archie became very ill again. He asked for a blessing and in it was told he would get well and that he would have fourteen years to make his preparations for the next life.

In conclusion, Archie said, "It has been many years since I had this experience. . . . Who am I, that I can deny having seen and heard these things? . . . I know the Gospel of Jesus Christ of Latter-day Saints is true. I know Jesus is my Savior and my Redeemer. . . . My humble and sincere prayer is that all who may read or hear this experience will do so with a prayerful heart, without prejudice. I am confident that if they do, they will know of the truth therein."[19]

Notes:

1. Rudger J. Clawson, Conference Report April 1933, 75–76.
2. George Q. Cannon, Conference Report April 1899, 19–20.
3. Brigham Young, *Journal of Discourses* (June 22, 1856), 3:372.
4. Ibid., 370.
5. Francis M. Lyman, Conference Report October 1909, 19.
6. Rudger J. Clawson, Conference Report April 1933, 75.
7. Brigham Young, "Preaching to Spirits in Prison," *The Contributor* 10 (July 1889), 321.

8. Peter E. Johnson, "A Testimony," *The Relief Society Magazine* 7, (1920), 450–455.
9. Zina Y. Card, "Manifestation to Mrs. Mary Hyde Woolf," *The Relief Society Magazine* 8 (August 1921), 492–93.
10. Hannah Adeline Savage, *Record of Hannah Adeline Savage* (Provo, Utah: L. Tom Perry Special Collections, Harold B. Lee Library, Brigham Young University), 3–5.
11. Brigham Young, *Journal of Discourses* (October 8, 1859), 7:333.
12. Brigham Young, *Journal of Discourses* (March 8, 1860), 8:10.
13. Orson Pratt, *Journal of Discourses* (October 15, 1854), 2:247.
14. William Wallace Raymond, "Vision 1881 Aug 12."
15. Harriet Ovard Lee, "A Remarkable Vision 1901."
16. *Biography of William Rufus Rogers Stowell 1893* (courtesy of the Church History Library, The Church of Jesus Christ of Latter-day Saints).
17. Orson F. Whitney, *Helpful Visions, The 14th Book of the Faith-Promoting Series*, 22.
18. Because of space considerations, this experience has been shortened.
19. Archie J. Graham, "A Visit Beyond the Veil" [n. d.].

> "A revelation of Jesus Christ unto his servant Joseph Smith. . . . Yea, the word of the Lord concerning his church, established in the last days for the restoration of his people, as he has spoken by the mouth of his prophets." (Doctrine and Covenants 84:2)

Chapter Eleven

The Restoration of the Gospel

*S*ome near-death experiences testify about the restoration of the gospel. When Jesus Christ lived on earth, He organized His Church "upon the foundation of the apostles and prophets, Jesus Christ himself being the chief corner stone" (Ephesians 2:20). After the Savior was crucified and the Twelve Apostles were killed, the priesthood was no longer on earth. The subsequent apostasy lasted until God called a new prophet in these latter days.

Joseph Smith was given all the priesthood keys, authority, and ordinances necessary to reestablish Jesus Christ's Church on earth. As the authorized representative of the Lord during his lifetime, Joseph Smith received God's word for mankind, which included revelations, prophecies, and commandments. Brigham Young testified, "Joseph Smith holds the keys of this last dispensation, and is now engaged behind the vail [sic] in the great work of the last days. . . . He holds the keys of that kingdom for the last dispensation—the keys to rule in the spirit world; and he rules there triumphantly."[1]

The early apostle Parley P. Pratt bore a powerful testimony of the Prophet Joseph Smith when he said, "I bear this testimony this day, that Joseph Smith was and is a Prophet, Seer, and Revelator—an Apostle holding the keys of this last dispensation and of the kingdom of God, under

Peter, James and John. And not only that he was a Prophet and Apostle of Jesus Christ, and lived and died one, but that he now lives in the spirit world, and holds those same keys to usward [sic] and to this whole generation. Also that he will hold those keys to all eternity; and no power in heaven or on the earth will ever take them from him; for he will continue holding those keys through all eternity, and will stand—yes, again in the flesh upon this earth, as the head of the Latter-day Saints under Jesus Christ, and under Peter, James and John."[2]

Martha Jane Boice

Many LDS near-death experiences testify of the restoration of the gospel and the divine role of Joseph Smith. One such experience is the account of Martha Jane Boice. Three years after joining The Church of Jesus Christ of Latter-day Saints, John and Martha Jane Boice moved to Kirtland, Ohio. In 1839, they tried to move to Missouri with their two children but were driven back by a mob. Instead, John and Martha Jane went to Illinois, where their third child, Benjamin, was born. While there, Martha became critically ill. When Martha realized she was dying, she became very bitter, blaming the Church for the grievous hardships she had endured and her imminent death.

Wanting to protect her children from the extreme trials she had suffered, Martha demanded that her three children be given to people in the area who were not members of the Church. However, after Martha died and went to the spirit world, she realized her grave mistake. She asked for and received permission from authorities to return to mortality long enough to give her husband an important message. A friend wrote the following account.

"It was in a log cabin of one large room that she [Martha] lay ill for over two months and then she seemed to have gone to her well earned rest on the evening of the 14th of Feb. 1840. Her form was laid upon a narrow bed draped in white at the far end of the room while tallow candles cast a restful glow upon a group of women which surrounded a table busily engaged in fashioning white material with which to clothe her form for its last sleep. A sorrowful husband sat there too. His only occupation thru the night being to keep alive the fire that flowed upon the hearth. It was when the wee hours of the night spread their stillness all around, that a voice called out from where the dead lay."

It was Martha. She whispered, "'John. John, raise me up.'

126

"John hastened to obey the command. He went to the couch where his wife lay and raised her up. She sat up on the board bed and said, 'Don't be afraid. I have been in the Spirit world but have obtained permission to return and to remain for two hours. I have come to rectify my mistake in willing away my children. You may keep two of them, the other will go with me. I made a mistake in growing weary of the Gospel. The Gospel is true. Joseph Smith is a prophet of the living God. You will do well to remain true to it all your life.'

"She remained the two hours allotted to her, bearing testimony to the Gospel and praising God for the beauties which she had seen in the Spirit world and for the joy of being able to return. She then instructed them to proceed with her funeral as they had already arranged for the following day. Then she bade her husband to lay her down again. This he did, and then her spirit took its flight again. She was buried the following day and her little son, Thomas was called away that same evening after a brief and sudden illness and he was laid by her side in a cemetery at Hudson, Ohio."[3]

Heroine Randall

Heroine Randall had only been married a short time when, in 1830, she had a near-death experience. A few years later when missionaries came to her door, she refused to attend their meetings. Then Heroine had a change of heart, and once she heard the gospel message, she accepted it and was baptized. A friend, Henry A. Stebbins, relates Heroine's experience.

"I well remember one dear old sister in Plano, Illinois . . . Heroine Randall. Her testimony I wrote down from her own lips, which was, that while young, soon after her marriage, while a member of the Baptist Church, she was stricken with a consuming fever and to all appearances died, so that her friends began preparations for her funeral.

"She related to others as well as to me, that at that time her spirit departed from her body, and rose above it, and that she looked down and saw her husband and friends weeping over it. Then a personage of beauty received her into his charge and conducted her beyond the confines of earth, even she realized to a great distance, until they came without the walls of a beautiful city, one that shone in splendor. The gates were open, and she looked within and saw its glory, and the throng of bright ones, a company of life, activity, and intelligence.

"As she gazed upon the glorious scene, she desired to enter, but her guide said she could not go in, the [sic] she was not yet prepared to enter there. When she asked him why she was not, he answered: 'You have not yet received and obeyed the gospel in its fullness, but if you return to the earth, to your mortal body, the time will come when you shall have the opportunity to hear the gospel of Christ preached in its completeness, and if you accept it and live faithful to the commandments, you will have the right to enter into the city that you have seen.'

"He then conducted her to earth again. She entered the room where her body was lying, and her spirit entered into it. Then her astonished friends saw her move, and her eyes open, and she spoke and said that they should not weep, for she would get well and remain with them. And very soon she received strength and speedily recovered from her sickness."

Henry concluded her story by saying, "This occurred in the state of New York, about the year 1830, and a few years later the elders of the latter-day work came into that neighborhood, preaching Christ's gospel restored with its full doctrines and blessings. For a time she would not attend the meetings, but finally went; and when she heard the plan of salvation unfolded as preached in New Testament times, when she considered its evidences, the words of her heavenly guide came to her memory, and as she listened her heart was filled with the divine Spirit, and she realized that the truth was being preached.

"She obeyed it; and all who knew her can truthfully say that she lived faithfully and reverently and bore as clear a testimony, sustained by as able arguments as very many of the elders can state in giving reasons for the hope that is within them when called to answer. And she continued ever in the hope of the promise made her by the bright attendant when her spirit was 'caught away' to see the city of God and be instructed."[4]

Notes:

1. Brigham Young, *Journal of Discourses* (October 9, 1859), 7:289.
2. Parley P. Pratt, *Journal of Discourses* (September 7, 1856), 5:195.
3. Samantha T. Brimhall, *Boice Family History* [ca 1930], (courtesy of the Church History Library, The Church of Jesus Christ of Latter-day Saints).
4. Alvin Knisley (comp.), *Infallible Proofs, A Collection of Spiritual Communications and Remarkable Experiences*, 37–38.

> "But behold, from among the righteous, he organized his forces and appointed messengers, clothed with power and authority, and commissioned them to go forth and carry the light of the gospel to them that were in darkness, even to all the spirits of men; and thus was the gospel preached to the dead." (Doctrine and Covenants 138:30)

Chapter Twelve

The Gospel Is Taught in the Spirit World

Since Heavenly Father is both merciful and just, it is only fair that the countless number of people who have died without hearing the gospel or learning about Christ will have that chance in the next life. There is a great missionary plan in place so that all souls, living or dead, can have the opportunity, if they desire, to hear the gospel and embrace the truth. Brigham Young taught, "All that have lived or will live on this earth, will have the chance to receive the gospel."[1]

The scriptures also bear this out. "For this cause was the gospel preached also to them that are dead, that they might be judged according to men in the flesh, but live according to God in the spirit" (1 Peter 4:6).

Speaking of deceased members of the Church, Brigham Young further declared, "What are they doing there [in the spirit world]? They are preaching, preaching all the time, and preparing the way for us to hasten our work in building temples here and elsewhere."[2]

President Wilford Woodruff explained further. "The Prophet Joseph Smith held the keys of this dispensation on this side of the veil, and he will hold them throughout the countless ages of eternity. He went into the spirit world to unlock the prison doors and to preach the gospel to the millions of spirits who are in darkness, and every apostle, every seventy, every elder, etc., who had died in the faith, as soon as he passes to the other side of the veil, enters into the work of the ministry, and there is a thousand times more to preach there than there is here."[3]

"Now, there are many of our ancestors who had no opportunity at all in life of hearing the Gospel," said Rudger J. Clawson during general conference. "That opportunity must come to them. How can it come to them? Only in one way, and that is by the preaching of the Gospel, and the Gospel will be preached to them, I am sure, by the apostles and prophets, high priests, seventies and elders who have lived and died and gone into the spirit world. The work to be done there is vastly greater than that which is done upon the earth by the Saints of God. There are millions and millions upon millions who have lived and died since the Savior was upon the earth, down to the present time. The work must be done for them."[4]

Men will not be the only ones preaching the gospel—women will also have an important role in sharing the message of the gospel. President Joseph F. Smith said, "Who is going to carry the testimony of Jesus Christ to the hearts of the women who have passed away without a knowledge of the gospel? Well, to my mind, it is a simple thing. These good sisters have been set apart, ordained to the work, called to it, authorized by the authority of the Holy Priesthood to minister for their sex, in the house of God for the living and for the dead, will be fully authorized and empowered to preach the gospel and minister to the women while the elders and prophets are preaching it to the men. The things we experience here are typical of the things of God and the life beyond us."[5]

Because of missionary work in the spirit world, any person who would have accepted Jesus Christ if they had heard about Him while on earth will have the opportunity to receive the highest degree of glory within the celestial kingdom. When the Prophet Joseph Smith saw the three degrees of glory in a vision, the Lord told him, "All who have died without a knowledge of this gospel, who would have received it if they had been permitted to tarry, shall be heirs of the celestial kingdom of God; Also all that shall die henceforth without a knowledge of it, who would have received it with all their hearts, shall be heirs of that kingdom; For I, the Lord, will judge all men according to their works, according to the desire of their hearts" (Doctrine and Covenants 137:7–9).

Many of those who have had near-death experiences saw the gospel being preached, and some saw their own loved ones—male and female—teaching spirits there. Some accounts make it clear that although missionaries work diligently to teach the gospel, people will not be forced to listen, nor will they be compelled to accept the gospel. Agency is an integral part of God's plan, and not everyone in the spirit world will accept the gospel.

When his guide took him to the spirit world, Henry Zollinger saw several members of his family preaching the gospel. "We then had the privilege of visiting with my brothers-in-law who had died. William who had been on a mission in Australia. He told me he was presiding over a large mission and was very happy in his labors . . . We next went to see his older brother John. I found him discussing the Gospel to a large congregation bearing a strong testimony to them, when he got through he told me he was very happy in his labors."[6]

During his near-death experience, David Lynn Brooks was asked by his departed wife if he recognized any of the people they had met. He replied, "I told her I didn't recognize any of them. She then asked me if I remembered the people we had done the temple work for in 1929 and 1930. She and I had worked the entire winter gathering genealogy of her people and then we did the temple work for them. She then told me she had been called by the priesthood to teach the gospel to those people and that she was very happy doing that work."[7]

John Peterson

John Peterson was twenty-two and living near Gottenberg, Sweden, when he died from consumption. After arriving in the spirit world, John attended a meeting where two distinguished apostles taught the gospel to a large crowd.

"I had joined the Church in the early part of 1857, and was ordained an Elder the same spring. Through the summer and fall I was very sick with the disease. I think about October, for five weeks, I could partake of no food, only drink. I lost my speech for three days. On the third day, in the afternoon, my attendants said the pulse in my wrists had stopped, but they could feel a slight pulsation in the head. My father and mother had concluded in their minds that I should die; that I was too far gone to be restored. Father told mother he would remain with me during the night. Mother therefore retired to her room, being fatigued and worn out.

"To while away the lonely hours, father sat reading to himself (Orson Pratt's Works). It was between ten and eleven o'clock that a visitor suddenly made his appearance in the room, and standing by the couch on which I lay, placed his hand on my head and asked if I was ready to go?

"I answered, 'Yes'; and just at that instant I seemed to stand upon the floor, my body lying on the bed. I looked around to see if my father could see us, but he seemed to have been too interested in reading to have noticed us. We started off on our journey through space, seemingly with the rapidity of lightning (for I can make no other comparison).

I asked my guide who he was. He answered he was one of the guardian angels sent to bring the dead."[8]

"We went some distance, and soon came to a great crowd of people, who seemed to be in an excited state of mind on account of something that was going to take place.

"My companion said: 'We will remain here, as there is going to be a meeting, and two Apostles are coming to preach to these people. These are mostly your progenitors, and are now in the lowest sphere in the spirit world.'"[9]

"There seemed to be a stand erected close by for the missionaries to preach in. They came as it were directly; part of the congregation were noisy and inclined to be troublesome.

"I asked my guide who these missionaries were, and he merely answered, 'The old man is the Apostle Matthias.' I understood by this it was the Apostle Matthias who had filled the place of Judas Iscariot who betrayed the Savior, and the young man, he further said, 'was an apostle from America who had lately been killed there,' but he did not tell his name, and which I subsequently learned to be Parley P. Pratt.

"It is some years since I happened to be in the company of one of Parley's wives, and was relating the incident to her, when she asked me to describe the kind of personage the young missionary was. I gave as near a description of him as I could recollect, for be assured I had never even heard his name, but his height, his being broad across the shoulders, the color of his hair, his eyes and gestures, that she instantly said it was Parley.

"But to return: The elder apostle stood up in the stand (for we were all seated there) and said to the people, 'Stop right there!' Then he sat down and perfect stillness prevailed, when the young apostle rose up to preach to the congregation, taking his text from the fourth chapter of Malachi, fifth and sixth verses, which he spoke upon at some length, as also upon temple building and the ordinances to be performed therein in redeeming the dead; which to me at that time was strange doctrine, for as I said, I had been in the Church but about six months.

"He further said, 'If they would receive the Gospel they should be redeemed by their children on the earth, and if they did not receive it they could not.'

"He then took his seat, when the elder apostle arose and told the people they could now retire, which they did, some of them in a noisy and boisterous manner, so that I thought they were as disorderly in the spirit world as here. All the form of the meeting that I could observe was when the apostle told them to 'stop right there,' they did so, seeming to be held as it were spellbound till the services were ended and he told them they 'could retire.'

"My guide then introduced me to the apostles by bowing his head, which was returned by them. No hand shaking took place; the elder apostle said to me, 'Would you as soon go back, for it seems to fall to your lot to redeem your forefathers?'

"I answered, 'Yes, but my lungs are gone.'

"He replied, 'It is easy to grow new lungs in a man; if you will go your guide will attend to this.'

"I answered, 'I will go.'

"With a bow we started to return and, seemingly, but a short space of time elapsed ere we reached my home, and standing by the bed, where my body lay, my guide touched my hands, the spirit entered the body at that instant, the blood commenced to circulate warmly though my veins, and in a few minutes I felt my lungs expanding.

"As I stood upon the floor I noticed the clock; the hands pointed to four o'clock in the morning, so I had been absent between five and six hours. My father was still reading.

"I spoke to him.

"Said he, 'My boy, I thought you were dead.'

"I said, 'I was, father.'

"He called my mother, and I then related to them where I had been, and that I should soon recover and be strong again, though I was but skin and bones, the consumption had so reduced me; and during the previous five weeks I had partaken of no solid food. I was weak, very weak. I asked my parents for something to eat, much to their surprise, and to this day I can well recollect the sensation I experienced in that sweet morsel of food.

"My mother, with unbounded joy and gratitude to God, provided for me. I felt no sickness after my return; the pain had all left me. I was only weak.

"It was four weeks before I was able to walk around the house, which was on the Christmas day of 1857. Since which time I have been what may be called a weakly man, but not a sickly one. I have worked at my trade (tailoring) the most of the time since. My parents also gathered to Utah and have since died here. My friends may think of this as they feel disposed, but it has been a strong testimony to me that there is an after life, and that the dead are being looked after as I have described it."[10]

Some Mortals Are Called to the Spirit World to Teach

Just as there is a great need for missionaries to spread the gospel throughout the world today, there is a need for worthy missionaries to teach the gospel in the spirit world. Some near-death experiences indicate that just as people are called in this life to positions of responsibility, mortals can be called to the spirit world specifically to work as missionaries or to perform other important duties. Brigham Young commented once that Joseph Smith was laboring in the spirit world and that "he is calling one after another to his aid, as the Lord sees he wants help."[11]

Wilford Woodruff taught the same principle. "I have felt of late as if our brethren on the other side of the veil had held a council, and that they had said to this one, and that one, 'Cease thy work on earth, come hence, we need help' and they have called this man and that man."[12] Apostle Melvin J. Ballard related one incident where a young missionary was called to the spirit world. "Some time ago a fine young elder, Elder Burt, received a call to go on a mission—he wanted to go to the South American Mission so he talked to me about it, and after conference it was decided to let him go to South America. On the way there he lost his life in the sinking of the Vesperous. I was distressed over his father and mother and I tried to comfort them, for the assurance came to me was that their son was still a missionary and that God needed him and was using him in a more effective way than if he had gone on his earthy mission."[13]

May Neville

Losing one child is painful, but losing two at the same time is excruciating. In January 1917, Merrill Neville and his sister, May Neville, passed away within one day of each other. May Neville was allowed to return briefly from the spirit world in order to comfort her mother's aching heart. She brought a message of hope and reassurance and told her mother that Merrill had been called to the spirit world to preach the gospel.

The day before nineteen-year-old Merrill died, his mother, Eliza Neville, was praying beside him when he took hold of her hands. "Mother, you won't feel bad if I die, will you?"

Startled, Eliza told him that she had felt impressed that he would *live* and go on a mission.

Merrill replied, "Yes, mother, I shall live; and I'm going on a mission . . . but the mission's not upon this earth. If I'm permitted to come back, mother, I'll come and tell you all I can."

The next day, Merrill died.

Later that night, Eliza was sitting beside May, who was very ill. May whispered, "Mother, Merrill is knocking for me."

Grief-stricken at already having lost one child, Eliza replied, "Oh, May, don't say that."

May said no more at the time, but the following evening, she whispered, "Mother, you didn't believe me last night when I told you Merrill was knocking for me. He is knocking again now."

Heartbroken, Eliza replied, "Oh May . . . I didn't disbelieve you, but I couldn't bear to think that it was so."

A short time later, May passed away. In her final moments, her parents clung to their daughter and tried in every way to restore life to the limp body, but it was not to be. While others stayed in the room with May's body, Eliza Neville wandered miserably from room to room. Finally, she returned to the bedroom and, closing her eyes, prayed aloud.

"Oh, Father in heaven, I don't see why I have been called upon to go through such trying scenes as this. I've had all the children I could have, and I've tried to raise them as near right as I knew how. Why have I been called upon to go through this?"

Just then, another daughter, Bessie, touched Eliza on the shoulder and said, "Mother, May wants you."

Confused, and thinking that May wanted her to go to heaven, Eliza replied, "Must I go, too?"

"No, Mother," Bessie said. "May has come back to life and wants to tell you what Merrill has said to her."

Rushing to her daughter's side, Eliza discovered that May was indeed alive. Although she wanted to talk, May was extremely weak. Afraid she might not be able to deliver the message Merrill had entrusted her to give,

May asked her mother to pray to the Lord on her behalf. Joining Eliza in prayer were her husband, May's sister and two brothers, a young friend, and a few Relief Society sisters from the ward. Everyone knelt around May's bed, placing their hands on her body and head while Eliza prayed.

As soon as Eliza said amen, May drew herself up on her pillow, her face shining with a special glow.

Eliza said, "She (May) said Merrill had come back to tell her what he wanted his mother to know. He told her that his grandparents had met him when he died, and he was with them now. They had a beautiful home, and were preparing a beautiful home for his mother and her family. He said it was always springtime over there.

"Merrill wished the family not to mourn for him. He said that so many of grandpa's people had been killed in the war that his grandfather needed Merrill to help him with his missionary work among his kindred dead. Merrill told her it was better for him to go while he was pure than to live and perhaps do something wrong. He said that if the family fretted and mourned for him he couldn't accomplish the work which his grandfather had for him to do. . . .

"May put her finger on each one of the family present and told them of their failings, which they must endeavor to overcome if they would go to that beautiful home which was being prepared for them. She said that all must go to Sunday School and to meeting; they should attend to their prayers, and pay their tithing. She said impressively to all present: 'Give to the poor; the more you give the more you will have to give.'

"Turning to her mother she finally said, 'Mother, you are going to live to be a real old lady; you will have better health than you have ever had.'"

The next morning, May was taken to the hospital. Ten days later, she went to the spirit world—this time to stay.[14]

The Gospel Is Taught to Those in Prison

After the death and Resurrection of Jesus Christ, He commanded the faithful to take the gospel to people in spirit prison. "And also they who are the spirits of men kept in prison, whom the Son visited, and preached the gospel unto them, that they might be judged according to men in the flesh; Who received not the testimony of Jesus in the flesh, but afterwards received it" (Doctrine and Covenants 76:73–74).

In his vision of the redemption of the dead, President Joseph F. Smith saw that righteous spirits, clothed with power and authority, were sent forth to preach the gospel to captives who were being held in spirit prison but who would repent of their sins and receive the gospel. "Thus was the gospel preached to those who had died in their sins, without a knowledge of the truth, or in transgression, having rejected the prophets. These were taught faith in God, repentance from sin, vicarious baptism for the remission of sins, the gift of the Holy Ghost by the laying on of hands, and all other principles of the gospel that were necessary for them to know in order to qualify themselves that they might be judged according to men in the flesh, but live according to God in the spirit" (Doctrine and Covenants 138:32–34).

Continuing, President Joseph F. Smith said, "I beheld that the faithful elders of this dispensation, when they depart from mortal life, continue their labors in the preaching of the gospel of repentance and redemption . . . among those who are in darkness and under the bondage of sin in the great world of the spirits of the dead" (Doctrine and Covenants 138:57).

There is much work to be done, and many worthy spirits in paradise are called as missionaries and sent to spirit prison to teach those who did not have the opportunity to hear the gospel while in mortality. President Brigham Young said, "The faithful Elders who leave this world will preach to the spirits in the spirit world. In that world there are millions and millions to every Elder who leaves here, and yet every spirit will be preached to that has had a tabernacle here on earth and become accountable."[15]

Apparently, missionaries sent to spirit prison to teach the gospel will meet with great success. President Lorenzo Snow said, "When the gospel is preached to the spirits in prison, the success attending that preaching will be far greater than that attending the preaching of our elders in this life. I believe there will be very few indeed of those spirits who will not gladly receive the gospel when it is carried to them. The circumstances there will be a thousand times more favorable."[16]

Brigham Young added, "The spirit of Joseph . . . is active in preaching to the spirits in prison, and preparing the way to redeem the nations of the earth, those who lived in darkness previous to the introduction of the Gospel by himself in these days."[17]

Notes:

1. Brigham Young "Preaching to Spirits in Prison," *The Contributor* 10 (July 1889), 321.

2. Brigham Young, *Journal of Discourses* (June 22, 1856), 3:370.

3. G. Homer Durham, comp., *Discourses of Wilford Woodruff*, (Salt Lake City: Bookcraft, 1946), 77.

4. Rudger J. Clawson, Conference Report April 1933, 76.

5. Joseph F. Smith, *The Young Woman's Journal* 23, (1912), 130.

6. Henry Zollinger, *Faith-promoting Collection 1882–1974*, box 2, folder 17 (courtesy of the Church History Library, The Church of Jesus Christ of Latter-day Saints).

7. Duane Crowther, *Life Everlasting* (Salt Lake City: Bookcraft, 1967), 59–60. Used with permission of Springville, Utah: Horizon Publishers & Distributors, Inc.

8. John Peterson, "Was Dead and Came to Life Again," *Juvenile Instructor* 41, (October 15, 1909), 609–610.

9. C.C.A. Christensen, "A Glimpse Of The Spirit World," *Juvenile Instructor*, vol. 28, (15, January, 1893), 56–57.

10. John Peterson, "Was Dead and Came to Life Again," *Juvenile Instructor*, vol. 41, (15 October, 1909), 609–610.

11. Brigham Young, "Preaching to Spirits in Prison," *The Contributor* 10 (July 1889), 321.

12. Wilford Woodruff, *Journal of Discourses* (October 8, 1881), 22:334.

13. Melvin J. Ballard, *Crusader for Righteousness* (Salt Lake City: Bookcraft, 1966), 272.

14. "Manifestations About Temple Work" [ca. 1918] (courtesy of the Church History Library, The Church of Jesus Christ of Latter-day Saints).

15. Brigham Young, *Journal of Discourses* (December 10, 1868), 13:76.

16. Lorenzo Snow, as quoted by Alma P. and Clea M. Burton in *For They Shall Be Comforted* (Salt Lake City: Deseret Book), 50.

17. Brigham Young "Preaching to Spirits in Prison," 321.

> "Therefore, cheer up your hearts, and remember that ye are free to act for yourselves—to choose the way of everlasting death or the way of eternal life." (2 Nephi 10:23)

Chapter Thirteen

Agency and Repentance

A fundamental part of the plan of salvation is agency—the ability and freedom to choose good or evil. "Wherefore, men are free according to the flesh; and all things are given them which are expedient unto man. And they are free to choose liberty and eternal life, through the great mediator of all men, or to choose captivity and death, according to the captivity and power of the devil" (2 Nephi 2:27).

Joseph F. Smith said,

> God has given to all men an agency, and has granted to us the privilege to serve Him or serve Him not, to do that which is right or that which is wrong, and this privilege is given to all men irrespective of creed, color or condition. The wealthy have this agency, the poor have this agency, and no man is deprived by any power of God from exercising it in the fullest and in the freest manner. This agency has been given to all. This is a blessing that God has bestowed upon the world of mankind, upon all his children alike.[1]

While in mortality, we are allowed to continue to exercise our sacred right of free agency. Dr. Elisabeth Kubler-Ross said, "The greatest gift God granted man is free will. Among living beings, free will is given only to man."[2]

Because we might be influenced by memories of the life we led before coming to earth, the Lord has provided safeguards and has put a veil over our minds during mortality—taking away memory of our previous existence. However, we can still see through the glass darkly and feel a sense of familiarity when we obey God's commandments and talk to God though prayer, which allows His Spirit to abide with us.

We should remember that once we pass through the veil and go to the Spirit World, we will be the same person in heaven that we are now. If we are righteous now, we will be righteous in the next life. "Spirits will have the same appetites and desires that they had when they lived on earth."[3]

Those that sin and choose evil here will have those same tendencies in the spirit world. Because we will still be able to make our own decisions and choices in the spirit world, that sphere will have the same cross section of diversity of righteousness or wickedness that exists now on earth. Brigham Young spoke of this when he said, "The wicked spirits that leave here and go into the spirit world, are they wicked there? Yes."[4]

Because there will be no sudden change in our personality when we die, we are told to overcome our imperfections while we are on earth. "For that same spirit which doth possess your bodies at the time that ye go out of this life, that same spirit will have power to possess your body in that eternal world" (Alma 34: 34).

Repentance is a natural component of agency. Since we are allowed to make our own decisions, everyone will make mistakes and sin. Knowing this, Heavenly Father developed the plan of salvation, whereby Jesus Christ, through the Atonement, will pay for our sins if we repent. Once we return to the spirit world, we will be judged according to the choices—good and bad—we made while on earth.

Repentance is also possible in the spirit world and is a necessary condition for exaltation. In the Book of Mormon, Christ teaches, "No unclean thing can enter into his [God's] kingdom; therefore nothing entereth into his rest save it be those who have washed their garments in my blood, because of their faith, and the repentance of all their sins, and their faithfulness unto the end" (3 Nephi 27:19).

Repentance is also a commandment. In the Book of Mormon, Alma told the people, "Behold, now I say until you that He commandeth you to repent; and except ye repent, ye can in nowise inherit the kingdom of God" (Alma 9:12).

During his near-death experience, Henry Zollinger said, "I noticed that people had their free agency there like we do here."[5]

During his visit to the spirit world, Archie Graham was shown lowly spheres where people who had not been valiant were living. He asked his guide if people on earth would make better choices if they knew what was waiting for them in the next life. "'That would never do,' he [the guide] said, 'as it would rob them of their full right to choose good or evil. Now they choose the thing they like most and the reward is waiting for them."[6]

Alpheus Cutler

It is natural to think that people who have near-death experiences will make righteous choices after seeing the next life. However, since people are allowed agency, this is not always the case. Even though he received a witness of the truthfulness of the gospel during his visit to the spirit world, Alpheus Cutler rejected it after returning to earth. His story is told by his grandson Abraham A. Kimball—son of Heber C. Kimball.

Alpheus Cutler traveled to Winter Quarters with other faithful saints but became bitter toward the Church and apostatized. He then started a new church and appointed himself as its leader. Many years later, his grandson Abraham A. Kimball, who had recently become converted to the Church, went east to visit with his brother, grandparents, and other relatives. While there, Abraham had a private talk with his grandfather, telling him that he had joined the Church.

As they talked, Alpheus said, "I know that Joseph Smith was a prophet of God, and I know that Brigham Young is his legal successor, and I always did know it. But the trouble with me was I wanted to lead, and could not be led. I have run my race and sealed my doom, and I know what I have got to meet.

"I died once, and was dead for some length of time. My spirit left my body and went to the land of spirits. I saw the crown that I should wear if I remained faithful, and the condemnation I should receive if I did not. I begged to remain but was informed that I must return and warn the people to repent, as my work on earth was not yet done.

"After my spirit returned to my body, those around discovered the appearance of life. The first words that I spoke were to Sidney Rigdon, who was stooping over me. I called upon him to repent of his sins, or he would be damned."

Abraham said, "My grandfather paused here, but continued by saying: 'I want you to go back to your father, taking your brother Isaac with you, as I know he is a good man, and remain steadfast to Mormonism. Let what may turn up, *never yield the point*; for it will save and exalt you in the kingdom of God.'

Continuing, Abraham said of his grandfather, "He wept like a child after saying this. He then said to me: 'One favor I wish to ask of you, namely, that you will not divulge this confession to those whom I lead while I live.' "[7]

Notes:

1. Joseph F. Smith, *Journal of Discourses* (April 8, 1883), (Liverpool, 1854–86), 24:175.
2. Elisabeth Kubler-Ross, *On Life After Death* (Berkeley, CA: Celestial Arts, 1991), 11.
3. *Gospel Principles* (Salt Lake City: The Church of Jesus Christ of Latter-day Saints, 1978), 242.
4. Brigham Young, *Journal of Discourses* (June 22, 1856), 3:370.
5. Henry Zollinger, *Faith-promoting Collection 1882–1974*, box 2, folder 17 (courtesy of the Church History Library, The Church of Jesus Christ of Latter-day Saints).
6. Archie J. Graham, *A Visit Beyond the Veil* [n. d.].
7. Abraham A. Kimball, *Gems For the Young Folks, Fourth Book of the Faith-Promoting Series* (Salt Lake City: Juvenile Instructor Office, 1881), 16–17.

"And I saw the dead, small and great, stand before God; and the books were opened: and another book was opened, which is the book of life: and the dead were judged out of those things which were written in the books, according to their works." (Revelation 20:12)

Chapter Fourteen

There Are Different Spheres in the Spirit World

A number of people who had near-death experiences reported seeing or visiting different spheres in the spirit world. They declared that although they saw people divided into different levels, money and power were not the determining factor, such as is often the case on earth.

When a person's physical body dies, its spirit goes to the spirit world, where it will be assigned a place in one of two main spheres: spirit prison or spirit paradise (see 1 Nephi 15:28–30).

President Joseph F. Smith, in his vision of the redemption of the dead, saw that these two spheres were separate from one another (see Doctrine and Covenants 138). Righteous people who have received gospel ordinances will go to paradise. *Paradise* is a term that simply means a place of departed spirits. Those who have not received the saving ordinances of the gospel and those that are unrighteous will go to spirit prison. Both of these spheres are temporary abodes where spirits will stay until the resurrection and the final judgment. *Spirit prison* is not to be confused with *hell*, which refers to the place where the wicked will live after the final judgment.

All of God's children will have a chance to hear the gospel. If a person did not have the opportunity while on earth, he or she will have that chance in the next life. If a person accepts the gospel in spirit prison, all necessary ordinances will be performed vicariously on earth by living proxies in the temple so the person can progress (see Doctrine and Covenants 138).

After the Resurrection, everyone will stand before Heavenly Father for the final judgment. God's judgment will be based on our acceptance of Christ as our Savior and our obedience to His commandments while we live on the earth. Melvin J. Ballard said, "We are reaping what we have heretofore sown, so shall we hereafter reap what we now sow."[1]

The scriptures tell us that if we do not live righteously on earth, we will not be able to live with God. "Therefore remember, O man, for all thy doings thou shalt be brought into judgment. . . . Wherefore, if ye have sought to do wickedly in the days of your probation, then ye are found unclean before the judgment-seat of God; and no unclean thing can dwell with God; wherefore, ye must be cast off forever" (Doctrine and Covenants 76:75, 77).

From a vision given to Joseph Smith, we know there are three kingdoms in heaven. Which one people go to after the final judgment will be determined by their conduct on earth. The highest degree of glory is the celestial kingdom. Within the celestial kingdom are three levels. To attain the highest level, where Heavenly Father and Jesus Christ dwell, one must receive the ordinance of marriage and be sealed as an eternal family in the temple. All little children who die before the age of accountability will be saved in the celestial kingdom. People who dwell in the celestial kingdom will have:

- Accepted Christ as their Savior.
- Repented and received a remission of their sins through the Atonement of Jesus Christ.
- Kept God's commandments.
- Received all the saving ordinances, such as baptism, the gift of the Holy Ghost, the temple endowment, and a temple sealing.

The second degree of glory is the terrestrial kingdom. Those who inherit this kingdom of glory were good people during life, but "were blinded by the craftiness of men. . . . These are they who receive of the presence of the Son, but not of the fulness of the Father" (Doctrine and

Covenants 76:75–77). People who will live in the terrestrial kingdom are those who:

- Died without the law
- Received not the testimony of Jesus in the flesh but afterward received it
- Those who were not valiant in the testimony of Jesus; wherefore, they obtain not the crown over the kingdom of our God (Doctrine and Covenants 76:72, 74, 79).

The telestial kingdom is the third kingdom. The telestial kingdom is for unrepentant sinners who did evil in this life. They will suffer for their sins and will not be redeemed from the devil until the last resurrection (see Doctrine and Covenants 76:85). People who will live in the telestial kingdom are those who:

- Received not the gospel of Christ, neither the testimony of Jesus.
- Those who deny not the Holy Spirit.
- Those who receive not of His fulness in the eternal world but of the Holy Spirit through the ministration of the terrestrial (Doctrine and Covenants 76:82–84, 86).

Another sphere, which has no glory, is outer darkness or hell, where the sons of perdition are sent. A son of perdition is someone who receives the truth but then denies the witness of the Holy Ghost. Hell is reserved for those who have rejected the gospel, have come out in open rebellion against God, are engaged in wickedness, and are completely subject to Satan. Only the willfully rebellious who knew the truth and rejected it will be cast into hell along with the devil (see Doctrine and Covenants 76:31–36, 43).

Thomas S. Thomas spoke of separate spheres when he wrote about people in the spirit world; "These souls are now busy, in the future existence, working in different habitations. Many are from different spheres."[2]

When John Peterson went to the spirit world and saw a large crowd, his guide told him, "These are mostly your progenitors, and are now in the lowest sphere in the spirit world."[3]

Charles R. Woodbury

While he was in the hospital, Charles R. Woodbury had a near-death experience and saw the celestial kingdom and hell. He writes:

"While I was in the L.D.S. Hospital in 1954, I was very weak. One day I saw a real bright light, brighter than noonday. In the light I saw people, men and women dressed in light clothing. Everyone was so happy, but all busy.

"A voice said to me, 'This is the Celestial Kingdom, the highest degree of glory. This is the reward of those who in mortal life complied with the new and everlasting covenant of marriage in the Temple of the Lord, and kept those covenants sacred, and if you and your wife continue as faithful as you have been, it shall be your privilege and joy to dwell together in the Celestial Kingdom, in the highest degree of glory, with your loved ones and the Father and Son forever.

"When this scene closed, the curtain dropped and what I saw before me was heart rending. I saw men and women, all dressed in dark clothing. Contention and strife existed there. They were searching for something they couldn't find.

"A voice said to me, 'This is what is spoken of in the Bible as Hell, or the bottomless pit. This is the reward of those who in mortal life disobeyed the laws of God, and the laws of the land, and created appetites and took things into their bodies which were contrary to the teachings of the Lord and detrimental to their physical health. In mortal life they could get things to satisfy this appetite and craving. Here they cannot get anything to satisfy it. In this condition they'll remain for the 1000 years during the Millennium, before their bodies are resurrected from the grave.'

"I was happy when this scene closed. I sure feel sorry for people in that condition. I hope and pray that myself or any of my loved ones will never be in that group . . . that they'll all be worthy to enjoy the blessings of the Celestial Kingdom."[4]

Children Are Saved in the Celestial Kingdom

Children who die will receive a celestial glory. When the Prophet Joseph Smith saw a vision of the three degrees of glory, he declared, "And I also beheld that all children who die before they arrive at the years of accountability are saved in the celestial kingdom of heaven" (Doctrine and Covenants 137:10). Speaking at the funeral services for King Follett, Joseph Smith said, "A question may be asked—'Will mothers have their children in eternity?' Yes! Yes! Mothers, you shall have your children; for they shall have eternal life."[5]

Joseph F. Smith explained why and how children are saved. "But, with little children who are taken away in infancy and innocence before they had reached the years of accountability, and are not capable of committing sin, the gospel reveals to us the fact that they are redeemed, and Satan has no power over them. . . . They are redeemed by the blood of Christ, and they are saved just as surely as death has come into the world through the fall of our first parents."[6]

Some people wonder how children will appear in the spirit world. The Prophet Joseph Smith taught, "Children will be enthroned in the presence of God and the Lamb with bodies of the same stature that they had on earth, having been redeemed by the blood of the Lamb; they will there enjoy the fullness of that light, glory and intelligence, which is prepared in the celestial kingdom."[7]

Joseph Smith's teachings are corroborated by the experiences of those who visited the spirit world and reported there were no children in lower spheres. Archie J. Graham, who visited a lower kingdom in the spirit world, said, "I was informed, however, there were no children under the age of eight years, as the atoning blood of Jesus Christ has paid for all children under that age, as they are sealed Christ's regardless of creed, or nationality." Later, when he went to a higher sphere, he said; "There were numerous parks and playgrounds, filled with happy and intelligent children."[8]

Harriet Salvina Beal Millet said she saw three of her siblings while in Paradise: "On the floor playing was our little darling William Francis that we buried on the plains. And with him were the twins."[9]

Occasionally, children who have died appear to loved ones on earth as adults. We do not fully understand how or why this occurs, but Joseph Smith taught that an infant child that died would come up in the resurrection as a child. He told a mother who had just lost her child, "You will have the joy, the pleasure, and satisfaction of nurturing this child, after its resurrection, until it reaches the full stature of its spirit."[10] Joseph F. Smith taught this same principle, saying, "The child that was buried in its infancy will come up in the form of the child that it was when it was laid down; then it will begin to develop . . . until it reaches the full measure of the stature of its spirit."[11]

Bertha Deusnup Elder

Tired, poor, and depressed at having to move time after time from a developed area to a bleak and barren one to open yet another new settlement, Bertha Deusnup Elder decided the world was too harsh to bring any more children into it. However, Bertha had a change of heart after she had a near-death experience in 1913. During her experience, Bertha saw a large group of children—two of whom seemed particularly beautiful. Janet Christensen, Bertha's granddaughter, tells Bertha's story.

When Bertha first became ill, her husband hired a nurse, Sister Edward, to watch over her. However, as the days passed, Bertha's condition worsened, and then she passed away. Bertha first became aware that she had died when she found herself rising above her bed. Then she noticed that all of the pain she had been suffering was gone.

The account states, "She [Bertha] was greeted by a woman who escorted her into a large room where she was greeted by many of her departed friends. One was a young man she had befriended and encouraged to develop his artistic talents. He was sitting in front of an easel, painting. Though he was very happy to see Bertha, he quickly returned to his work as though his time was very precious.

"Bertha was then taken into another room where there were many children. On the far side of the room she saw two little girls, whom she did not know. They were so beautiful she could not look away from them.

"'Do you want them?' the guide asked.

"'Yes. Oh, yes,' she responded quickly. 'Can I return to earth life and have them?'"

The escort told Bertha that she could have them and explained, "That is the purpose of this visit, to let you see them. Now we must return."

Bertha then returned to her body and in time, recovered fully from her illness. Then Bertha told Jonathan she wanted more children. They moved again, this time to Oakley, Idaho, where Bertha had a baby girl whom she named Alberta. Two years later, Bertha had another daughter, LaVirle. Bertha always felt strongly that these two daughters were the little girls she had seen in heaven.[12]

Notes:

1. Melvin J. Ballard, *Crusader for Righteousness* (Salt Lake City: Bookcraft, 1966), 108.
2. Thomas S. Thomas, *A Glimpse of the Future.*
3. C. C. A. Christensen, "A Glimpse of the Spirit World," *The Juvenile Instructor* 28, (January 15, 1893), 56–57.
4. Charles R. Woodbury, *Faith Promoting Experiences of Patriarch Charles R.*

Woodbury (courtesy of the Church History Library, The Church of Jesus Christ of Latter-day Saints).

5. Joseph Smith, *History of the Church*, April 7, 1844 (Salt Lake City: The Church of Jesus Christ of Latter-day Saints, 1950), 6:316.
6. *Gospel Doctrine, Selections From the Sermons and Writings of Joseph F. Smith*, 13th ed. (Salt Lake City: Deseret Book, 1963), 452–56.
7. Joseph Smith, *History of the Church*, March 20, 1842, 4:555–56.
8. Archie J. Graham, *A Visit Beyond the Veil*.
9. Cora Anna Beal Peterson, [biographical sketch of William Beal, n. d.] (courtesy of the Church History Library, The Church of Jesus Christ of Latter-day Saints).
10. *Gospel Doctrine, Selections from the Sermons and Writings of Joseph F. Smith*, 455–56
11. *Gospel Doctrine, Selections from the Sermons and Writings of Joseph F. Smith*, 24.
12. Lee Nelson, *Beyond The Veil*, vol. 1 (Springville, Utah: Cedar Fort, Inc., 1988), 37–40. Used with permission.

> "Behold, mine house is a house of order, saith the Lord God, and not a house of confusion." (Doctrine and Covenants 132:8)

Chapter Fifteen

The Spirit World Is Organized and Is Governed by the Priesthood

A number of people who had near-death experiences commented that the spirit world was perfectly organized and that people appeared to be subject to laws and rules. Brigham Young said, "Every departed spirit is subject to the laws that govern the spirit world."[1]

Heavenly Father is a God of order, and the same divinely appointed priesthood that provides organization and the authority to govern on earth will exist in the spirit world in accordance with God's will (see Doctrine and Covenants 138:30). Joseph Smith taught, "I would just remark, that the spirits of men are eternal, that they are governed by the same Priesthood that Abraham, Melchizedek, and the Apostles were: that they are organized according to that Priesthood which is everlasting, 'without beginning of days or end of years,'—that they all move in their respective spheres, and are governed by the law of God."[2] Speaking of the spirit world, President Brigham Young said, "They will have apostles, prophets and ministers there, as we have here, to guide them in the ways of truth and righteousness, and lead them back to God."[3]

Every righteous man who holds the priesthood here on earth, whether he is a deacon or a high priest, will hold the same priesthood when he goes to the spirit world. Brigham Young explained, "When the faithful Elders, holding this Priesthood, go into the spirit world they carry with them the same power and Priesthood that they had while in the mortal tabernacle."[4] Apostle Rudger Clawson said, "They who have gone before us, who bear the priesthood, have taken the means with them which represents divine authority."[5] President Wilford Woodruff said the same thing. "The same priesthood exists on the other side of the veil. Every man who is faithful is in his quorum there."[6]

"Now a man who is an apostle here will be an apostle there," Rudger Clawson confirmed when speaking at general conference. "A man who is a high priest here, or a seventy, or an elder, or a patriarch, when he dies, will still be in possession of the office he held on earth. . . . All that divides . . . is the veil, and the principles of the Gospel that govern here in the Church of Christ will surely govern there in the Church of Christ. So the men holding various offices in the priesthood in this life will pass into their proper quorums in the life to come. No doubt it will all be done in perfect order. There will be no confusion, and the good work will go on."[7]

Although people will be divided into different levels in the spirit world, money and power will not be the determining factor, as it often is in worldly matters. After his visit to the spirit world William Wallace Raymond commented on how it was organized, saying that society there is governed by ability and position in the holy priesthood. He further declared, "They all live in perfect order such as I have never seen on earth."[8]

Jedediah M. Grant

As second counselor to Brigham Young, forty-year-old Jedediah M. Grant worked tirelessly during the Mormon Reformation of 1856, traveling throughout Utah and calling people to repentance. It was generally thought at the time that Jedediah contracted pneumonia because he neglected his health in his fervor to serve the Lord. His condition became critical and shortly before passing away, Jedediah had two near-death experiences. When Jedediah related some of things he had seen to President Heber C. Kimball on December 1, 1856, he mentioned that everyone in the spirit world was "organized in perfect harmony" and that there was no disorder anywhere.

When President Heber C. Kimball visited Jedediah on that December day, the first thing he did was give his friend a blessing. Shortly afterward, Heber said Jedediah "raised himself up and talked for about an hour as busily as he could, telling me what he had seen and what he understood until I was afraid he would weary himself, when I arose and left him.

"He [Jedediah] said to me, 'Brother Heber, I have been in the spirit world two nights in succession, and of all the dreads that ever came across me, the worst was to have to again return to my body, though I had to do it. But O,' says he, 'the order and government that were there! When in the spirit world, I saw the order of righteous men and women'; beheld them organized in their several grades, and there appeared to be no obstructions to my vision; I could see every man and woman in their grade and order.

"'I looked to see if there was any disorder there, but there was none, neither could I see any death, nor any darkness, disorder or confusion.' He said that people he saw were organized in family capacities, and when he looked at them, he saw grade after grade, and all were organized in perfect harmony. He would mention one item after another, and say: 'Why it is just as Brother Brigham says it is; it is just as he has told us many a time. . . .'

"He saw the righteous gathered together in the spirit world, and there were no wicked spirits among them. He saw his wife; she was the first person that came to him. He saw many that he knew, but did not have conversation with any except his wife Caroline. She came to him, and he said that she looked beautiful and had their little child, that died on the plains, in her arms, and said, 'Mr. Grant, here is little Margaret; you know that the wolves ate her up, but it did not hurt her; here she is all right.'"

Jedediah continued, "'To my astonishment,' he said, 'when I looked at families there was a deficiency in some, there was a lack, for I saw families that would not be permitted to come and dwell together, because they had not honored their calling here.

"He asked his wife Caroline where Joseph and Hyrum and Father Smith and others were; she replied, 'They have gone away ahead, to perform and transact business for us. . . .'

"He also spoke of the buildings he saw there, remarking that the Lord gave Solomon wisdom and poured gold and silver into his hands that he might display his skill and ability, and said that the temple erected by Solomon was much inferior to the most ordinary buildings he saw in the spirit world.

"In regard to gardens, says brother Grant, 'I have seen good gardens on this earth, but I never saw any to compare with those that were there.

I saw flowers of numerous kinds and some with from fifty to a hundred different colored flowers growing upon one stalk. . . .'

"After mentioning the things that he had seen, he spoke of how much he disliked to return and resume his body, after having seen the beauty and glory of the spirit world, where the righteous spirits are gathered together.

"Some may marvel at my speaking about these things, for many profess to believe that we have no spiritual existence. But do you not believe that my spirit was organized before it came to my body here? And do you not think there can be houses and gardens, fruit trees, and every other good thing there? The spirits of those things were made, as well as our spirits, and it follows that they can exist upon the same principle.

"After speaking of the gardens and the beauty of every thing [sic] there, brother Grant said that he felt extremely sorrowful at having to leave so beautiful a place and come back to earth, for he looked upon his body with loathing, but was obliged to enter it again."

Jedediah M. Grant passed away later that day, on December 1, 1856.[9]

Requests Made to Priesthood Authorities

A few people who had near-death experiences mentioned receiving permission from priesthood authorities for certain actions, such as returning to earth to visit or comfort a loved one.

An example of this is when David Lynn Brooks' wife came back and was allowed to talk to her husband. She told David, "I have wanted to come to you before this, but only tonight was I given permission by the priesthood to visit with you."[10]

Martha Jane Boice had been dead for some time when she returned briefly to give a message to her husband, John. The account states; "It was when the wee hours of the night spread their stillness all around, that a voice called out from where the dead lay."

It was Martha. She whispered, "'John. John, raise me up.'

"John hastened to obey the command. He went to the couch where his wife lay and raised her up. She sat up on the board bed and said, 'Don't be afraid. I have been in the Spirit world but have obtained permission to return and to remain for two hours.'"[11]

Joseph R. Murdock

When Joseph R. Murdock entered the spirit world and met his

ancestors, they let him know how displeased they were with him. Some even turned their backs on him. Joseph found out they were unhappy because he had neglected to do ordinance work for them. He then asked for permission to return to mortality so he could do the necessary work. Joseph related his experience to A. F. Bennett of the Genealogical Society of Utah, who wrote the following:

Joseph related, "I have always been active in the church and in business pursuits, having taught school, served on a mission to the Northern States, in a Bishopric and as Stake President of Wasatch Stake. I have engaged in farming, stock raising, merchandising, and was a leader in the organization of several irrigation companies. In politics I was a member of a constitutional convention and a state senator. I was a leader in fighting the liquor traffic. In addition, I was president of the Bank of Heber City. My time was so fully occupied that I felt there was none of it left for genealogical research and temple work.

"Then one day I passed away; my spirit left my body and entered the spirit world. Quite a number of people were there to greet me, relatives, some of them dressed in Scottish costumes.

"I expected them to greet me warmly and welcome me to their midst. Instead they were not at all glad to see me; some even turned their backs abruptly upon me in distinct displeasure.

"'Why have you not done the work for us?' they demanded. 'We depended upon you, and you have failed us.'

"I was heartbroken. Now all my many activities and responsibilities on earth seemed to be of little consequence. Their interest was to have the work done which would bring blessings to them. I had failed them, and they were not at all happy about it. In my great distress I sought for and obtained permission to return to life and make up for my past neglect. Now I have done all I can in research and temple work, and, Brother Bennett, I am making sure that when I meet these relatives again, I shall receive a better welcome from them."[12]

Notes:

1. Brigham Young, *Journal of Discourses* (December 10, 1868), 13:76.
2. Joseph F. Smith and his assistants, comp., *Teachings of the Prophet Joseph Smith*, 208.
3. Brigham Young, "Preaching to Spirits in Prison," 321.

4. Brigham Young, *Journal of Discourses* (June 22, 1856), 3:371.

5. Rudger Clawson, Conference Report April 1933, 76.

6. G. Homer Durham comp., *Discourses of Wilford Woodruff* (Salt Lake City: Bookcraft, 1946), 77.

7. Rudger Clawson, Conference Report April 1933, 76.

8. William Wallace Raymond, "Vision 1881 Aug 12" (courtesy of the Church History Library, The Church of Jesus Christ of Latter-day Saints).

9. Heber C. Kimball, *Journal of Discourses* (December 4, 1856), (Liverpool, 1854–86), 4:135–137.

10. Duane Crowther, *Life Everlasting* (Salt Lake City: Bookcraft, 1967), 59–60. Used with permission of Springville, Utah: Horizon Publishers & Distributors, Inc.

11. Samantha T. Brimhall, *Boice Family History* [ca 1930] (courtesy of the Church History Library, The Church of Jesus Christ of Latter-day Saints).

12. A. F. Bennett, *Faith-promoting Collection 1882–1972*, box 2, folder 8 (courtesy of the Church History Library, The Church of Jesus Christ of Latter-day Saints).

"Behold, I will reveal unto you the Priesthood, by the hand of Eliljah the prophet, before the coming of the great and dreadful day of the Lord. And he shall plant in the hearts of the children the promises made to the fathers, and the hearts of the children shall turn to their fathers. If it were not so, the whole earth would be utterly wasted at his coming." (Doctrine and Covenants 2:1–3)

Chapter Sixteen

The Importance of Ordinance Work

According to the above scripture in the Doctrine and Covenants, the earth will be wasted if our hearts are not turned to our ancestors. Joseph F. Smith explains this doctrine. "Why would the earth be wasted? Simply because if there is not a welding link between the fathers and the children—which is the work for the dead—then we will all stand rejected."[1]

How do we weld that link? For the work of God to have meaning, we must find our ancestors through genealogy work and be linked to them through sealing ordinances. The ordinances of the gospel are:

- Baptism
- Confirmation
- Aaronic and Melchizedek Priesthood ordinations
- Washings and Anointings (cleansing ordinances that prepare people for the priesthood and authority in the celestial kingdom)
- Temple Endowment (this ordinance teaches basic information that is required to enter advanced spheres in the celestial kingdom)
- Eternal Marriage (a marriage that continues beyond the grave)
- Sealing of Families (this binds families together eternally, making family units complete)

There will be people in spirit prison who, after listening to missionaries, will repent and accept the gospel of Jesus Christ. However, they need to have the necessary saving ordinances performed in their behalf. Because those in spirit prison lack a physical body, they cannot perform those ordinances themselves—their work must be done vicariously on earth. Mortals who are worthy can do this work in temples so people in the spirit world can receive the subsequent blessings.

The Apostle Rudger J. Clawson said, "The Savior stands for us. He has given His life's blood, that precious blood, that we might be saved. So we must stand for our ancestors. We must do for them the work that they cannot do for themselves. I call your attention to this fact, that that particular work is perhaps the most benevolent, the most charitable work in all the world, because they find themselves in a position where they cannot move. Their progress is stopped."[2]

Because ordinance work is so important, the Lord has commanded his servants to build temples. President Gordon B. Hinckley said of temple work, "I know of no other work to compare with it. It more nearly approaches the vicarious sacrifice of the son of God in behalf of all mankind than any other work of which I am aware. . . . It is a service which is of the very essence of selflessness."[3]

During his near-death experience, Archie Graham saw people in spirit prison learn about and accept the gospel. However, that wasn't enough to allow them to go to paradise. Archie said, "Even though they may repent, progress in wisdom and knowledge . . . they are still held in prison . . . until someone has been baptized, confirmed and has received all other sacred ordinances pertaining to the endowment of the Holy Priesthood for them in the Temple of the Lord on the earth. This is the only power that can release them."[4]

When Harriet Salvina Beal Millet was in the spirit world, her mother gave her many instructions regarding genealogy. Harriet said, "She told me of temple work she wanted done and wanted Father to do it with me to help him. She said there were sealings to be done." Later on, when Harriet saw a room full of men busily working, she asked her mother what they were doing. Her mother said they were "Preparing genealogy so that the work can be done on earth for those who have died without having the privilege of hearing the gospel themselves."

Brother Cox

For weeks, Brother Cox had been unable to get out of bed or even speak. When his wife, Elnara, checked on him the morning of February 25, 1939, she was surprised to find him able to speak. He then told her that he had been to the spirit world and found out that his ancestors were anxious to have their ordinance work done. His experience is told by his wife, Elnara Cox. Like many older couples of this era, they referred to each other as "Ma" and "Pa."

When Elnara walked into the bedroom and saw her husband awake, she said, "Oh my Pa, you have had a good sleep you ought to feel better now."

Brother Cox was overcome with sudden emotion. Elnara said, "Tears Rolled [sic] down his cheeks and he could hardly speak; but when he got hold of him self [sic] so he could speak he said, 'I had a dream. I saw my mother'; I said, 'Did your mother look natural'; and he said, 'Oh yes my mother looked so good and she has the Best of health.' Then I ask[ed] him if his mother talked to him and he said, 'No but she Beconed [beckoned] me and I knew by the sign she gave what she wanted me to do':

"I thought when he said she Becond [beckoned] him I though[t] he ment [meant] she wanted him to come with her. But he said, 'She wants me to have my work done.' We was married in the Temple but he had not been sealed to his Parents; so then he said between his sobs; ma, will Eli [their son] have the athority [sic] to do that work for me [?]

"I said 'Sure he will Pa, or any of the Boys that has been through the Temple will have that athority [sic] Nelson Harrison or any of the Boys that has been through the Temple if that is your request.'

"He said 'I want Eli to do it for me.' Then he said 'oh the wealth that is over there, there is no wealth on this Earth that can compare With the wealth that is over there';

"Then I ask him if he saw any one [sic] else that he knew.

"He said, 'No, my mother came to me I did not go to her: he says, 'Oh the nice place my mother was in and the nice things she had.'

"Then I said, 'I thought you just told me your mother came to you.'

"He said, 'Oh yes, but I saw where my mother was and she looked so nice and she was so happy.' Then he said, 'Ma I want you to tell Lewis I want him to join the church for it is the only true church on this Earth and I want him to stay with it and I want you all to stay with it.

"I said 'no Pa, don't tell me to tell Lewis, you tell him your very own self. Do you realize that you can talk now you can say any thing [sic] you want to say now and you have been for months you could not think of words you wanted to say and now you can say anything you want to.

"He then says, 'Will you call Lewis and tell him I want to talk to him.'

"I said, 'Sure I will' and I went and called Lewis and told him his father wanted to talk to him.

"He said, 'Alright mother, I will be right down,' and he was there in five minutes."

While Lewis was talking to his father, his sister, Hazel, came. Elnara said that as they stood by their father's bed, "Tears rolled down his cheeks and he said, 'Oh Hazel you look like my mother:' and then he told her the same thing he had told the rest of us all about seeing his mother.

"I ask Pa if he did not wish he had of went when I wanted him to when I went to Salt Lake to do my mother's work and he said, 'Oh I have wished a Thousand times I had.' Written by his wife, Elnara Cox."[6]

Ancestors Are Anxious to Have Ordinance Work Done

Family relationships extend beyond death. In the plan of salvation, mortals can perform saving ordinances that allow family members—living and dead—to be linked together. Baptism is one of those ordinances, and it provides entrance into the kingdom of God. Sealing ordinances join a woman with a man in eternal marriage, and when their children are born, they are automatically tied to their parents throughout eternity. Sealings can also be performed to tie children who are born outside the covenant of eternal marriage to their parents.

Many of those who visited the spirit world saw spirits who were being held in prison because they had not yet had their ordinance work done. A few people who had near-death experiences were asked by their ancestors to return to mortality so they could do genealogy work and temple work. One man was even given a chilly reception because he had failed to do temple work for his ancestors. He promised to do better when he returned to earth. Others were instructed about the importance of genealogical work.

We cannot achieve perfection and exaltation until our ancestors have had an opportunity to accept the gospel. "They without us cannot be made perfect" (Hebrews 11:40). In order for us to progress, we must see that ordinance work is done for our ancestors. Joseph Smith said, "For we without them [our dead] cannot be made perfect; neither can they without us be made perfect. . . . It is necessary in the ushering in of the dispensation of the fulness of times, which dispensation is now beginning to usher in, that a whole and complete and perfect union, and welding together of dispensations, and keys, and powers, and glories should take place. . ." (Doctrine and Covenants 128:18).

Heavenly Father has laid a great responsibility upon Church members to seek after our dead. Everyone has an obligation to help their deceased ancestors by performing genealogy and temple work for them. President Ezra Taft Benson said, "The need for each of us to perform temple and genealogical work has never been more urgent. We must redouble our efforts to accomplish this great and holy work. We cannot hope for perfection without being linked to our forefathers. Neither can they hope for perfection without us. My brothers and sisters, it is up to each of us to see that this work is done."[7]

Joseph F. Smith said, "There isn't anything so great and so glorious in this world as to labor for the salvation of the living and for the redemption of the dead."[8]

During his near-death experience, Peter E. Johnson was asked many times by his ancestors if he was going to stay or if he was going to return to mortality. Wondering why they seemed so anxious about it, Peter turned to his guide. "I then inquired why it was that I was asked so often if I was satisfied and if I desired to remain. I was then informed that my progenitors had made a request that if I chose I might be granted the privilege of returning, to again take up my mortal body, in order that I might gather my father's genealogy and do the necessary work in the temple for my ancestors." Peter then decided to return. His guide said, "'Good. Your progenitors will be pleased with your decision.' I asked the question why, and I was told that it was their desire that I should return to the body, hunt up my father's genealogies and do their work in the temple."[9]

When Joseph Murdock went to the spirit world, he received a chilly welcome from his relatives. Joseph said, ". . . some even turned their backs abruptly upon me in distinct displeasure.

"'Why have you not done the work for us?' they demanded. 'We depended upon you, and you have failed us.'

"I was heartbroken. . . . Their interest was to have the work done which would bring blessings to them. I had failed them . . . In my great distress I sought for and obtained permission to return to life and make up for my past neglect. Now I have done all I can in research and temple work."[10]

Lorena Wilson

Lorena Wilson was already weak and ill with blood poisoning when she caught a cold that settled in her lungs. She was lying in bed when her departed parents and other relatives visited her. Her father told Lorena it was important that the temple work be done for their ancestors. Later that night, he returned and took Lorena to the spirit world where she met some of her ancestors who were waiting for their ordinances to be done. Lorena writes about her illness and subsequent near-death experience:

"On the morning of November 7, 1914, I met with an accident which resulted seriously. [sic] During a period of two weeks or more my mind had been troubled with foreboding of something terrible that was going to happen to me. That morning the feeling became so intense that, after starting to my work, I retired again to my room and offered a special prayer in these words: 'O, Lord, if it is possible let this bitter cup pass, for I feel like I could not endure it.'

"I got no relief to my feelings, however, and went to my work at my cutting table, (in our school of dressmaking), even sadder in spirits. Almost immediately, in brushing off the table, a rusty needle was thrust into my right hand, and an inch of it was broken off in my hand. I soon saw it was necessary to call a doctor and doing so, I went at once to his office to have the needle extracted. The operation of finding and extracting the needle without destroying essential ligaments was, as could be expected, a delicate and difficult task.

"While at first thought it would seem to be the work of a few minutes, the doctors were baffled for the needle would change position. In short the second day was declining and the operation had not yet been successful, my vitality was then so low from the repeated administration of chloroform that my life was in danger. It seemed like I could not rally from the chloroform. I was so near death's door that the gates of the other world opened to my view, and I saw a vast congregation of people shut up within an enclosure. I was about to enter but they motioned for me to go back. One of the doctors told me afterward that he would not at that time, have given a straw for my chances of life. . . ."

Finally, the doctors took an x-ray and were able to locate and remove the needle.

"Blood poison [ing] had developed, however. I remained at the hospital two weeks and suffered much. The case became so serious that consulting physicians advised the amputation of my hand."

A prayer in the temple was offered for Lorena, and she became well enough to go home. However, her difficulties had not ended.

"I had not been home again very long before I contracted a severe cold which settled upon my lungs. . . . The pain and distress became severe to an alarming degree. My breath became short and difficult till I feared it would stop altogether. . . . A fear of death came over me, for I did not feel prepared to die. . . . Now I prayed, with all the fervent faith I could exercise, for relief. While in that attitude, lying upon my bed at about midday, I noticed my room filling with soft bright light.

"Immediately following the light, my father, who had been dead seven years, came into my room. He was accompanied by my mother, who had been dead thirty years, and by my sister and her daughter-in-law who had both been dead two years. . . . Father told me about our ancestors, how they had always stood up for the right. They were a good, worthy people, he said, and had accepted the Gospel in very large numbers, and were waiting with anxious hope for the ordinance of baptism. . . .

"Father then said the time had come for these ordinances to be performed for our kindred in the spirit world, and he desired me to take up the work and see that it was done. I told him that I would."

Then Lorena's father said, "I will come for you at one o'clock. I was left in wonderment as to what was going to happen, but that night I went to sleep as usual. While asleep, as I believe, though it seemed real and natural, my visitors came again and took me with them. We went and saw a large congregation of people, shut up within walls—the same as I saw while on the operating table, as before mentioned. There were so many that it seemed like there were millions of them.

"Father introduced me to our people as we stood on an elevated stand where they could see me, and he told them I had promised to attend to the temple work for them. He then desired me to address them. I felt humiliated that I did not know anything to say, but I said this much, that I would do all in my power for their redemption. . . . These people did not look like any I have ever seen on the earth. Their manner of dress and the texture of the materials from which their clothing was made, and their mode of dressing their hair were entirely different.

"When my visitors were about to bid me good bye, I asked father to give me a sign that I might know that what I had seen and heard was a reality.

"He said, 'This will be your sign, you will be afflicted in your other hand. . . .'"

"When I awoke in the morning, to my surprise and relief, my sickness had all left me. I had not so much as a cough. I was healed entirely, except my hand and it was better. I was even able to get up and go to work. But the promised sign had been given. My other hand was afflicted. It was not entirely paralyzed, but was affected with numbness which has remained to the present writing. I am hoping to so far prove my faithfulness that I can again be trusted with the full use of my hands. . . .

"After this experience, I was light hearted and lifted up with a heavenly feeling impossible for me to describe. Such joy can only be understood by those who have passed through some such experience. This spirit remained with me for many days and only gradually drew away and left me to myself. Salt Lake City, November, 1915."

Notes:

1. Joseph Fielding Smith, *Doctrines of Salvation* (Salt Lake City: Bookcraft, 1955), 2:122.
2. Rudger Clawson, Conference Report April 1933, 77.
3. Gordon B. Hinckley, "The Salt Lake Temple," *Ensign*, March 1993, 5.
4. Archie J. Graham, *A Visit Beyond the Veil* [n. d.].
5. Cora Anna Beal Peterson, [biographical sketch of William Beal, n. d.].
6. Elnara Cox, *Faith-Promoting Collection 1882–1974*, box 2, folder 102.
7. Ezra Taft Benson, Regional Representatives Seminar, April 3, 1981, 2, as quoted by Michele R. Sorensen and Dr. David R. Willmore in *The Journey Beyond Life*, vol. 1 (Salt Lake City: Sounds of Zion, 1988), 181.
8. Joseph F. Smith, *Young Women's Journal* (March 1912), 130.
9   John Peterson, "Was Dead and Came to Life Again," *Juvenile Instructor* 41, (October 15, 1909), 609–610.
10. A. F. Bennett, *Faith-Promoting Collection 1882–1972*, box 2, folder 8 (courtesy of the Church History Library, The Church of Jesus Christ of Latter-day Saints).
11. Lorena A. Wilson, *An Open Vision: An Afternoon With My Deceased Parents*.

Chapter Seventeen

Those in the Spirit World Ask What People on Earth Are Doing

few near-death experiences mention people in the spirit world who ask for news of loved ones on earth. This would seem to indicate that spirits do not have an unrestricted view of mortals. Conversely, a few near-death accounts indicate that those on the other side know a great deal about their loved ones on earth.

President Joseph F. Smith said our departed loved ones are greatly concerned about our well-being. He declared that people in the spirit world "are as deeply interested in our welfare today, if not with greater capacity, with far more interest behind the veil, than they were in the flesh."[1]

President Wilford Woodruff also testified of this. "I believe the eyes of the heavenly hosts are over this people; I believe they are watching the elders of Israel, the prophets and apostles and men who are called to bear off this kingdom. I believe they watch over us all with great interest."[2]

Shortly after he arrived in the spirit world, Tom Gibson was asked to speak in a meeting about conditions on earth. "I got the impression, while I was in the auditorium, that . . . people there are interested in the progress in ours [mortality]."[3]

William Wallace Raymond spoke of people in the spirit world, saying, "The people are acquainted with our doings on earth, but they said it was not wisdom for us to know to know much about them."[4]

Ella Jensen

Critically ill from scarlet fever, Ella Jensen hovered between life and death. One morning, Ella's departed uncle, Hans, appeared and told Ella that messengers from heaven would come for her soon. When Ella passed away, her father went to see President Lorenzo Snow, who quickly came to the house and commanded Ella to come back to life. While in the spirit world, Ella had a number of people ask about their friends and relatives on earth. Leah Rees, a neighbor who had come to sit with Ella, relates the first part of Ella's experience.

"About three or four o'clock in the morning I [Leah] was suddenly awakened by Ella calling me. I hurried to her bed. She was all excited and asked me to get the comb, brush and scissors, explaining that she wanted to brush her hair and trim her finger nails and get all ready, 'for,' she said, 'they are coming to get me at ten o'clock in the morning.'

"I asked who was coming to get her.

"'Uncle Hans Jensen,' she replied, 'and the messengers. I am going to die and they are coming at ten o'clock to get me and take me away.' I tried to quiet her, saying that she would feel better in the morning if she would try to sleep.

"'No,' she said, 'I am not going to sleep any more, but spend all the time getting ready.' She insisted that I get the comb, hair-brush and scissors, which I did, but she was so weak that she could not use them.

"As I was brushing her hair, she asked me to call her parents. I explained that they were tired and asleep and that it would be better not to disturb them.

"'Yes,' Ella replied, 'you must call them. I want to tell them now.'

"The parents were called and as they entered the room, the daughter told them that her Uncle Hans, who was dead, had suddenly appeared in the room, while she was awake, with her eyes open, and told her that messengers would be there at ten o'clock to conduct her into the spirit world. The father and mother feared that the girl was delirious and tried to get her to be quiet and go to sleep.

"She knew their thoughts and said: 'I know what I am talking about. No, I am not going to sleep any more. I know that I am going to die and that they are coming to get me.'"

Leah left the house at eight o'clock. Ella's parents remained at their daughter's bedside while relatives and friends came to see her. At ten, Ella's father, Jacob, was holding her hand when her pulse weakened.

A few moments later, Jacob said to his wife, "Althea, she is dead. Her pulse has stopped." Jacob and Althea wept at the loss of their daughter.

Jacob Jensen gives his own account of his daughter's death. "Ella had been sick for several weeks. She awoke one morning with the idea that she was about to die, and told us that her Uncle Hans had appeared in her room and said he was coming for her that morning. We kind of put her off and told her we thought she must have been dreaming and not to pay much attention to it, to go to sleep and she would feel better in the morning; but she said: 'No, I know I am going, because he told me he would be here for me at ten o'clock in the morning.'

"She wanted to see all the folks and bid them good-bye. All who were near came in, all but Grandma Jensen. She was in town and I sent for her. She arrived just when the others of us had said good-bye. It was not more than a minute after that when her pulse stopped and she passed away. I was holding her hand and felt the pulse stop.

"We talked the matter over and wondered what we should do. I told my wife that I would go to town, more than a mile from home, and see President Snow, tell him about her death and have him arrange for the funeral. . . ."

When Jacob told President Lorenzo Snow about his daughter, President Snow asked President Rudger Clawson to go with him to the Jensen home, which was approximately a mile south of Brigham City. When they entered the house, President Snow asked Jacob if he had any consecrated oil.

Jacob said, "I was greatly surprised, but told him yes and got it for him. He handed the bottle of oil to Brother Clawson and asked him to anoint Ella. . . . During the administration I was particularly impressed with some of the words which he used and can well remember them now.

"He said: 'Dear Ella, I command you, in the name of the Lord, Jesus Christ, to come back and live, your mission is not ended. You shall yet live to perform a great mission.' He [President Snow] said she should yet live to rear a large family and be a comfort to her parents and friends. . . .

"After President Snow had finished the blessing, he turned to my wife and me and said, 'Now, do not mourn or grieve any more. It will be all right. Brother Clawson and I are busy and must go, we cannot stay, but you just be patient and wait, and do not mourn, because it will be all right.'"

News of Ella's death had spread and friends began to call at the home, expressing their sympathy.

Jacob said, "Ella remained in this condition for more than an hour after President Snow administered to her, or more than three hours in all after she died. We were sitting there watching by the bedside, her mother and myself, when all at once she opened her eyes. She looked about her room, saw us sitting there, but still looked for someone else, and the first thing she said was: 'Where is he? Where is he?'

"We asked, 'Who? Where is who?'

"'Why, Brother Snow,' she replied. 'He called me back.'

"We explained that Brother Snow and Brother Clawson were very busy and could not remain, that they had gone. Ella dropped her head back on the pillow, saying: 'Why did he call me back? I was so happy and did not want to come back.'"[5]

Ella related her experience in her own words. "On the 1st of March, 1891, I was taken severely ill with the scarlet fever, and suffered very much for a week. It was on the morning of the 9th that I awoke with a feeling that I was going to die. As soon as I opened my eyes I could see some of my relatives from the other world. They were engaged in conversation, and when they disappeared I heard the most beautiful singing, far superior to anything I had ever heard before. I then asked my sister to assist me in getting ready to go into the spirit world. She combed my hair, washed me, and I brushed my teeth and cleaned my nails that I might be clean when going before my Maker. All this time and for six hours, I could hear the singing still. I then bade my dear ones good by, and my spirit left my body."

Ella continues, "At ten o'clock my spirit left my body. It took me some time to make up my mind to go, as I could hear and see the folks crying and mourning over me. It was very hard for me to leave them, but as soon as I had a glimpse of the other world I was anxious to go and all care and worry left me.

"I entered a large hall. It was so long that I could not see the end of it. It was filled with people. As I went through the throng, the first person I recognized was my grandpa, H.P. Jensen, who was sitting in one end of the room, writing.

"He looked up, seemed surprised to see me and said: 'Why! There is my grand daughter, Ella.'

"He was very much pleased, greeted me and, as he continued with his writing, I passed on through the room and met a great many of my relatives and friends. It was like going along the crowded street of a large city where you meet many people, only a very few of whom you recognize.

"The next one I knew was Uncle Hans Jensen with his wife, Mary Ellen. They had two small children with them. On inquiring who they were, he told me one was his own and the other was Uncle Will's little girl. Some seemed to be in family groups. As there were only a few whom I could recognize and who knew me, I kept moving on.

"Some inquired about their friends and relatives on the earth. Among the number was my cousin. He asked me how the folks were getting along and said it grieved him to hear that some of the boys were using tobacco, liquor and many things that were injurious to them. This proved to me that the people in the other world know to a great extent what happens here on the earth.

"The people were all dressed in white or cream, excepting Uncle Hans Jensen, who had on his dark clothes and long rubber boots, the things we wore when he was drowned in the Snake River in Idaho. Everybody appeared to be perfectly happy. I was having a very pleasant visit with each one that I knew. Finally I reached the end of that long room. I opened a door and went into another room filled with children. They were all arranged in perfect order, the smallest ones first, then larger ones, according to age and size, the largest ones in the back rows all around the room. They seemed to be convened in a sort of Primary or Sunday School presided over by Aunt Eliza R. Snow. There were hundreds of small children.

"It was while I was standing listening to the children sing 'Gladly Meeting, Kindly Greeting' that I heard . . . President Lorenzo Snow, call me. He said: 'Sister Ella, you must come back, as your mission is not yet finished here on earth.' So I just spoke to Aunt Eliza R. Snow and told her I must go back.

"Returning through the large room, I told the people I was going back to earth, but they seemed to want me to stay with them. I obeyed the call, though it was very much against my desire, as such a perfect peace and happiness prevailed there, no suffering, no sorrow. I was so taken up with all I saw and heard, I did hate to leave that beautiful place.

"This has always been a source of comfort to me. I learned by this experience that we should not grieve too much for our departed loves ones and especially at the time they leave us. I think we should be just as calm and quiet as possible. Because as I was leaving, the only regret I had was that the folks were grieving so much for me. But I soon forgot all about this world in my delight with the other.

"For more than three hours my spirit was gone from my body. As I returned I could see my body lying on the bed and the folks gathered about in the room. I hesitated for a moment, then thought, 'Yes, I will go back for a little while.' I told the folks I wanted to stay only a short time to comfort them."

Ella's oldest sister, Meda, said Ella told her about the terrible suffering she experienced when her spirit again entered her body. Ella said there was practically no pain on leaving the body in death, but it was nearly unbearable when coming back to earth.

One of Ella's aunts, Harriet Wight, who had lost two daughters, came to visit Ella after she had come back from the spirit world. When her Aunt Harriet began to cry, Ella said, "Why, Aunt Harriet, what are you crying for. [sic] You need not cry for your girls who have gone. I saw and talked with them, and they are very happy where they are."

When other relatives visited Ella, she told them the same thing, that she had met many of their relatives and friends in the spirit world and that they were happy there and asked about their loved ones on earth. Two of those Ella spoke with were Alphonzo H. Snow and his wife, Minnie.

When Ella saw them, she said, "Oh! Come here, Alphonzo and Minnie, I have something to tell you. After my return to earth I told my parents of some of the remarkable experiences which I had while in the spirit world. But there was one experience that seemed very strange, and I could not understand it.

"You know your little son, Alphie, has been in my Sunday School class in the First ward. I have always loved him very much. While I was in Aunt Eliza R. Snow's class of children in the spirit world, I recognized many children. But all of them had died excepting one, and this was little Alphie. I could not understand how he should be among them and still be living.

"When I told this to mother, she said, 'Yes, Ella, little Alphie is dead, too. He died early this morning while you were so very sick. We knew you loved him and that it would be a shock to you, so we did not tell you about his death.'"

Alphonzo said, "It was very consoling, indeed, to hear Ella tell of seeing our dear little boy and that he was very happy. She said it was not right for us to grieve and mourn so much for him and that he would be happier if we would not do so."

President Rudger Clawson, who helped President Snow administer to

Ella, added another interesting piece to this experience, regarding Ella's Uncle, Hans Peter Jensen. President Clawson said that when Ella saw Hans in the spirit world, it cleared up a mystery that had been plaguing his family for years.

President Clawson said, "Sometime before this [Ella's] advent into the spirit world, her Uncle Hans, who lived in Brigham City . . . left for the north [Snake River in Idaho] and at once turned his attention to salmon fishing. One morning he went from the home where he was staying, clothed in a jumper and overalls, with gum boots, to fish; but he never returned. His oldest brother, Jacob Jensen [Ella's father] came to me greatly alarmed, said that no word had been received from Hans for some time and nobody seemed to know where he was. He was greatly excited about it and feared that his brother had been drowned in the Snake River.

"Jacob organized a posse of men and at once instituted a search covering a period of some two or three weeks, at the Snake River, but their efforts were fruitless. No trace could be found of Hans and he was never again heard from until his niece, Ella Jensen, met him in the spirit world. She said that he was dressed in a jumper and overalls with gum boots. The mystery [of where and how he had died] was solved.

"There seemed to be no doubt thereafter that Hans Jensen was drowned in the Snake River. It is said that when the dead manifest themselves to the living they usually appear as they were last seen on earth so that the living will recognize them. If that be true, it accounts for the strange habit that her uncle was wearing."

Lorenzo Jensen tells one more interesting incident in regards to Hans's disappearance. "The night that Hans Jensen disappeared, his mother . . . awakened her youngest son, Willard, and asked him to go open the door and let Hans come in the house. Willard went to his mother's bedside and said, 'Why, mother, Hans cannot be here, he is up in Idaho fishing, you know.'

"'Yes, but I know he is here, I heard him calling me. I have not been asleep. I know he is outside and wants to come in.'

"Willard went to the door, opened it, walked entirely around the house, returned to his mother and said he was sure that Hans was not there. The mother replied: 'Then Hans is dead, because I know that he came to me and called me.' A few days later, word came telling of Hans' disappearance."[7]

Returning to Ella's story, President Clawson said that when Ella first returned to her body, her parents doubted her story. After Ella told them about being in the spirit world, Elder Clawson heard Jacob whisper to his wife, "Do you hear what she is saying? Why, the girl is certainly delirious. She is out of her mind."

President Clawson said, "Ella looked up and said: 'Father, you think then that I am out of my mind, do you? I will very soon prove to you that I am perfectly rational.'

"She turned to her mother: 'While in this large building in the spirit world, I met a woman who greeted me and said she was Aunt Mary and told me that she died while I was a baby.'

"The mother asked: 'Can you describe her?'

"The answer was: 'Yes, she was a tall woman with black hair and dark eyes and thin features.'

"'Yes,' the mother answered, 'surely you have described your Aunt Mary.'

"'I also met another woman there, who said she was my Aunt Sarah and had died just before I was born.'

"'Will you describe her?'

"'Yes, she was rather short and somewhat fleshy, with round features, light hair and blue eyes.'

"'Why, yes, Ella, that is your Aunt Sarah. You have described her perfectly.'

"Ella turned to her father saying: 'Do you now think that I am out of my mind?'

"'No,' he answered, 'you have had a very wonderful experience.'"

Ella later became president of the Young Ladies' Mutual Improvement Association in Brigham City. In time, she married Henry Wight, and they had eight children.[8]

Notes:

1. Joseph F. Smith, Conference Report April 1916, 2.
2. Wilford Woodruff, *Journal of Discourses* (October 19, 1880), 21:317.
3. Arvin S. Gibson, *Margaret and Marshall Gibson, An Old-fashioned Love Story: A Biography.*
4. William Wallace Raymond, "Vision 1881 August 12."

5. LeRoi C. Snow, "Raised from the Dead," *Improvement Era* 32, (September 1929), 881–86.
6. Ella Jensen, "Remarkable Experience," *Young Woman's Journal* 4, (January 1893), 165.
7. LeRoi C. Snow, "Raised from the Dead," 973–79.
8. LeRoi C. Snow, "Raised from the Dead," 972–80.

Chapter Eighteen

See Someone They Didn't Know Was Dead

In a few near-death experiences, visitors to the spirit world saw people they didn't know had died. After returning to mortality, they were told that the person they saw in the spirit world had indeed passed away. When David P. Kimball visited the spirit world, he said, "There were thousands of the Saints presented to me, many who had died at Nauvoo, in Winter Quarters, on the plains and in Utah. I saw Brother Pugmire and many others whom I did not know were dead."[1]

During his near-death experience, John Peterson saw Parley P. Pratt speaking to a large congregation. When John returned to mortality and told others about this, they didn't know what to make of it. Although they lived in Sweden, as far as they knew, Parley was still alive and well. It was only later that word finally reached them that Parley P. Pratt had been murdered shortly before John's visit to the spirit world.[2]

W. W. Merrill was asked to give a blessing to a young woman who was ill. Soon after, he had a near-death experience. While in the spirit world, W. W. Merrill saw the young woman to whom he had given a blessing. When he came back, Elder Merrill discovered that the young woman had—like himself—died but came back to mortality.[3]

Woman Sees Her Brother and Mother

President David O. McKay, the ninth prophet of the Church, tells about the near-death experience of a woman who was in the last stages of a terminal illness. This woman had always been very close to her brother, William, and during her illness asked about him every day. Then, unknown to her, William died unexpectedly. Since she was so sick herself, no one wanted to cause her anguish. Everyone felt it would be better if she did not know. However, when she visited the spirit world, she saw William and knew he had passed away. President McKay relates this experience as follows:

"I spoke at the funeral service of a mother in Logan only recently. That good mother, before she died, as she lay on the bed of illness, was wont to inquire about her brother. Nearly every night she would say, 'How is he getting along?' mentioned his name, but, suddenly, one day that brother left his mortal existence almost instantly.

"That afternoon as the sister awoke from sleep, she made no inquiry as to the condition of her brother, didn't ask about him, but stated, 'I have seen William and Mother together. How happy they seem. They wanted me to go with them, but I was not ready. How happy they will be.'

"She knew he was gone. Nobody had said a word to her, but a consciousness had come to her that her brother William was with her mother, who had been dead for many years. The sister, however, was not quite ready. In two more days she, too, joined them. Her body was weakened by disease, suffering; her physical strength was wasted, but the spirit was responsive to another environment to which her loved ones, in the prime of physical life and health, were unresponsive."[4]

Discover That a Mortal Is Going to Die Soon

There are several accounts that relate a person visiting the spirit world discovering that someone they know on earth is going to leave mortality soon. When Martha Jane Boice returned from the spirit world for a short time, she talked with her husband about their three children, saying; "You may keep two of them, the other will go with me." The account states, "She [Martha] was buried the following day and her little son, Thomas was called away that same evening after a brief and sudden illness."[5]

Walter P. Monson

Walter P. Monson was speaking in church when he was stricken with sudden pain and taken to the hospital. After being operated on, Walter had a near-death experience where he learned that although he would return to life, his mother and his six-year-old son, Richard, would soon be taken. Walter relates his experience as follows:

"On the evening of the 23rd day of December 1923, while addressing an audience at the old Farmers' Ward chapel, on South State Street, in Salt Lake City, Utah, I was stricken with intense pain from strangulated [sic] hernia. That night I underwent an abdominal operation at the Holy Cross hospital at 10 p.m. Part of the strangulated intestine was in such a condition and so badly discolored and my chances of living so slight, that the doctors did not remove the afflicted section. They simply sewed up the outer skin of the wound, feeling that it was only a matter of a few hours at most before I would die.

"My first consciousness returned at eight o'clock the next morning. When I awoke my family and others were kneeling about my bed and Bishop LeGrand Richards of the Sugarhouse Ward was praying for my recovery.

"At midnight of the 24th, Christmas Eve, I was conscious and fully awake. I heard the Christmas chimes and knew of the nurse taking my pulse and temperature. Suddenly, I was stricken with a coldness that attacked my feet and hands. It moved up my limbs and up my arms towards my body. I felt it reach my heart. There was a slight murmur. I gasped for breath and lapsed into unconsciousness, so far as all things mortal were concerned. Then I awoke in full possession of all my faculties in another sphere of life.

"I stood apart from my body and looked at it. I saw it lying upon the bed. I noticed that its eyes were partly closed and that the chin had dropped. I was now without pain, and the joy of freedom I felt and the peace of mind that came over me were the sweetest sensations I have ever experienced in all my life. I lost all sense of time and space. And the law of gravitation had no hold upon me.

"As I turned my head in the direction I intended to go, I saw my little daughter, Elna, who died in infancy, twenty-one years before. She was more mature than when she passed away, having the intelligence of an adult, and was most beautiful to my eyes, so full of life and so intelligent and sweet.

"As she came towards me she raised her right hand and said, 'Go back, papa, I want Richard first. Then grandma must come, and then mama is coming, before you.'"

"The next thing I knew was my body gasping for breath. I felt my heart action start and I was conscious of the coldness leaving my body just as it had come. All numbness left me and the natural warmth returned.

"I felt the nurse shaking me and heard her say, 'Mr. Monson, you must not let yourself slip like that again.'

"The house doctor came in and gave me a hypo of some heart stimulant. During the eleven days that followed not a drop of water nor a morsel of food passed my lips, for the doctors were certain that the discolored section of my intestine would break any moment and that death would follow.

"For five weeks I remained in the hospital, gaining a little strength each day. I was administered to frequently by Brothers James E. Talmage, George Albert Smith, Patriarch Kirkham and my family exercised all the faith within their power in my behalf. Mrs. Monson visited me every day with my son Richard. She was told by the doctor, C. F. Wilcox, that there was no hope for my recovery, and, of course, her visits were attended with deep emotion.

"Many times little Richard, for he was barely six years old, took my hand and pressed it affectionately against his cheek.

"'Daddy,' he would say anxiously, 'you're not going to die, are you?'

"I could not control my emotions, try as I would, but I managed to say, 'No, Dick, it is not my turn.'

"Four weeks after I returned home, my boy, Richard, passed away. During the last hours of his life he sat up his bed, opened his big blue eyes and looked toward the door with intense interest.

"'Come in, Elna,' he said, 'there's only papa and mama here.'

"I asked him whom he could see and he answered, 'Elna is there. It's funny you can't see her. And there are a whole lot of people with her who want me to come.'

"He called his mother to the bed and put his arms around her neck. 'Can I go with Elna?' he asked.

"'Yes, my dear,' she answered, 'you have suffered enough.'

"'Then I'll go. And I'll be happy if you will promise not to cry once for me,' he pleaded.

"Mrs. Monson gave him the promise he wished and left the room.

"'Daddy,' he said to me, 'come here. I guess mama has gone out to cry.'

"He paused a moment, then turned and looked in the direction of the door and listened intently at something he evidently heard.

"'Dear old daddy,' he went on at length, 'so you promised at the hospital I could go. Now I know why you cried when I said, 'You are not going to die, are you, daddy?'

"Three hours later his eyes closed in eternal sleep. How he knew that I wept because I had been told by Elna that he was to go first and that my coming back was equivalent to a promise that he might precede me to the great beyond, can only be explained though knowledge given him from Elna herself, for he knew nothing of the circumstance of what I saw and heard while my spirit was separated from my body at the hospital.

"Three weeks after his passing, I visited my mother, Ellen Monson, at Preston, Idaho. Mother had been a sufferer for many years, but her constitution was strong and the doctor had told her that she had every chance of living for ten or fifteen years. She lamented the fact that she was spared, while my boy was taken. She said she had desired to die for twenty-two years.

"Without realizing what I said, I made her this promise: 'Mother, you haven't twenty-two days to suffer.'

"Nineteen days from that time, mother left us. And six years from the time of mother's death, Mrs. Monson passed away.

"The experience I had during my consciousness in another sphere I related to Doctor Talmage, who came to administer to me at the hospital. I also told it to Bishop LeGrand Richards and Alec Curtis of Sugarhouse, and to Doctors C. F. Wilcox and Clonge and other members of the doctors' staff at the hospital. This I did while I was still at the hospital.

"The sight of my daughter, Elna, and the words she spoke to me on the occasion I have referred to, and the consciousness of my looking upon my lifeless body, as I have described, are as real to me today as any other experience I have had in my lifetime. Dated November 20, 1934."[6]

James G. Marsh

James G. Marsh was the nine-year-old son of Thomas B. Marsh, a member of the original Twelve Apostles. When James became seriously ill, he left his body and went to the spirit world, where he learned that a young woman who lived near him on earth was going to die soon. This account was printed in the *Elders' Journal*.

"It seems that the Lord had respect unto this lover of righteousness; for when he [James] was but about nine years of age, he had a remarkable vision, in which he talked with the Father and many of the ancient prophets face to face, and he beheld the Son of God coming in his glory.

"He said that the Lord showed him his own name written in the book of life in the mansions of celestial glory, and he saw his own mansion there. And the Lord informed him that the righteous did not die, but fell asleep to rise again in the resurrection of the Just, although the world calls it death; and to show him that there is no bitterness in the death of the righteous, he was permitted to see, in the vision, the departure of a young sister, in the church, who was the daughter of Brother Hezekiah Peck, who was then living a neighbor to him, but she died shortly after he had had the vision. And he said that he saw angels conduct her spirit to the celestial paradise.

"He saw bloody wars among all people accompanied with earthquakes, pestilences and famines. And he saw all the cities of the nations crumble and fall to rise no more. He saw the church of Christ ready to ascend on high, and when they were ready, Zion from above hovered in sight, accompanied by the Lord and all the holy prophets. The church on beholding them, arose triumphantly and met them in the expanse above.

"These are a few of the things which he related of his vision to his parents, suffice it to say, he saw the beginning and end of all things and he never after appeared to be afraid of death. During his illness, which lasted but four days, he constantly manifested a desire to depart and be with the Lord." [7]

Notes:

1. Orson F. Whitney, *Helpful Visions, The 14th Book of the Faith-Promoting Series*, 22.

2. John Peterson, "Was Dead and Came to Life Again," *Juvenile Instructor* 41, (October 15, 1909), 609–610.

3. J. Berkeley Larsen, "The Reality of Life After Death," *BYU Speeches of the Year*, October 6, 1953 (1953–1955), 4.

4. David O. McKay, *Gospel Ideals*, abridged edition (Salt Lake City: Improvement Era Publication, 1953), 54.

5. Samantha T. Brimhall, Boice Family History [ca. 1930] (courtesy of the Church History Library, The Church of Jesus Christ of Latter-day Saints).

6. Jeremiah Stokes, *Modern Miracles* (Salt Lake City: Bookcraft, 1945), 78–81.

7. "Obituary," *Elders' Journal* (courtesy of the Church History Library, The Church of Jesus Christ of Latter-day Saints).

Chapter Nineteen

Message Is Given

*I*t is common for visitors to the spirit world to be given messages, either for themselves, for loved ones on earth, or for as many people on earth as they can contact. Most often, these messages have to do with telling others to repent and to be watchful and prayerful.

Some people were admonished by departed relatives to live more righteously, to work harder on overcoming faults, and to do all the good they could when they returned to mortality. A few people were told they needed to return to earth and finish the work they had promised to do in the preexistence before they returned to the spirit world.

Sometimes people were allowed to return only briefly so they could deliver an important message to someone else—usually to warn others or to admonish them to stay true to the gospel. The most common messages were exhorting people to do genealogy and temple work for their ancestors.

The Savior gave Lovisa Tuttle a message for her friends and relatives. "He told me that I must return again to warn the people to prepare for death; that I must exhort them to be watchful as well as prayerful; that I must declare faithfully unto them their accountability before God and the certainty of their being called to stand before the judgment seat of Christ."[1]

When Lorena Wilson went to the spirit world, she was told to return and do temple work for her ancestors. "Father then said the time had come for these ordinances to be performed for our kindred in the spirit world, and he desired me to take up the work and see that it was done. I told him that I would."[2]

When May Neville went to the spirit world shortly after her brother, Merrill, died, he asked her to return and warn their family that they needed to overcome their failings.[3]

The message given to Herman Stulz was, "Go back and finish the work that you promised you would do before your spirit left here." Herman was also told that in the future, he would hear about and accept the gospel and be able to go to the temple and do ordinance work for his ancestors.[4]

Richard H. Hamblin Jr.

When Richard H. Hamblin Jr. returned to life after his visit to the other side, he said he had been given three messages. One was a personal message from his departed wife, and two were from departed friends who wanted Richard to give the messages to their families. Richard's friend, Bernard Morton, recorded his account.

"The following is an account and history of the strange events that happened to Richard H. Hamblin Jr. and . . . has been written at the expressed wish of Richard H. Hamblin before he died and has been written by Bernard Morton of Kaysville, Utah. . . ."

"On June 2nd 1937, Mr. Hamblin had a heart attack after shearing a sheep. . . . The doctors could not extend any hope of recovery. On July 9, 1937, he got so bad he passed over to the other side and came back and called his family and told the children he had been on the other side and had talked to their mother, said she was just as beautiful as the day they layed [sic] her away during the flu epidemic of 1918–19.

"He begged to be allowed to stay with her but she said no, that he had some important work to do for their children and must come back to do this as the children had strayed away and would be lost to them if he did not come back and lead them back.

"He also told of other people that he talked to over on the other side and brought messages back from some of them to their families—told Mrs. Clif. Barber that her son who died about a year before this told him to tell his mother to quit grieving over him as he was all right and for her to quit feeling badly. Said to tell his mother that he had a far more beautiful home than any mansion that you could imagine here. He also told W. O. Thurgood of a message from his dead wife.

"He first told Elton, his son, all that had happened and when his daughter Mattie and son Ray got there next morning he had Elton repeat all he had said while he listened to correct anything that was not exactly right. This arrangement on account he was so weak he could hardly talk and doing it this way would save his strength. He told them about this mission for his children that he had to do and told them that their mother had told him what had to be done for him to get better. . . .

"She [his wife] said she would help him from that side and with the children's help from this side he would get better. . . . He said it had been made known to him that he would have a very bad sick spell before many days [which] would pass and that this would culminate in an immediate healing—that he would stand up out of this invalid's chair perfectly healed.

"When W. O. Thurgood came to see him that day he gave him the message from his dead wife and Thurgood disbelieved him. Rich [Richard] then told him that he would believe him when he saw him raise from the dead out of that chair as he was to be one of them present when this miracle should happen.

"About 12 Noon July 12, 1937, his [Richard's] daughter Mirla, Hazel, his present wife were with him and by all appearances he died as his head dropped forward and he fell out of the chair on his face on the floor.

"He was immediately raised up on his feet by some power and turned to his family and said, 'see I told you I would come back.' The ones present were so astonished they could not believe what had happened. To convince them he did body exercises to show them that he was perfectly healed."[5]

Tell Loved Ones to Stop Grieving

Occasionally, visitors to the spirit world are asked to deliver a message from departed family members to loved ones on earth, asking them to stop mourning their death. A few spirits said they were even hindered in their work in the spirit world because their relatives on earth were grieving so much. Others simply wanted their loved ones to cheer up and know they were happy and well.

May Neville came back briefly from the spirit world to deliver a message to her mother from her brother, Merrill, who had died the day before. "Merrill wished the family not to mourn for him. He said that if the family fretted and mourned for him he couldn't accomplish the work which his grandfather had for him to do."[6]

Richard H. Hamblin Jr. came back from the spirit world with a message for a friend, Mrs. Barber. Richard "told Mrs. Clif. [sic] Barber that her son who died about a year before this told him to tell his mother to quit grieving over him as he was all right and for her to quit feeling badly."[7]

When Ella Jensen returned from the spirit world, she told her friends, Alphonzo H. Snow and his wife, Minnie, that she had seen their young son, Alphie. Alphonzo said, "It was very consoling, indeed, to hear Ella tell of seeing our dear little boy and that he was very happy. She said it was not right for us to grieve and mourn so much for him and that he would be happier if we would not do so."[8]

Henry Zollinger

While Henry Zollinger was in the spirit world, he saw two of his brothers-in-law, who asked him to tell their loved ones to stop grieving for them. Henry's near-death experience occurred when he was accidentally electrocuted while working on his farm in 1920. He writes:

"On August 7, 1920, I was moving a hay derrick under a live electric wire, the derrick pole caught on the wire, and the consequence was I received a shock that threw me in the air, then I fell under the derrick frame and the boys that were with me seeing the situation urged the horses up a few feet which left me pinned under the frame, until they received help.

"The boys who were with me with Henry Merchant, a hired man, LeGrande Stirland a brother-in-law and my two boys Lyman and Ray, they all said I was dead. LeGrande took my boys away from the terrible scene while the Merchant boy went to the nearest house to telephone for a Doctor and for help. I lay there about an hour before the Doctors Eliason and Wallace Budge came. They at once lifted me out from under the derrick and took me to the Utah Idaho Hospital.

"After LeGrande had got the children quieted down a little he came to see me again and he says he saw me breathe, he then took my hat to the creek and brought water and put it on my face and hands until the Doctors came. While my body was under the derrick and they thought me dead I had an experience in the Spirit World which I wish to relate.

"My Spirit left the body and I could see it lying under the derrick and at that moment my Guardian angel, my mother and my sister Annie were beside me. My mother died January 31, 1918 and my sister at the age of four years. I saw that her spirit was full grown in stature and also seemed very intelligent. We then visited many the vicarious work that had be[en] done for by father, and although some still remained dormant she hoped they would obey the Gospel.

"She then warned me to be very careful and keep the faith. Also told me to warn my brothers and sisters to live more closely to the Gospel and not let worldly things lead them astray as that is the way the Nephites of old were led away. Mother informed me that my brother John, who has been somewhat careless in a religious way would some day take a turn in regard to him and his family.

"Also at the death of father my brother William would have the privilege of being in charge of the records.

"My mother then introduced me to the heads of five generations of my father's people, all of whom were in the Gospel. I noticed that people had their free agency there like we do here and that by gaining knowledge was the only way to progression. My mother also informed me that my father would receive another large record of our dead kindred.

"My guide then took me and showed me the spirits of the children that would yet come to my family if we would be faithful, they were full grown but not in the same sphere as those who had lived upon this earth. I could see many of the spirits that had been refused the privilege of having a body, there was much sorrow.

"We then had the privilege of visiting with my brothers-in-law who had died. William who had been on a mission in Australia. He told me he was presiding over a large mission and was very happy in his labors and to tell his parents and his people not to mourn about him as he was losing nothing but doing much good. We next went to see his older brother John. I found him discussing the Gospel to a large congregation bearing a strong testimony to them, when he got through he told me he was very happy in his labors and had no regrets that he was there and to tell his people not to mourn.

"My guide made known to me that my brother Oliver and two brothers-in-law could go on missions, Christian not for some time but Byron would be called among the Indians and would perform a wonderful mission among that people.

"Then as we were coming back I saw a man who had been a Campbellite Minister down in Texas when I was upon my mission there three years ago. He was a great friend to us and has opened his house many times for us to preach in. He had died while I was still in the mission field. He asked me if I could do the work in the Temple that was necessary for his salvation. I told him I would and he seemed pleased.

"I then met a man whom I had never seen before, his wife had come into the Church and was baptized after he had died, she spoke to me while I was on my mission in regard to having the work done for him in the Temple, but as she had already spoken to other Elders about it I thought it was already done but the man told me it was not done yet and he was anxious for it to be done. I told him I would see to it. Then my guide told me Thomas Stirland would get a record of his dead relations. I then returned to my body and I understood all the time I was away from it that I would return to it as the guide told me that in the beginning. Henry Zollinger."[9]

Notes:

1.   Cora Anna Beal Peterson, [biographical sketch of William Beal, n. d.].
2.   Lerona A. Wilson, *An Open Vision; An Afternoon With My Deceased Parents.*
3.   "Manifestations About Temple Work [ca. 1918], (courtesy of the Church History Library, The Church of Jesus Christ of Latter-day Saints).
4.   Herman Stulz, *Autobiography.*
5.   Richard H. Hamblin Jr., *Faith-Promoting Collection 1882–1974*, box 2, folder 27.
6.   "Manifestations About Temple Work [ca. 1918], (Courtesy of the Church History Library, The Church of Jesus Christ of Latter-day Saints).
7.   Richard H. Hamblin Jr., *Faith-Promoting Collection 1882–1974*, Box 2, Folder 27, (Courtesy of the Church History Library, The Church of Jesus Christ of Latter-day Saints).
8.   LeRoi C. Snow, "Raised from the Dead," *Improvement Era* (September 1929), 32:973–979.
9.   Henry Zollinger, *Faith-Promoting Collection 1882–1974*, box 2, folder 17.

> "And again, it shall come to pass that he that hath faith in me to be healed, and is not appointed unto death, shall be healed."
> (Doctrine and Covenants 42:48)

Chapter Twenty

Given Choice to Stay
or Return to Mortality

Many people who had near-death experiences were allowed to choose between staying in the spirit world or returning to mortality. Usually, they were surprised to learn this, as most didn't think they would have any choice in the matter. However, agency has always been an important part of Heavenly Father's plan, and the ability to make our own decisions is a cornerstone of not only this life but the life to come.

While in the spirit world, Peter E. Johnson was taken by his guide to meet with a group of latter-day Apostles. Peter said, "As soon as I came into their presence, I was asked if I desired to remain there. This seemed strange, for it had never occurred to me that we would have any choice there in the spirit world, as to whether we should remain or return to the earth life."[1] Peter then decided to return to mortality.

Archie Graham was also given a choice to stay or return by his guide, who said, "The Lord, our Master, has given me charge concerning you, that you may choose for yourself, after knowing the things that are in store for you over there. You may come and enjoy these things in the Spirit World, or you may remain upon the earth."[2]

In order to make an informed decision, visitors to the spirit world were sometimes given additional information about what they could accomplish

in mortality if they were to return. Some were told about the importance
of having children, and others were told about the need to do genealogy
and complete temple work for themselves or their ancestors. Occasionally,
ancestors who wanted their ordinances done were influential in persuad-
ing visitors to return to mortality. Other times, people were gently asked
to make the decision to return because they had a specific mission that had
not yet been completed. Quite often, those who decided to return acted
unselfishly and came back to mortality to help their loved ones.

Such was the case with Flora Mayer. She was perfectly happy in the
spirit world and didn't want to leave, even when her guide explained Flora
was free to return if she wished. However, Flora was advised to go back
because her children and husband needed her and because it was not yet
her time to be there. Flora then decided to return.[3]

Marriner Wood Merrill

Traveling by horseback could be dangerous during a heavy rain,
which made the ground slippery and unstable, but there was no time to
be lost as Marriner Wood Merrill and a group of men were hurrying to
defend a group of settlers from an Indian attack. As they rode, Marriner's
horse slipped and fell, fatally injuring Marriner. After his spirit left his
body, Marriner was given the choice of either going on to the spirit world
or returning to his body. Marriner's son, Amos N. Merrill, tells his father's
story.

"The following incident transpired a short time after Father settled
in Richmond, Cache County: Indians were never very troublesome in
Cache Valley and the country north, yet at times threatening situations
arose. It was during one of these occasions that Father and a number of
other men from northern Cache Valley were called to go to the protection
of the settlers further north.

"A heavy rain fell just before their departure which made the roads
and the countryside extremely muddy and slippery. As Father took a
detour, he had gone out a short distance from the company when his horse
slipped and fell with Father under him. When the other men of the party
reached the scene Father was motionless and from all appearance, dead.

"Father relates that his spirit left his body and stood, as it were, in
the air above it. He could see his body and the men standing around and
he heard their conversation. At his option he could re-enter his body or
remain in spirit.

"His reflection upon his responsibility to his family and his great desire to live caused him to choose to enter his body again and live. As he did so, he regained consciousness and experienced severe pains incident to the injuries which he had suffered from the accident."[4]

Phoebe Woodruff

On October 9, 1838, Phoebe and Wilford Woodruff, along with their baby, started out on a journey of two thousand miles. Wilford was in charge of leading a company of fifty-three people from Maine to Illinois. The company spent three months traveling in wagons through rain, mud, snow, and frost—traveling as far as they could go each day before camping wherever night overtook them. On October 24, Phoebe and her baby were stricken with what was thought to be cholera. Phoebe then had a near-death experience and was told she could return to mortality if she was willing to go through all the trials and tribulation that her husband would be called upon to endure for the gospel's sake. Wilford relates his wife's experience:

"On the 23rd of November my wife, Phoebe, was attacked with a severe headache, which terminated in brain fever. She grew more and more distressed daily as we continued our journey. It was a terrible ordeal for a woman to travel in a wagon over rough roads, afflicted as she was. At the same time our child was also very sick.

"The 1st of December was a trying day to my soul. My wife continued to fail, and in the afternoon, about 4 o'clock, she appeared to be struck with death. I stopped my team, and it seemed as though she would breath her last lying in the wagon. Two of the sisters sat beside her, to see if they could do anything for her in her last moments.

"I stood upon the ground, in deep affliction, and meditated. I cried unto the Lord, and prayed that she might live and not be taken from me. I claimed the promises the Lord had made unto me through the prophets and patriarchs, and soon her spirit revived, and I drove a short distance to a tavern, and got her into a room and worked over her and her babe all night, and prayed to the Lord to preserve her life.

"In the morning the circumstances were such that I was under the necessity of removing my wife from the inn, as there was so much noise and confusion at the place that she could not endure it. I carried her out to her bed in the wagon and drove two miles, when I alighted at a house and carried my wife and her bed into it, with a determination to tarry there until she either recovered her health or passed away. This was on Sunday morning, December 2nd.

"After getting my wife and things into the house and wood provided to keep up a fire, I employed my time in taking care of her. It looked as though she had but a short time to live. She called me to her bedside in the evening and said she felt as though a few moments more would end her existence in this life. She manifested great confidence in the cause she had embraced, and exhorted me to have confidence in God and to keep His commandments. To all appearances, she was dying. I laid hands upon her and prayed for her, and she soon revived and slept some during the night.

"December 3rd found my wife very low. I spent the day in taking care of her, and the following day I returned to Eaton to get some things for her. She seemed to be gradually sinking and in the evening her spirit apparently left her body, and she was dead.

"The sisters gathered around her body, weeping, while I stood looking at her in sorrow. The spirit and power of God began to rest upon me until, for the first time during her sickness faith filled my soul, although she lay before me as one dead.

"I had some oil that was consecrated for my anointing while in Kirtland. I took it and consecrated it again before the Lord for anointing the sick. I then bowed down before the Lord and prayed for the life of my companion, and I anointed her body with the oil in the name of the Lord. I laid my hands upon her, and in the name of Jesus Christ I rebuked the power of death and the destroyer, and commanded the same to depart from her, and the spirit of life to enter her body.

"Her spirit returned to her body, and from that hour she was made whole; and we all felt to praise the name of God, and to trust in Him and to keep His commandments.

"While this operation was going on with me (as my wife related afterwards) her spirit left her body, and she saw it lying upon the bed, and the sisters weeping. She looked at them and at me, and upon her babe, and, while gazing upon this scene, two personages came into the room. . . . One of these messengers informed her that she could have her choice: she might go to rest in the spirit world, or, on one condition she could have the privilege of returning to her tabernacle and continuing her labors upon the earth.

"The condition was, if she felt that she could stand by her husband,

and with him pass through all the cares, trials, tribulation and afflictions of life which he would be called to pass through for the gospel's sake unto the end.

"When she looked at the situation of her husband and child she said: 'Yes, I will do it!'

"At the moment that decision was made the power of faith rested upon me, and when I administered unto her, her spirit entered her tabernacle. . . .

"On the morning of the 6ᵗʰ of December, the Spirit said to me: 'Arise, and continue thy journey!' and through the mercy of God my wife was enabled to arise and dress herself and walked to the wagon, and we went on our way rejoicing."[5]

Told They Must Return

Although some people were allowed to choose whether or not they would stay in the spirit world, others were simply told they had to return to mortality. Sometimes a person was told that God wanted them to gain further knowledge or that they needed more time in mortality to work on overcoming faults and failings.

Others were told they had not completed their mission or else it was not their appointed time to die. Lorenzo Dow Young was surprised when his guide told him they were going to return. Lorenzo said, "I could distinctly see the world from which we had first come. . . . I was filled with sad disappointment, I might say horror, at the idea of returning there. . . . I plead [sic] with my guide to let me remain. He replied that I was permitted to only visit these heavenly cities, for I had not filled my mission in yonder world; therefore I must return and take my body."[6]

After Jacob Hamblin fell from a tree and had a near-death experience, he was told he had to return to mortality. Jacob saw his father, who told him that it was not time for him to come. His father said simply, "'Your work is not yet done.' I attempted to speak to him again, but he motioned me away with his hand and in a moment I was back to this earth."[7]

Others were told they had an important work to do, such as Richard H. Hamblin Jr., who was overjoyed to be reunited with his wife. Richard said, "He begged to be allowed to stay with her but she said no, that he had some important work to do for their children and must come back to do this as the children had strayed away and would be lost to them if he did not come back and lead them back."[8]

When Alpheus Cutler was told he had to return to mortality, he said,

"I begged to remain but was informed that I must return and warn the people to repent, as my work on earth was not yet done."[9]

Lovisa Tuttle

In 1784, Lovisa Tuttle, the sister of Lucy Mack Smith, became very ill. After suffering for several years, Lovisa was just beginning to recover when she had a violent reoccurrence. Her younger sister, Lovina, went to stay with and care for her. Lovisa's condition worsened and she became so ill that she could not even speak. The only nourishment she could tolerate was a little rice water. Then Lovisa's spirit left her earthly body. However, after arriving in the spirit world, Lovisa was told she had to return and warn people to prepare for the time when they would die and stand accountable before God.

When Lovisa suddenly returned to her body and sat up in bed, she badly startled her sister. Lovisa then said, "The Lord has healed me, both soul and body—raise me up and give me my clothes, I wish to get up."

Lovisa's husband, Joseph, was convinced that his wife's energy and unusual vitality was a prelude to her death but decided to humor his wife. He told Lovina to go ahead and help Lovisa get dressed. After sitting on a chair for a time, Lovisa said she wanted to go see her father-in-law, who was sick in bed and lived across the street.

Having been informed that Lovisa was near death, Mr. Tuttle cried out when he saw her walk into his room because he was sure he was seeing a ghost. Lovisa reassured him that she was there in the flesh and after a short visit, returned home.

News quickly spread about Lovisa's amazing recovery. Friends and neighbors flocked to her home. Lovisa told everyone that she would speak in church on Sunday and explain more about the strange way in which she had been healed.

That Sunday a large congregation gathered. After a short greeting, the minister turned the time over to Lovisa. After singing a hymn, Lovisa began to relate her near-death experience.

"I seemed to be borne away to the world of spirits, where I saw the Savior, as through a veil, which appeared to me about as thick as a spider's web, and he told me that I must return again to warn the people to prepare for death; that I must exhort them to be watchful as well as prayerful; that I must declare faithfully unto them their accountability before God and the certainty of their being called to stand before the judgment seat of

Christ; and that if I would do this my life should be prolonged."

Lovisa then spoke about the uncertainty of life. When she sat down, her husband and sister stood and testified that Lovisa had truly been near death shortly before her amazing recovery.

For three years, Lovisa continued to speak as often as she could, urging people to repent and to prepare for the next life. Then Lovisa became ill once again, this time with consumption. She passed away in 1789.[10]

Notes:

1. Peter E. Johnson, "A Testimony," *The Relief Society Magazine* 7 (1920), 450–455.

2. Archie J. Graham, *A Visit Beyond the Veil.*

3. Marba Peck Hale, Papers [ca. 2000], folder 6 (courtesy of the Church History Library, The Church of Jesus Christ of Latter-day Saints).

4. Bryant S. Hinckley, comp., *The Faith of Our Pioneer Fathers* (Salt Lake City: Bookcraft, 1956), 183.

5. Wilford Woodruff, *Leaves From My Journal, Third book of the Faith-Promoting Series* (Salt Lake City: Juvenile Instructor Office, 1882), 52–55.

6. Lorenzo Dow Young, *Fragments of Experience, Sixth Book of the Faith-Promoting Series* (Salt Lake City: Juvenile Instructor Office, 1882), 27–30.

7. James A. Little, *Jacob Hamblin, Fifth Book of the Faith-Promoting Series, second edition* (Salt Lake City: *Deseret News* Press, 1909), 61–62.

8. Richard H. Hamblin Jr., *Faith-Promoting Collection 1882–1974,* box 2, folder 27 (courtesy of the Church History Library, The Church of Jesus Christ of Latter-day Saints).

9. Abraham A. Kimball, *Gems For the Young Folks, Fourth Book of the Faith-Promoting Series* (Salt Lake City: Juvenile Instructor Office, 1881), 16–17.

10. Lucy Mack Smith, *History of Joseph Smith by His Mother, Lucy Mack Smith* (Salt Lake City: Stevens & Wallis, Inc., 1945), 12–15.

"And all wept, and bewailed her: but he [Jesus] said, Weep not; she is not dead, but sleepeth. And they laughed him to scorn, knowing that she was dead. And he put them all out, and took her by the hand, and called, saying, Maid, arise. And her spirit came again, and she arose straightway: and he commanded to give her meat." (Luke 8:52–55)

Chapter Twenty-One
Coming Back to Mortality

Return Occurs Because of Prayer or a Priesthood Blessing

There are many scriptural accounts of people being called back to earth through the power of the priesthood or because of prayer. Jesus called back the twelve-year-old daughter of Jairus (Mark 5:35–42), the son of the widow of Nain (Luke 7:12–16), and Lazarus (John 11:1–44).

In many near-death experiences, faithful prayers and the administration of the priesthood brought departed loved ones back from the spirit world when the person had not been appointed to death. In many cases, the departed spirit watched as men holding the priesthood blessed their bodies.

Wilford Woodruff, who later became the fourth president of the Church, exercised the power of the priesthood on the behalf of his wife, Phoebe, when she died. Wilford said, "I anointed her body with the oil in the name of the Lord. I laid my hands upon her, and in the name of Jesus Christ I rebuked the power of death and the destroyer. . . . Her spirit returned to her body, and from that hour she was made whole."[1]

Hannah Adeline Savage was told that because of the prayers of her loved ones, she would return to mortality. Hannah said, "I was extreamly [sic] happy while in the spirit world and asked my guide that I might remain but my guide told me my family and friends were praying for my return and I must come back."[2]

Through a priesthood blessing, Peter E. Johnson was restored to his mortal body. He says, "Just how my spirit entered the body I cannot tell, but I saw the apostle place his hands upon the head of my prostrate body, and almost instantly I realized that the change had come and I was again in the body."[3]

Told by Matthew Cowley

Elder Matthew Cowley, who later became an apostle, served a mission to New Zealand in 1914 and tells a humorous story about a native's near-death experience. The man was revived after receiving a priesthood blessing. Elder Cowley relates the story as follows:

"I was called to a home in a little village in New Zealand one day. There the Relief Society sisters were preparing the body of one of our saints. They had placed his body in front of the big house, as they call it, the house where the people came to wail and weep and mourn over the dead, when in rushed the dead man's brother."

The brother said, "'Administer to him.'

"And the young natives said, 'Why, you should do that; he's dead.'"

"'You do it!'" the brother insisted.

So one of the young men anointed the dead man. Then an old gentleman knelt and blessed the man and commanded him to rise.

Elder Cowley said dryly, "You should have seen the Relief Society sisters scatter."

"The man sat up and said, 'Send for the elders; I don't feel very well. . . .'

"Well, we told him he had just been administered to, and he said, 'Oh, that was it.'

"He said, 'I was dead. I could feel life coming back into me just like a blanket unrolling.'"

Elder Cowley concluded his story by saying that this "dead man" outlived the brother that had asked the elders to administer to him.[4]

Brigham Smoot

When Brigham Smoot was called on a mission to Samoa in June 1889, his mother made him promise that he would not go swimming in the sea. However, the day after he arrived, Brigham's senior companion, Edward J. Wood, coaxed him to join the elders for their usual daily bath at sea. Disregarding his promise, Brigham went with the other elders and, after falling into a hole, drowned. After his spirit left his body, Brigham watched the other elders pull him from the water and try to resuscitate him. He wondered why they didn't administer to him. Finally, Elder Wood used the priesthood and gave him a blessing, after which Brigham returned to his body. Edward J. Wood related Brigham's experience during a talk he gave in general conference.

Elder Wood began by talking about the coral reefs around Samoa. "These islands are surrounded by a coral reef, and in the reef there are large holes, ten to eighteen feet deep, and when the tide is out, we wind our way, guarding ourselves from the holes, until we come to the edge of the reef."

Brigham was winding his way along one of these coral reefs with the others when he slipped and fell into a deep hole. Unable to swim, he struggled wildly at first and then began to sink. When Elder Wood noticed Brigham was missing, he called to the other elders, who began searching frantically for the new elder. Elder Wood felt a particular sense of responsibility since he had promised to be responsible for the new missionary's safety.

Elder Wood said, "We swam to the reef and hunted around and saw the young man in about twelve feet of water, in the attitude of prayer. His limp body was dragged from the hole and carried to the beach. Blood was flowing from his eyes, nose and mouth. He was perfectly lifeless and dead."

The elders tried to restore him, but nothing worked. As the natives gathered around to watch, they told the missionaries that a native boy had previously drowned in that same hole.

"You can hardly imagine my feelings, feeling myself almost responsible for the death of that young man," Elder Wood said, "We worked for over forty minutes with that young man's body, carried him onto the beach with his head down, his feet on my shoulders. No sign of life at all."

Elder Wood suggested to the mission president that Brigham be taken into a house, dressed in garments and administered to, feeling this was the only way his companion's spirit could reenter his body. The natives objected, saying that it was sacrilegious to tamper with a body after it was dead. Despite their objections, the missionaries carried Elder Smoot into a house and, laying his body on a table, dressed him in clean garments and a clean shirt and pants. The natives watched as Brigham was anointed.

After sealing the blessing, Elder Wood said, "I felt his eyes move under my hands, and he awoke and came to, and asked us to place him up on the table and he would tell us what he saw, 'before I forget it . . . for I can feel it is going from me."

When he was able to speak, Elder Smoot told the others about his experience. "I called, when I got into deep water. You paid no attention to me, and the last thing that I thought of was my mother's admonishing me to always pray in time of danger.

"When you took my body out of the water I was with you. When you walked up and down the beach I walked up and down with you. I saw my body. I prayed to God with all my soul that you would not bury me nor consider me dead until you exercised the power of your priesthood. I was told by something that it was the priesthood that had the power to return my spirit to my body. I watched you all the time. I wondered why you did not do it, having this glorious ordinance in the Church.

"You elders apparently were going to forget all about it. And oh, how glorious, when you exercised your priesthood and anointed me with oil in the name of the Son of God and through the priesthood which you had! As soon as you said that, my spirit body entered my physical body."[5]

Another account adds additional information to Brigham's experience. "He [Brigham] told of how, in the spirit, he had watched them recover his body from the hole, take it to the beach, and try to restore it to life. He also told of touching Elder Wood on the shoulder and telling him that the only way to bring life back into the body was to use the Priesthood which he bore. The natives were thoroughly impressed by the whole affair and became more friendly to the elders and the Church. Elder Wood recorded that the ordeal was 'terribly frightening,' and acknowledged the 'hand of the Lord in sparing life.'"[6]

Mitchell Dalton

After eleven-year-old Mitchell Dalton died, his heartbroken father's prayer allowed him to return briefly to mortality. The account states:

"A stirring testimony of life after death is told by Mrs. Hannah Daphne Dalton . . . mother of President Don Mack Dalton of the South Africa mission. Mrs. Dalton, who is a regular temple worker in Salt Lake relates the following incident that occurred in Manassa, Colorado, while her husband, John Dalton, was bishop of the Manassa Ward.

"Mitchell was a sweet boy of 11 years, with brown eyes and light brown hair. Bright in school and was a favorite among all who knew him. His general health was good, but this winter (December, 1895), he became sick and got worse and worse. Nothing seemed to do him any good. He was resting easy as we thought and we were all sitting quietly and close to the bed side.

"I got up and looked at him and said, 'Oh! John, Mitchell is dead,' and he was. His father took him in his arms and begged and prayed to God to let his boy live. They were preparing to wash him and his father was still pleading and praying for him to live. His eyes commenced to open and his lips began to move.

"He opened his eyes and said, 'Oh, Papa and Mama, why did you call me back. I have been to such a beautiful place.'

"He told of the people he had met, also of people he had never seen before. Then he would say to his Papa, 'Won't you let me go back. I have been to such a beautiful place,' but we could not.

"The people in the town commenced hearing about him and about the wonderful things he was saying. Our big house was crowded with people who had come far and near to hear him tell of the marvelous things he had seen. His father held him constantly in his arms.

"Occasionally he would say, 'Papa, lay me down a few minutes and let me rest and then I will talk to these good people some more.' All night he talked with great wisdom.

"Just as the sun was coming up, he said, 'Papa, lay me on the lounge and pull up the blind.' He looked up in his father's eyes and said, 'Papa, may I go now?'

"His father said, 'Yes, Mitchell,' and he died instantly.

"His father was so stricken that his hair was perfectly white and he looked like an old man, but we never forgot Mitchell's testimony of the reality of the future life."[7]

Physical Sensations upon Re-entering Physical Body

Although a person feels no pain after his or her spirit leaves its physical body, many of those who came back reported it was painful to return to their body. Some even said it was agony to reenter their physical body. A few reported feeling only an unpleasant tingling sensation, similar to what is felt when blood has been cut off from an arm or leg and then restored again. For others, the pain they felt when returning to their physical bodies apparently came from the physical injuries or illnesses that had caused them to die.

It was very painful for Charles John Lambert to return to his body. "I began to recover sensibility in my body, to which I had returned in the interval that appeared blank. My agony while recovering was fearful. It seemed as if the suffering of an ordinary life-time had been concentrated into a few minutes duration. It appeared as if every sinew of my physical system was being violently torn out. This gradually subsided."[8]

Earl Stowell said it was painful and difficult to re-enter his body. Earl stated, "I felt myself sinking back into my room. It was painful and took quite a bit of effort to work myself back into the cold and stiff body that lay on the bed. More than a few minutes passed before I could drive the cold out of it."[9]

Ella Jensen said she suffered terribly when her spirit re-entered her body. There was practically no pain on leaving the body in death, Ella said, but it was nearly unbearable when coming back to earth.[10]

George Washington Brimhall

George Washington Brimhall—whose son, George H. Brimhall, later became president of Brigham Young University—crossed the plains with his family in 1850. He settled in southern Utah and served in the Territorial Legislature until he was called in 1864 to "strengthen the settlements on the Rio Virgen [sic] river." The sun in southern Utah could be fierce, and on several occasions, George had severe reactions to the heat and drought. Once he suffered from heatstroke and had a near-death experience. When he was allowed to return to his physical body, George suffered a great deal of pain.

Suffering from heat stroke and believing that his time on earth was about to end, George said, "I told my little boy, George H. to take my body back with him when he went to Salt Lake. He promised he would, which was all I wished. I said good-bye to my wife and children. My spirit arose out of my body and was ascending from it very slowly, feeling perfectly happy and without pain. Looking down I saw Thomas Rhoades and another man with their hands upon my head, and I heard Brother Rhoades say, 'In the name of Jesus Christ come back into your body and live again.'"

George stated, "I began to settle down, my spirit entering my body again, but not without much pain. In a few days I was well."[11]

Don't Want to Return—Body Appears Loathsome

In a number of cases, people who were told they needed to go back to mortality didn't want to because they were repulsed by their physical body. Several commented that their physical body was loathsome in appearance and that they were reluctant to return. Such was the case with Jedediah M. Grant, who said, "Of all the dreads that ever came across me, the worst was to have to again return to my body, though I had to do it." Jedediah told his friend, Heber C. Kimball about his feelings. Heber later said; "After mentioning the things that he [Jedediah] had seen, [in the spirit world] he spoke of how much he disliked to return and resume his body." Heber added, "After speaking of the gardens and the beauty of every thing [sic] there, brother Grant said that he felt extremely sorrowful at having to leave so beautiful a place and come back to earth, for he looked upon his body with loathing, but was obliged to enter it again."[12]

While still in the spirit world, Peter E. Johnson was asked if he was satisfied being in the spirit world or if he wanted to return to mortality. "I informed them that I was, and had no desire to return to the fever and misery from which I had been suffering while in the body."[13]

After his spirit left his physical body, Herman Stulz described it as a torture chamber. "So this is what is called death, but I was more full of life than I was heretofore in my mortal life, why should we fear death, I was freed from all suffering, death was a welcome visitor, to get my spirit out of that sick body lying on the bed which was only a torture chamber for me and I had no more use for it and I wanted to get away from it."[14]

Jacob Hamblin

Jacob Hamblin served for many years as a missionary and peacemaker among the Indians in southern Utah before having a near-death experience in 1858. When Jacob was told to return to his physical body, he did so with the greatest reluctance, saying his body looked "loathsome." He relates his experience as follows:

"During the summer of 1858, when I was at my home on the Santa Clara [near St. George, Utah] one morning about 9 o'clock, while engaged in cutting some of the large branches from a cottonwood tree, I fell a distance of twenty or thirty feet to the ground. I was badly bruised, and was carried to my house for dead, or nearly so.

"I came to my senses about 8 o'clock in the evening, and threw off from my stomach quite a quantity of blood. I requested the brethren who were standing around to administer to me, and they did so. From the time I fell from the tree until then consciousness was lost to me, so far as earthly matters were concerned.

"During the time my body lay in this condition, it seemed to me that my body went up from the earth and looked down upon it, and it appeared like a dark ball. The place where I was, seemed very desirable to remain in. It was divided into compartments by walls from which appeared to grow out vines and flowers, displaying an endless variety of colors.

"I thought I saw my father there, but separated from me. I wished him to let me into his compartment, but he replied that it was not time for me to come to him.

"I then asked why I could not come. He answered, 'Your work is not yet done.'

"I attempted to speak to him again, but he motioned me away with his hand and in a moment I was back to this earth. I saw the brethren carrying my body along, and it was loathsome to me in appearance.

"A day or two after my fall from the tree, I was carried to the Mountain Meadows, where I was fed on goat's milk and soon recovered."[15]

Notes:

1. Wilford Woodruff, *Leaves From My Journal, Third Book of the Faith-Promoting Series* (Salt Lake City: Juvenile Instructor Office, 1882), 52–55.

2. *Record of Hannah Adeline Savage* (Provo, Utah: L. Tom Perry Special Collections, Harold B. Lee Library, Brigham Young University), 3–5.

3. Peter E. Johnson, "A Testimony," *The Relief Society Magazine*, vol. 7, (1920), 450–455.

4. Matthew Cowley, *BYU Speeches of the Year* (February 18, 1953), 9.

5. Edward J. Wood, Conference Report, April 1917, 130–131.

6. Melvin S. Tagg, "The Dead Restored to Life," *The Life of Edward James Wood, Church Patriot, Master's Thesis*, Brigham Young University, (copy on file at the Church History Library, Salt Lake City: The Church of Jesus Christ of Latter-day Saints, 1959). Used with permission.

7. Joseph Heinerman, *Spirit World Manifestations* (Salt Lake City: Magazine Printing and Publishing, 1978), 117–18.

8. Charles John Lambert, as told to J. N., "A Curious Experience in Drowning," *Juvenile Instructor* 21 (December 1, 1886), 359.

9. *Biography of William Rufus Rogers Stowell 1893*, (copy on file at the Church History Library, Salt Lake City: The Church of Jesus Christ of Latter-day Saints, 1959).

10. LeRoi C. Snow, "Raised from the Dead," 975.

11. Orson F. Whitney, *History of Utah*, vol. 4 (Salt Lake City: George Q. Cannon & Sons Co., Publishers, 1904), 170.

12. Heber C. Kimball, *Journal of Discourses* (December 4, 1856), 4:135–137.

13. Peter E. Johnson, "A Testimony," *The Relief Society Magazine* 7, (1920), 450–455.

14. Herman Stulz, *Autobiography* [ca.1971], (copy on file at the Church History Library, Salt Lake City: The Church of Jesus Christ of Latter-day Saints, 1959).

15. James A. Little, *Jacob Hamblin, Fifth Book of the Faith-Promoting Series*, 2nd ed. (Salt Lake City: Deseret News, 1909), 61–62.

Chapter Twenty-Two

How People Were Affected By Their Near-Death Experiences

*M*ost people who had near-death experiences were deeply affected by them and had their lives profoundly changed. After her experience, Bertha Elder changed her mind about not bringing any more children into the world and had two more girls—those she had seen in the spirit world.

After Harriet Salvina Beal Millet was shown the spirit world by her mother, Clarissa, she stopped her incessant arguing with her sister. However, Harriet's life was not the only one that changed. When she came back to her body, Harriet delivered a message from her mother to her father. He was instructed to complete temple work and to stop criticizing Church leaders, especially Brigham Young. After relaying the message, Harriet later helped him do the ordinance work. Also, Harriet wrote, "From that time forth I never heard my Father speak ill of anyone in authority and he would not allow anyone to do so in his hearing or in his house."[1]

Being in the spirit world made David Kimball feel guilty about the life he had led. Because he didn't feel he was ready to stay in the spirit world, David asked if he could return to mortality so he could repent, do better, and provide for his family. He was then given two more years on earth to accomplish those things.

A number of people who had near-death experiences said they lost all fear of death. James G. Marsh commented that after his visit to the spirit world he was no longer afraid of death and the same was true for Dr. Wiltse. Victoria McCune said that she no longer feared death because she now knew that there is an afterlife. After seeing how miserable people were in a lower sphere, Charles Woodbury came away with a fervent desire that he and his loved ones live worthily so they could be in the celestial kingdom.

A number of people who had near-death experiences felt a need to tell others about the next life, so they would feel a desire to live more righteously. Thomas S. Thomas said, "I feel it is a duty, which has impressed itself upon me, to give to the world a clear and concise description of what I have seen."[2]

An angel told Lovisa Tuttle what she was expected to do after her return to mortality. Lovisa reported, "He told me that I must return again to warn the people to prepare for death; that I must exhort them to be watchful as well as prayerful; that I must declare faithfully unto them their accountability before God and the certainty of their being called to stand before the judgment seat of Christ." Lovisa did all of those things faithfully for three years before returning to the spirit world to stay in 1789.[3]

When Lorenzo Dow Young was told he had to return to his body, he begged to stay in the spirit world. He was only comforted when his guide told him he could return if he did certain things. Lorenzo reported, "[My guide told me that,] if I would bear a faithful testimony to the inhabitants of the earth of a sacrificed and risen Savior, and His atonement for man, in a little time I should be permitted to return and remain. . . . I felt that a great mission had been given me, and I accepted it in my heart. The responsibility of that mission has rested on me from that time until now." Lorenzo said he did his best after returning to mortality "to fill the important mission I had received. . . . As I had opportunity, I continually exhorted the people, in public and private, to exercise faith in the Lord Jesus Christ, to repent of their sins and live a life of righteousness and good works."[4]

After her return to mortality, Heroine Randall lived faithfully and continually bore her testimony to the truth of the gospel and the reality of life after death. The same was true of a man (whose name is not given) who married sometime after he returned from the spirit world. The account states that he and his wife lived together happily in the knowledge that God loved them and that there was life after death.

Joseph R. Murdock's priorities changed after his near-death experience. When Joseph met with his ancestors in the spirit world, they were very unhappy that he had not done their temple work. Feeling ashamed that he had let his extensive responsibilities in church, business, and civic duties take precedence over genealogical work, Joseph went to work and, to make up for his past neglect, did all he could thereafter to complete temple work for his relatives.

While in the spirit world, Mary Hyde Woolf also learned about the importance of temple work and, after she returned, worked for a time on completing work for her ancestors before she passed away.

After writing about his near-death experience, Charles Lambert said, "The incident narrated above made an indelible impression upon my mind, and doubtless has more or less influenced my life since it occurred. . . . The effect produced upon me has been to cause me to avoid ever disobeying my parents. I have never, from that time to the present, so far as I know, acted contrary to their expressed wishes, and I trust I never shall."[5]

A few people did not change their lives after their near-death experience, showing that a mere visit to the spirit world is not enough to change a person unless he decides to change. This is shown by Alpheus Cutler, who was given a charge to fulfill after he returned to his body. Although Alpheus was shown the crown he would wear if he remained faithful and the condemnation he would receive if he did not, he turned away from the gospel after returning to mortality. Alpheus said that while he was in the spirit world, "I begged to remain but was informed that I must return and warn the people to repent."[6]

Notes:

1. Cora Anna Beal Peterson, Biographical sketch of William Beal.
2. Thomas S. Thomas, *A Glimpse of the Future.*
3. Lucy Mack Smith, *History of Joseph Smith by His Mother, Lucy Mack Smith* (Salt Lake City: Stevens & Wallis, Inc., 1945), 12–15.
4. Lorenzo Dow Young, *Fragments of Experience, Sixth Book of the Faith-Promoting Series* (Salt Lake City: Juvenile Instructor Office, 1882), 27–30.
5. Charles John Lambert, as told to J. N., "A Curious Experience in

Drowning," *Juvenile Instructor* 21, (December 1, 1886), 359.

6.   Abraham A. Kimball, *Gems For the Young Folks, Fourth Book of the Faith-Promoting Series* (Salt Lake City: Juvenile Instructor Office, 1881), 16–17.

"And these things doth the Spirit manifest unto me; therefore I write unto you all. And for this cause I write unto you, that ye may know that ye must all stand before the judgment-seat of Christ, yea, every soul who belongs to the whole human family of Adam; and ye must stand to be judged of your works, whether they be good or evil; And also that ye may believe the gospel of Jesus Christ, . . . And I would that I could persuade all ye ends of the earth to repent and prepare to stand before the judgment-seat of Christ." (Mormon 3:20–22)

Chapter Twenty-Three
Comparing Modern-Day and Early-Church Near-Death Experiences

There are many similarities and a few differences between modern-day near-death experiences and those in early Church history. In his book *The Light Beyond*, Dr. Raymond A. Moody Jr., MD, identifies ten traits that define a near-death experience. One or more of the following attributes need to be present to qualify the incident as a near-death experience.

A sense of being dead—people find themselves floating, then become aware they are dead.

Peace and painlessness—pain ends when leaving the body and is replaced by peace.

Out-of-body experience—when a person finds himself rising and sees his body below.

The tunnel experience—a portal or tunnel opens and the person is propelled into darkness.

People of light—people (sometimes relatives) are surrounded by a bright light.

The Being of light—a supreme Being who radiates total love.

The life review—panoramic review of everything the person has done in life.

Rising rapidly into the heavens—leaving their physical body behind.

Reluctance to return—most want to stay in this new existence.

Different time and space—time seems compressed and is unlike time on earth.[1]

All of these features can be found, in varying degrees, in LDS near-death experiences. The first and third elements—a sense of being dead and an out-of-body experience—occur frequently in LDS accounts and usually occur at the beginning of the near-death experience. Usually the first indication a person has that he is dead is when he finds himself rising and sees his own lifeless body below. The second element—peace and painlessness—also occurs frequently in LDS accounts. A sense of peace and painlessness is also common to both modern-day and early Church history accounts.

The fourth element—seeing a tunnel—is one of the most common features of modern experiences yet is mentioned rarely in LDS episodes. In fact, only one LDS account mentions having a "tunnel-like" incident. However, it is possible that this difference could be due to semantics, because a slight change in wording makes this element more similar to LDS accounts. For example, in *The Light Beyond*, some people describe the "tunnel" element as going through a "portal," through which "they are propelled into darkness," or a "'floating experience,' in which they rise rapidly into the heavens."[2] Another person described it as "being pulled very rapidly through a dark space of some kind." These types of descriptions are much more in keeping with LDS experiences, which frequently mention "going through darkness"[3] before arriving in the brightly lit spirit world. Also, arriving at a world of light might easily be construed as seeing a light at the end of a dark tunnel, which would make it more similar to LDS experiences.

The fifth and sixth elements—seeing people of light and a being of light—are frequently seen in LDS accounts. In fact, having a personage escort a person to heaven is one of the most commonly mentioned elements of the LDS near-death experience. Often, the guide appears in glory and is surrounded by brilliant light. A number of LDS accounts mention seeing God or Jesus Christ, who are surrounded by a bright light.

Although light is one of the most common elements of the LDS experience, it is usually only mentioned in connection with guides, Heavenly Father, Jesus, or the spirit world itself, rather than something at the end of a tunnel.

Element seven—the life review—was mentioned only rarely in LDS experiences. The reason behind this is not clear. One possible explanation is that the majority of people who had modern-day experiences were interviewed and might have felt pressed to recall every element. In *Gaze Into Heaven*, no one was interviewed—they only wrote down those elements that were of significance to them.

The last three elements in Dr. Moody's list—rising rapidly to the heavens, a reluctance to return, and noting that time and space are different—were also mentioned frequently in LDS accounts. To sum up, there are many more similarities than differences between near-death experiences that occurred long ago and those that have taken place recently. The spirit world is stable and constant.

Notes:

1. Raymond A. Moody, Jr., MD, with Paul Perry, *The Light Beyond* (New York: Bantam Books, 1988) 7–20.
2. Ibid., 11, 15.
3. Raymond A. Moody, Jr., MD, *Life After Life* (New York: Bantam Books, 1975), 30.

> "So when this corruptible shall have put on incorruption, and this mortal shall have put on immortality, then shall be brought to pass the saying that is written, Death is swallowed up in victory. O death, where is thy sting? O grave, where is thy victory? . . . Thanks be to God, which giveth us the victory through our Lord Jesus Christ."
> (1 Corinthians 15:54–57)

Chapter Twenty-Four

What Can Be Learned by Gazing Into Heaven

The remarkably undeviating accounts in *Gaze Into Heaven* correspond to the doctrine of The Church of Jesus Christ of Latter-day Saints and teach us living truths regarding the gospel. They are consistent with what Joseph Smith, Brigham Young, and other prophets have taught. When Jedediah Grant, who served as second counselor to Brigham Young, returned from his visit to the spirit world, he declared, "Why it is just as Brother Brigham says it is; it is just as he has told us many a time."[1] Following is a list of what these near-death experiences tell us about death and the spirit world.

At death, the spirit rises and looks down on its lifeless physical body. People who have left their body often report seeing loved ones crying or people trying to restore life. Looking down and seeing their lifeless body helps the deceased people realize they have died.

There is no pain after death. Whatever discomfort or pain a person may have been experiencing due to injury, illness, or disease ceases when the spirit leaves the physical body.

We do not go through the process of dying alone. Newly departed spirits are met by a spiritual guide to ease the transition from mortality to the spirit world. Often, this guide is a loved one or a guardian angel.

Life continues, feeling natural and real. Death does not terminate our existence. The spirit lives on, for it is eternal. The spirit world will seem normal, familiar, and real.

Our identity and personality will carry through with us into the next life. Every part of our personality will remain intact. In the next life, we will be the same person we are now.

There are great feelings of peace, love, and happiness in the spirit world. One of the most commonly reported elements in near-death experiences is the great love and happiness people feel upon entering the spirit world.

There will be a reunion with family and loved ones. Family relationships continue beyond the grave. At some point after death, we will meet and be reunited with departed family members and friends.

Some people see Heavenly Father, Jesus Christ, or other religious leaders. Visitors to the spirit world saw Joseph Smith and other prophets, as well as modern and ancient apostles.

Occasionally, there is a full review of a person's life. This review does not seem to be an unpleasant experience. Some people indicated that the love Christ proffers during this experience offsets the pain of seeing how and when he or she could have done better.

Light is an integral feature of the spirit world. Personages coming to earth are almost always surrounded by light. The more exalted the person, the more light surrounds them. God the Father and Jesus Christ have an incredible amount of light emanating from them, which appears to be the source of illumination in the spirit world.

There are no disabilities of any kind in the spirit world. Our spiritual body, which looks like our physical body, will be in perfect condition. If we have lost a limb, been scarred, or been blind on earth, we will find our limbs restored, our skin smooth, and our sight perfect in the spirit world. In addition, those who have been mentally handicapped on earth will have minds that function perfectly. There appear to be a few special exceptions to this physical perfection, such as the Savior and Hyrum Smith. However, these imperfections appear to exist for a reason. The Savior showed the scars He suffered during the Crucifixion to His disciples and also to people in the new world as a witness that He was indeed Jesus Christ. It could be that these scars will remain—at least temporarily—as identifying marks or a testimony against those who inflicted them.

We will have increased mental capacities, be able to move with the speed of light, and have increased powers of vision. Not only will our minds be sharper and able to process information more quickly, but we will also be able to move effortlessly and see great distances.

Spirits do not have to talk to communicate. While we will be able to talk, we will also be able to perceive each other's thoughts without verbal communication.

Memory will be restored. The veil of forgetfulness that was placed on us at birth will be removed. We will be able to remember that we used to live in a spiritual sphere before coming to earth and that we are returning to our heavenly home. Some people remember promises they made in the premortal world to do specific things on earth.

The spirit world is beautiful beyond description. The spirit world is filled with lovely gardens, shrubs, trees, foliage, and flowers, as well as magnificent buildings and temples.

There are animals in the spirit world. Birds, fish, and all kinds of animals were created spiritually and then physically and will be present in the spirit world.

The spirit world is close by. Some people indicate that the spirit world is on this earth, although it remains invisible to our mortal eyes, but it might also extend to other areas.

Time is different in the spirit world. Time and its importance are earthly concepts and will exist in a different form in the next life.

Music is an important part of life in the spirit world. Music of all kinds will be provided for our pleasure and inspiration.

All is well with children who die on earth. After the resurrection, a child's body will grow to match the stature of the spirit. Children that die before the age of accountability are cared for lovingly until they are reunited with their parents. After the resurrection, a child's body will grow to match the stature of the spirit.

People are busy with meaningful work. People are actively engaged in a variety of labors and activities in the next life.

We will be engaged in many activities we are familiar with on earth. Various accounts reveal that activities such as reading, gardening, and constructing homes and buildings are common in the spirit world. A few people reported that eating and sleeping (most likely by resurrected beings) are part of normal activities in the spirit world.

Education is an important, ongoing process. An important function of the next life will be to learn and gain knowledge. Children and adults will be provided with educational opportunities.

The gospel will be taught in the spirit world. Missionaries will teach those who want to learn more about Jesus Christ and His Church. Missionaries will be called and sent to spirit prison to teach those who did not have a chance to hear the gospel while on earth.

Mortals are sometimes called to the spirit world in order to teach the gospel. Missionaries are sometimes called to the spirit world to preach, just as they are called here on earth to teach others the gospel. In addition, missionaries in the spirit world will be called to preach the gospel to people in paradise and in spirit prison.

The spirit world is divided into two main spheres: paradise and spirit prison. God determines which sphere people will be sent to, and His determination depends upon the type of life the person lived while on earth.

After the final judgment, most people will be sent to one of three kingdoms of glory. After being judged by God, people will go to the celestial, terrestrial, or telestial kingdom. A few will be sent to another sphere—hell or outer darkness—which has no glory and is where sons of perdition are sent.

Race doesn't matter. People are not judged according to the color of their skin but by their good works and their obedience to God's commandments.

The type of life we lead on earth determines our condition in the next life. Everything we do here directly influences where we will live in the next life. Mortality is a time for us to gain knowledge, overcome faults, learn to love and serve others, and fulfill the mission that was given us in the premortal world.

It is more difficult for spirits to overcome weaknesses than for mortals. It is important to grow and develop Christlike traits as much as possible while on earth because it is much harder for spirits to overcome weaknesses without a physical body. Also, spirits have a difficult time overcoming physical addictions acquired during mortality.

The priesthood will be the governing authority. Heavenly Father is a God of order, and the priesthood will provide an efficient, smoothly run governing body in the spirit world.

We will be able to make requests to priesthood authorities. Just like on earth, people can go to priesthood authorities with requests and to receive counsel.

Ordinance work is an important part of the spirit world. Because of the importance of family relationships, spirits will be actively engaged in genealogy to provide a welding link between generations. Physical ordinance work will be done in temples on earth.

Our ancestors are anxious to have ordinance work performed on their behalf. Because spirits who accept the gospel in spirit prison cannot progress until their ordinance work is done on earth, they are eager for this important work to be done.

Some people in the spirit world have already been resurrected. Although a few important Church leaders have already been resurrected so they can more easily perform their duties, most people will be resurrected at a later time.

Spirits will have their agency. Although the gospel will be taught to all people, no one will be forced to accept it. Agency always has been and always will be an integral part of life throughout eternity.

Repentance will be possible in the next life. We can repent, be forgiven, and progress in the spirit world.

Joseph Smith will be recognized and honored as the Prophet who helped restore the gospel of Jesus Christ in the latter days. Just as God has called prophets, such as Noah, Abraham, and Moses, to declare His word since the beginning of time, He speaks in our day to modern-day prophets. As the first prophet of this dispensation, Joseph Smith was instrumental in restoring the gospel to the pattern Jesus Christ established.

Spirits ask newcomers about conditions on earth. Although there are a few exceptions, most spirits are not able to freely view the earth and their loved ones. They are eager to find out from new arrivals how their loved ones are doing and how the Church is progressing.

Occasionally, visitors to the spirit world see someone they didn't know had died. Also, visitors sometimes discover that a person (or several persons) on earth will soon be called to the spirit world.

Those in the spirit world often give messages to people who visit. Spirits may give visitors words of counsel or messages of warning, or advise them to live more in accordance with God's will. The most common message is to attend to genealogical work and to do temple work. Sometimes, visitors are asked to relay messages to other people on earth.

A spirit's ability to work can be hampered if loved ones on earth mourn for them too much. Spirits want their loved ones on earth to know they are happy. They are grieved when family and friends sorrow too much over their temporary separation.

People who have near-death experiences are sometimes given the choice of remaining in the spirit world or returning to mortality. Others are told they must return to earth.

Everyone on earth has a specific mission to perform. Heavenly Father sent each one of us to earth with a specific mission. Visitors to the spirit world are sometimes told that because their mission has not yet been completed, they must return to mortality.

Through the power of the priesthood, a person can be called back to mortality. Prayer, as well as priesthood blessings, can be determining factors as to whether a person returns to earth.

When spirits are told they must return to mortality, their body is healed enough to sustain life. When a person who has a fatal disease or injury is told to return, their body will be healed enough that life can be sustained. In some cases, people are healed completely.

Returning to one's physical body can be painful. While some people describe the physical sensation of returning to their body as a tingling—similar to when an arm or leg awakens after being asleep—many others describe the process as being very painful.

Most people who have near-death experiences want to stay in the spirit world. People do not want to leave because they feel such joy and happiness. Some are reluctant to return to mortality because their physical body appears loathsome to them.

People who have seen the spirit world often exhibit an increased spirituality. Many feel a keen resolve to live better and want to have their loved ones live more righteously so they can enjoy the blessings they saw in the spirit world. Some have a great desire to educate others about the importance of showing love, being more diligent in obeying God's commandments, and doing everything they can to prepare for the next life.

Notes:

1.   Heber C. Kimball, *Journal of Discourses* (December 4, 1856), 4:136.

"They never did look upon death with any degree of terror, for their hope and views of Christ and the resurrection; therefore, death was swallowed up to them by the victory of Christ over it." (Alma 27:28)

Chapter Twenty-Five

Near-death Experiences Are of Great Worth

Near-death experiences have a purpose and can be of great worth. They provide credible evidence that life continues beyond death and show that how we live our lives here and now will determine what blessings we receive in the next life.

These experiences can teach many things, but first and foremost, they confirm that Heavenly Father and Jesus Christ are actual divine beings who love us and who are vitally interested in each and every one of us. These accounts testify in a convincing manner that Heavenly Father is loving, kind, and just, and that His Son, Jesus Christ, came to earth and died for us so that we can live again with him once more.

Each person whose experience is recorded in this book bears a profound and personal witness that life continues beyond the grave and that mortality is only one phase of our eternal journey. Life did not begin with our birth any more than it ends with death. Dr. Elisabeth Kubler-Ross said, "Dying is a human process in the same way that being born is a normal and all-human process. The dying experience is almost identical to the experience at birth. . . . Dying is only moving from one house into a more beautiful one."[1]

While life is precious and we should live it to the fullest, we don't have to be afraid of death because we will continue to exist even after our physical body is laid in the grave. When the physical body dies, the spirit will return to heaven, from whence it came, to await the time when it will be reunited with a perfect body during the resurrection. "Therefore the grave hath no victory and the sting of death is swallowed up in Christ" (Mosiah 16:8). Those who have faith and believe in Christ know that life continues. Death is not something to be dreaded; rather it can be thought of as a graduation from a world of hardships. "It shall come to pass that those that die in me shall not taste of death, for it shall be sweet unto them" (Doctrine and Covenants 42:46).

In speaking about death, President Spencer W. Kimball said, "To the unbeliever it [death] is the end of all, associations terminated, relationships ended, memories soon to fade into nothingness. But to those who have knowledge and faith in the promise of the gospel of Jesus Christ, death's meaning is also the same as formerly: a change of condition into a wider, serener sphere of action; it means the beginning of eternal life, a never-ending existence. It means the continuation of family life, the reuniting of family groups, the perpetuation of friendships, relationships, and associations."[2]

It stands as a testimony of the truth of the gospel that so many near-death experiences testify of the four-fold purposes of the Church, which is to teach the restored gospel to every nation, kindred, tongue, and people; to build up faith and encourage people to walk in obedience to the commandments of the Lord; to redeem the dead; and to care for the poor and needy. Despite this, these experiences are not meant to "prove" that the Church is true. Rather, they are meant to open our eyes to the fact that life will continue, that our sojourn on earth is momentary, and that we ought to refocus our priorities and spend our time productively, with an eye toward the next life.

By expanding our understanding of what lies ahead, we can choose—if we will—to reassess our lives so we can use our time in mortality wisely and make good choices that will benefit us both in this life and in the life to come. Near-death experiences remind us that mortality is the time to learn to master ourselves and show us the importance of using our time on earth to improve ourselves and prepare for the next life. We must never forget the vital importance of repentance. Although we all make mistakes, we can, through Jesus Christ and His atoning sacrifice, be forgiven. Everyone has sins to repent of, faults to change into strengths, and frailties to overcome. Alma said:

For behold, this life is the time for men to prepare to meet God; yea, behold the day of this life is the day for men to perform their labors. And now, as I said unto you before, as ye have had so many witnesses, therefore, I beseech of you that ye do not procrastinate the day of your repentance until the end; for after this day of life, which is given us to prepare for eternity, behold, if we do not improve our time while in this life, then cometh the night of darkness wherein there can be no labor performed. Ye cannot say, when ye are brought to that awful crisis, that I will repent, that I will return to my God. Nay, ye cannot say this; for that same spirit which doth possess your bodies at the time that ye go out of this life, that same spirit will have power to possess your body in that eternal world. For behold, if ye have procrastinated the day of your repentance even until death, behold, ye have become subjected to the spirit of the devil, and he doth seal you his . . . and the devil hath all power over you; and this is the final state of the wicked. (Alma 34:32–35)

Knowing the reasons for this life and what lies ahead in the next can help us endure to the end. A calm assurance that great rewards can be ours can help us patiently bear the trials and burdens we face on earth. "Have patience, and bear with those afflictions, with a firm hope that ye shall one day rest from all your afflictions" (Alma 34:39–41). As we try to bear our burdens with humility and meekness, we show our willingness to submit to Heavenly Father's will, thereby proving ourselves worthy of eternal glory in the life to come.

Gaze Into Heaven is not meant as light entertainment—it is intended to inspire and motivate us to action. If we are wise, we will take the insights and knowledge gained from these near-death experiences to enrich our spiritual lives. When we understand that love, kindness, and good works follow us into the next life, we will want to work harder to become better. We will have a greater desire to learn, study, and increase our knowledge. We can work on improving our relationships with others and repairing those that may be damaged or broken.

These experiences clearly teach us that the most important thing about living is learning to love others and treating them kindly. Life is not a competition and should not be about acquiring power, position, or possessions, for none of that can be taken to the next life. What counts in this life is our own good works, learning to master ourselves by overcoming our faults, and gaining knowledge. Those are the things we will take with us beyond the veil.

There is something innately persuasive about these near-death experiences. As we ponder them, we may feel whisperings of the Spirit of God, giving us a desire to prove ourselves worthy and to increase in light and knowledge. If we will turn our lives over to Heavenly Father, we will grow and progress until the time comes for us to pass through the veil, where we will be able to partake of the glories awaiting us there.

While these near-death experiences can provide us with inspiration, they will not save us. We must work to improve ourselves and put more effort into developing divine qualities of kindness, mercy, love, and charity. We must seek to complete our missions on earth and endure to the end. It is everyone's calling in life to "bring to pass much righteousness" (Doctrine and Covenants 58:27).

Let us all follow the admonition of Nephi: "Wherefore, ye must press forward with a steadfastness in Christ, having a perfect brightness of hope, and a love of God and of all men. Wherefore, if ye press forward, feasting upon the word of Christ and endure to the end, behold, thus saith the Father: Ye shall have eternal life" (2 Nephi 31:20).

Notes:

1. Elisabeth Kubler-Ross, *On Life After Death* (Berkeley, CA: Celestial Arts, 1991), 10.
2. Edward L. Kimball, ed., *The Teachings of Spencer W. Kimball* (Salt Lake City: Bookcraft, 1982), 39.

Common Elements
in LDS Near-Death Experiences with
a List of Corresponding Accounts

What Happens First During a Near-Death Experience

See Lifeless Mortal Body

Mr. Bertrand—"I was astounded to recognize my own envelope [body]." (25)

Albert M. Boyce—"He found himself standing next to his own body." (12)

George W. Brimhall—"My spirit arose out of my body . . . looking down I saw." (200)

Bertha Deusnup Elder—Bertha said she found herself rising above her bed. (148)

Joseph Eldridge—"I looked down on my body and could see myself lying there." (11, 109)

Tom Gibson—"My spirit was standing looking at my body." (88)

Loisie Goates—"I could see my body . . . in bed." (48)

Archie J. Graham—"I arose . . . leaving my body behind." (115)

Jacob Hamblin—"I saw the brethren carrying my body along." (202)

Ella Jensen—"I could see my body lying on the bed and the folks gathered about." (170)

Peter E. Johnson—"I . . . saw my body lying on the bed." (11, 62)

Charles John Lambert—"I looked into the water and beheld my body." (32, 55)

Harriet Ovard Lee—"I saw . . . people in the room . . . crying . . . over my lifeless body." (12, 40)

Victoria McCune—"I knew that body belonged to me." (69)

Marriner Wood Merrill—"His spirit left his body and stood, as it were, in the air." (188)

Walter P. Monson—"I stood apart from my body and looked at it." (177)

No name, told by Frederick Babbel—The man's spirit rose above his body. (50)

John Peterson—"I seemed to stand upon the floor, my body lying on the bed." (132)

Heroine Randall—"Her spirit departed from her body, and rose above it." (127)

Brigham Smoot—"When you took my body out of the water . . . I saw my body." (198)

Earl Stowell—"I found myself just below the ceiling looking down at a body." (16)

Herman Stulz [1st experience]—"I saw myself . . . watching little Herman spinning." (13)

Thomas S. Thomas—"The doctor . . . gave me up for dead. . . My wife hugged . . . me." (98)

Phoebe Woodruff—"Her spirit left her body, and she saw it lying upon the bed." (190)

Henry Zollinger—"My Spirit left the body and I could see it lying under." (184)

Pain Is Gone

George W. Brimhall—"My spirit arose . . . feeling perfectly happy and without pain." (15, 200)

Bertha Deusnup Elder—Bertha said she soon realized that all of the pain was gone. (15)

Ella Jensen—"There was practically no pain on leaving the body in death." (170)

Harriet Ovard Lee—"All pain . . . left me." (40)

Walter P. Monson—"I was now without pain." (177)

Earl Stowell—"I felt well, very well. Until then I had not realized how much pain . . ." (16)

Herman Stulz [2nd experience]—"I was released from all pains." (74)

Dr. Wiltse—"How well I feel. . . . Only a few minutes ago I was horribly sick." (56)

Met by a Spiritual Guide

David Lynn Brooks—"I saw in the opening . . . my lovely wife." (50)

Bertha Deusnup Elder—"She [Bertha] was greeted by a woman who escorted her." (148)

Joseph Eldridge—"[An] angel took me and carried me." (109)

Tom Gibson—"Looking closer at the person standing near me, I saw . . ." (88)

Loisie M. Goates—"when two personages came." (48)

Archie J. Graham—"A messenger, a man in white, stood before me." (115)

Ella Jensen—"I could see some of my relatives from the other world." (168)

Peter E. Johnson—"Turning around I beheld a personage." (62)

Charles John Lambert—"There were spiritual persons with me." (32)

Harriet Ovard Lee—"My guide called me by name, commanding me to follow." (40)

Flora Mayer—"A man came from that light and acted as a guide for her." (20)

Harriet Salvina Beal Millet—"I was overjoyed to see my Mother there by me." (57)

May Neville—May said of her brother, "His grandparents . . . met him when he died." (136)

John Peterson—"I asked my guide who he was." (132)

Heroine Randall—"Then a personage of beauty received her into his charge." (127)

Hannah Savage—"There was a guide close by my side." (25)

Jennie Schnakenberg—Saw an angel, who soon "passed away from my sight. (80)

Earl Stowell—"Two beings placed themselves on each side of me." (16)

Herman Stulz [2nd experience]—"The strange personage watched me." (75)

Eliza Ursenbach—"My father, who had previously died, had come for her." (20)

J. R. Williams—"A messenger came and took me by the hand." (81)

Lorena Wilson—"My father, who had been dead seven years, came into my room." (163)

Phoebe Woodruff—"Two personages came into the room." (190)

Mary Hyde Woolf—"After the spirit withdrew . . . she saw a Guide by her side." (20)

Lorenzo Dow Young—"At once, a heavenly messenger, or guide was by me." (20)

Henry Zollinger—"My Guardian angel . . . mother and my sister Annie were beside me." (184)

Arrival In The Spirit World

Life Continues, Feeling Natural and Real

Mr. Bertrand—"I never was as alive as I am." (25)

Tom Gibson—"It was as real as . . . as anything I have seen or felt on earth." (90)

David P. Kimball—"It was so real." (105)

Peter E. Johnson—"I felt perfectly natural . . . the same in the spirit as I had been in the body." (62)

Charles John Lambert—"What I have described . . . was as real as anything could be." (33)

Walter P. Monson—". . . are as real to me today as any other experience." (179)

William Wallace Raymond—"[The inhabitants] are . . . natural . . . move quite natural . . ." (84)

Hannah Adeline Savage—"He . . . showed me the spirits who were beings real as we are." (25)

Herman Stulz [2nd experience]—"Everything functioned like it did in mortality." (74)

Thomas S. Thomas—"The soul's movements through space was natural." (99)

Lorena Wilson—"It seemed real and natural." (163)

Dr. Wiltse—"I have died . . . and yet I am as much a man as ever." (55)

Lorenzo Dow Young—"Beings . . . as naturally human as those among whom I had lived." (28)

Same Person as Before Death

Peter E. Johnson—"I turned my head . . . realized that it was I myself . . . I was the same." (27)

Thomas S. Thomas—"All your faculties are intact, memories of your past are . . . plain." (73, 99)

Dr. Wiltse—"Here am I still a man, alive and thinking . . . as clearly as ever." (56)

Lorenzo Dow Young—"I thought and acted as naturally as I had done in the body." (27)

Feel Joy, Peace, Love, and Happiness

George W. Brimhall—"My spirit arose out of my body . . . feeling perfectly happy." (15)

Martha Jane Boice—"Praising God for . . . the joy of being able to return." (127)

Joseph Eldridge—"I felt supremely happy." (109)

Tom Gibson—"I felt completely at peace." (90)

Archie J. Graham—"Everything seemed to be love and smiles." (118)

Ella Jensen—"Perfect peace and happiness prevailed there, no suffering, no sorrow." (169)

Harriet Ovard Lee—"The people who lived on it looked . . . happy." (41)

Flora Mayer—"She was happier than she had ever been." (30)

Victoria McCune—"A feeling of peace was upon me . . . a greater happiness was mine." (70)

Walter P. Monson—"The peace of mind that came over me were the sweetest." (177)

Hannah Adeline Savage—"I was extreamly [sic] happy." (113, 195)

Herman Stulz [2nd experience]—"It was a feeling of ecstasy." (75)

Thomas S. Thomas—"You read from their cheerful countenances a . . . contentment." (100)

Charles R. Woodbury—"Everyone was so happy." (108)

Mary Hyde Woolf—"She felt she could never depart . . . so great was her happiness." (21)

Lorenzo Dow Young—"The people . . . seemed contented and happy." (28)

Review of Life

> Tom Gibson—"I became conscious of my past life being reviewed for me." (89)
>
> Charles John Lambert—"Every action . . . was clearly before my comprehension." (31, 32)
>
> George Albert Smith—"Everything I had ever done passed before me." (31, 83)

Meet with Loved Ones

> David Lynn Brooks—"I saw . . . my lovely wife." (50)
>
> Bertha Deusnup Elder—"Greeted by many of her departed friends." (36, 148)
>
> Loisie Goates—"I saw my own little ones." (49)
>
> Archie Graham—"This radiant young instructor was my dead brother." (116)
>
> Jedediah M. Grant—"He saw his wife . . . and had their little child." (153)
>
> Mary Hales—"It was my brother, Howard . . . When we reached my sister." (93)
>
> Jacob Hamblin—"I saw my father there." (202)
>
> Richard H. Hamblin Jr.—"He . . . told the children he had . . . talked to their mother." (182)
>
> Ella Jensen—"The first person I recognized was my grandpa . . . " (168)
>
> Peter E. Johnson—"My mother and other sisters and friends came to see me." (63)
>
> David P. Kimball—"When my mother came to me." (105)
>
> Iva Langford—"I was shown my grandfather, brother, and sister, and . . . relatives." (36)
>
> Flora Mayer—"She saw many people she knew who were dead, both friends and family." (30)
>
> W. W. Merrill—The woman Elder Merrill blessed went to heaven and saw her mother. (37)
>
> Harriet Salvina Beal Millet—"I was overjoyed to see my Mother." Also sees brothers. (57)
>
> Walter P. Monson—"I saw my little daughter, Elna." (177)
>
> Joseph R. Murdock—"Quite a number of people were there to meet me, relatives." (155)

May Neville—"His grandparents had met him when he died." (136)

No name, told by Frederick Babbel—". . . entering . . . spirit world where he met loved ones." (50)

William Wallace Raymond—"I also saw my parents, children and many . . . neighbors." (84)

George Albert Smith—"I recognized him as my grandfather." (83)

Earl Stowell—Earl met an old man who he later discovers is his grandfather. (18–20)

Thomas S. Thomas—"The grand greeting you first receive is from your closest of kin." (35)

Eliza Ursenbach—Her husband came to meet her. (20)

Lorena Wilson—"We . . . saw a large congregation of people [her ancestors]." (163)

Lorenzo Dow Young—"There I met my mother, and a sister." (29)

Henry Zollinger—"My mother then introduced me to . . . my father's people." (185)

See Jesus, Joseph Smith, or Other Prophets and Leaders

Tom Gibson—"When we got close to the Savior." (89)

Archie J. Graham—Archie saw Joseph and Hyrum Smith, Lorenzo Snow, and others. (119)

Jedediah Grant—Jedediah's wife told him that Joseph and Hyrum had gone ahead. (153)

Mary Hales—"We saw . . . homes. He pointed out . . . the one Joseph Smith lived in." (94)

Peter E. Johnson—"The guide [said] I was wanted by some of the apostles." (63)

Harriet Ovard Lee—"That is our Prophet Joseph Smith and his brother Hyrum." (42)

James Marsh—"The Lord showed him." (180)

Harriet Salvina Beal Millet—"Surprised to see the Prophet Joseph Smith." (38)

Jennie Schnakenberg—". . . my eyes upon my blessed savior." (80)

John Peterson—"It was the Apostle Matthias . . . the young man . . . Parley P. Pratt." (132)

William Wallace Raymond—"Brother Joseph Smith presides over the Latter-day Saints." (84)

Lovisa Tuttle—"I saw the Savior, as through a veil." (192)

Lorenzo Dow Young—"Jesus and the ancient apostles were there. I saw . . . Paul." (28)

Light in the Spirit World

Tom Gibson—"It was a city of light." (48)

Loisie Goates—"I was told to follow a light." (48)

Harriet Ovard Lee—"There seemed to be a silvery light in this place." (44)

Heroine Randall—Heroine saw a city that "shone in splendor." (88)

Earl Stowell—"Everything was well but not brilliantly lighted, but I saw no shadows." (17)

Herman Stulz [2nd experience]—"I entered a well lighted room." (76)

Charles R. Woodbury—"I saw a real bright light, brighter than noonday." (146)

Mary Hyde Woolf—"They rose upward from sphere to sphere, which grew lighter." (72)

Lorenzo Dow Young—"It was clothed in the purest light, brilliant but not glaring." (28)

Light around Spiritual Personages

David Lynn Brooks—"Light filling the room . . . I saw my lovely wife." (50)

Tom Gibson—"He was bathed in light." (50)

Archie Graham—"His presence seemed to illuminate the room." (115)

Flora Ann Mayer—"She saw a very bright light. A man came from that light." (20)

No name, told by Frederick Babbel—". . . said the voice in the . . . dazzling white light." (51)

Heroine Randall—In a city, Heroine saw "a throng of bright ones." (88)

Lorena Wilson—"Immediately following the light, my father . . . came into my room." (163)

Charles R. Woodbury—"In the light I saw people." (48, 146)

Attributes of the Spirit Body

Vision Is Increased

> Mr. Bertrand—"I see better than ever, and I am dead." (25)
>
> Jedediah Grant—"There appeared to be no obstruction to my vision." (153)
>
> Peter E. Johnson—"I could see clearly and distinctly the people on the street." (64)
>
> Charles John Lambert—"I saw clear through the log." (31)
>
> Thomas S. Thomas—"My visionary powers were more than they are on earth." (101)
>
> Dr. Wiltse—"I never saw that street more distinctly than I saw it then." (56)
>
> Lorenzo Dow Young—"I could see everything with the most minute distinctness." (28, 55)

Able to Move Quickly and Effortlessly

> Tom Gibson—"All I had to do was think of where I wanted to be, and I could go there." (88)
>
> Archie J. Graham—"I could move about with the least exertion, as though in thought." (57, 119)
>
> Charles John Lambert—"I could move about without the slightest effort." (32)
>
> Harriet Ovard Lee—"I felt as light as a feather and as free as a bird on the wing." (40)
>
> Harriet Salvina Beal Millet—"I followed her . . . and floated through the air." (58)
>
> Walter P. Monson—"The law of gravitation had no hold upon me." (57, 177)
>
> John Peterson—"We started off . . . seemingly with the rapidity of lightning." (132)
>
> William Wallace Raymond—"They . . . move quite natural from place to place." (84)
>
> Earl Stowell—"Our speed of travel increased." (16)
>
> Thomas S. Thomas—"My mode of travel was as fast as thought." (98)
>
> Dr. Wiltse—"He traveled at a swift but pleasant rate of speed upward." (56)

Mary Hyde Woolf—"They rose upward from sphere to sphere." (72)

Lorenzo Dow Young—"Almost instantly [we] were in another world." (28)

Resurrected Personages

Peter E. Johnson—"I was told that the Prophet Joseph Smith has his body." (63)

John Peterson—When John was introduced to two apostles, they did not shake hands. (132)

Mental Characteristics of the Spirit Body

Mental Faculties Are Quickened

Thomas S. Thomas—"My mental faculties were much brighter." (101)

Victoria Clayton McCune—"In life I never possessed the keen intelligence . . . I had then." (70)

Able to Read Thoughts

Tom Gibson—"It was as if we could communicate with each other without speaking." (89)

Peter E. Johnson—"While I did not ask the question, they read it in my mind. . ." (63)

Victoria Clayton—"[My intelligence] could read their thoughts." (70)

Mary Hyde Woolf—"The guide read her thoughts." (72)

Memory Is Restored

Herman Stulz [2nd experience]—"Memory of my pre-mortal life came back to me. . ." (76)

Thomas S. Thomas—"The fond memories of the past returned in all their splendor." (99)

General Appearance of the Spirit World

Martha Jane Boice—"The beauties which she had seen in the Spirit world." (70, 127)

Mitchell Dalton—"I have been to such a beautiful place." (70, 199)

Loisie M. Goates—"I followed and was taken to a place heavenly to me." (49)

Mary Hales "Started walking . . . through a place . . . like earth but . . . more beautiful." (79, 93)

Ella Jensen—"I did hate to leave that beautiful place." (169)

Iva Langford—"I was shown . . . the beautiful place they were in." (37)

Harriet Ovard Lee—"I . . . gazed . . . on the grandeur and loveliness of my surroundings." (40)

Flora Ann Mayer—"It was so beautiful and peaceful there she didn't want to leave." (30)

May Neville—"It was always springtime over there." (136)

Heroine Randall—"They came without the walls of a beautiful city." (88, 127)

Jennie Schnakenberg—"I beheld beauty everywhere." (80)

Eliza Ursenbach—". . . testify of the beauty of the Spirit World." (21)

J. R. Williams—"We approached a beautiful place." (81)

Lorenzo Dow Young—". . . more beautiful and glorious than anything I had . . . seen." (28, 79)

Trees, Flowers, Rivers, and Lakes

Joseph Eldridge—"filled with water clear as Crystal." (109)

Tom Gibson—"I noticed a profusion of flowers and trees . . . more colors than on earth." (89)

Archie Graham—"Nestled among trees, vines and flowers, and had a . . . terraced lawn." (120)

Jedediah Grant—"I saw flowers of numerous kinds." (154)

Mary Hales—". . . with many beautiful flowers of many colors and many green plants." (93)

Jacob Hamblin—"Vines and flowers, displaying an endless variety of colors." (202)

Harriet Ovard Lee—"We came to another river, which shone as clear as crystal." (41)

William Wallace Raymond—"[There are] lovely parks." (84)

George Albert Smith—"A large and beautiful lake, facing a great forest of trees." (82)

Jennie Schnakenberg—"Green, green hills, birds, [and] flowers." (80)

Earl Stowell—"I could see those buildings and a well kept lawn and garden." (16)

Thomas S. Thomas—"Rivers were most beautiful. . . . The ground was a carpet of green." (101)

J. R. Williams—"By the chapel was a grove." (81)

Mary Hyde Woolf—"Spacious grounds . . . [and] a broad road bordered with trees." (72)

Animals, Fish, and Birds

Archie J. Graham—"There were many . . . lakes, ponds, fish, birds and pet animals." (119)

William Wallace Raymond—". . . abounded with all kinds of animals." (84)

Jennie Schnakenberg—"Green, green hills, birds, [and] flowers." (80)

Thomas S. Thomas—"Birds perched and sang their sweet songs." (101)

Cities in the Spirit World

Tom Gibson—"Daniel next led me to a city." (48)

Archie Graham—"We now came into the center of this massive city." (118)

Charles John Lambert—"In a twinkling, as it were, I was in the city." (32)

Heroine Randall—"They came without the walls of a beautiful city." (88)

William Wallace Raymond—"Outside of the cities." (84)

Thomas S. Thomas—"Cities are most beautiful with all colors and shadings." (88)

Lorenzo Dow Young—"The city was grand and beautiful beyond anything I can describe." (28)

Buildings

Tom Gibson—"The buildings and paths appeared to be built of . . ." (89)

Loisie M. Goates—"I entered the building with two guides." (103)

Archie J. Graham—". . . painted and stone houses . . . large chapels for worship." (117)

Jedediah Grant—"Temple erected by Solomon was . . . inferior to . . . buildings." (153)

Mary Hales—"We saw many beautiful homes." (94)

Richard H. Hamblin Jr.—"He had a far more beautiful home than any mansion." (182)

David P. Kimball—"The richness, grandeur and beauty of it [house] defied description." (105)

Harriet Ovard Lee—"I . . . beheld a massive building of indescribably magnificence." (42)

Harriet Salvina Beal Millet—"We came to a beautiful building, very large." (58)

May Neville—"They had a beautiful home." (92, 136)

William Wallace Raymond—"They live in beautiful cities with fine streets, paved." (84)

Earl Stowell—"The building on my left was a mansion . . . on the right . . . a cottage." (17)

Thomas S. Thomas—"There I saw beautiful homes." (101)

Mary Hyde Woolf—"They passed glorious mansions and spacious grounds." (72)

Other Aspects of the Spirit World

Time Is different

Tom Gibson—"Time doesn't seem to work the same as here." (91)

Walter P. Monson—"I lost all sense of time and space." (177)

Herman Stulz [2nd experience]—"The time element did not matter." (75)

Thomas S. Thomas—"Time is endless." (100)

Music

Joseph Eldridge—"Then I heard very beautiful singing." (109)

Loisie M. Goates—". . . the music being lovely." (49)

Archie J. Graham—"Wonderful pipe organ, the music of which sounded like . . . angels." (119)

Ella Jensen—"I heard the most beautiful singing." (168)

David P. Kimball—"I heard the most beautiful singing I ever listened to in all my life." (104)

Harriet Ovard Lee—"I heard the most beautiful singing." (44)

Thomas S. Thomas—"You will find there is a busy place for the musician." (101)

Clothing

> Joseph Eldridge—"He clothed me with beautiful white garments and robes." (109)
>
> Tom Gibson—"They were dressed in clothes that looked . . . similar to what we wear." (90)
>
> Loisie M. Goates—"There was William Goates . . . in his earthly clothing." (49)
>
> Archie Graham—"A man in white, stood before me." (115)
>
> Mary Hales—". . . amphitheater filled with rows and rows of soldiers in uniform." (93)
>
> Ella Jensen—"The people were all dressed in white or cream, excepting Uncle Hans." (169)
>
> Harriet Ovard Lee—"They were all dressed in white." (44)
>
> Joseph Murdock—"Some of them dressed in Scottish costumes." (155)
>
> William Wallace Raymond—"They dress quite natural . . . material looks like white silk." (84)
>
> Earl Stowell—"He was wearing old fashioned clothing." (17)
>
> Lorena Wilson—"The texture of the materials . . . was entirely different." (163)
>
> Dr. Wiltse—"I examined the fabric . . . some kind of Scotch material." (56)
>
> Charles Woodbury—"Men and women dressed in light clothing." (108)
>
> Lorenzo Dow Young—"The personage with me was dressed in the purest white." (27)

People in the Spirit World Are Active and Busy

> Bertha Deusnup Elder—"He quickly returned to his work." (148)
>
> Tom Gibson—"There are many people involved in a lot of work expanding the gospel." (90)
>
> Loisie M. Goates—"They were so busy and happy." (49)
>
> Archie J. Graham—"Most of the people were happy and busy at something." (117)
>
> Peter E. Johnson—"I observed that the people there were busy." (66)
>
> Harriet Ovard Lee—"There seemed to be millions of men who were at work." (44)

Harriet Salvina Beal Millet—"Many men sat writing as fast as they could." (59)

Heroine Randall—"A company of life, activity, and intelligence." (88)

Hannah Adeline Savage—"I saw they were very busy." (113)

Thomas S. Thomas—"These souls are now busy, in the future existence." (145)

Charles Woodbury—"I saw people . . . everyone was so happy, but all busy." (146)

Mary Hyde Woolf—"All were busy, but the people in different places would bow." (72)

Lorenzo Dow Young—"The people, men and women . . . seemed contented and happy." (28)

"Earthly" Activities in the Spirit World

Archie J. Graham—"Caretakers were . . . engaged in pruning and . . . cultivating the flowers." (116)

Mary Hales—"The children were sitting on logs while women instructed them." (93)

Ella Jensen—"They seemed to be convened in a sort of Primary or Sunday School." (169)

David P. Kimball—"Building . . . was unfinished . . . workmen were busy upon it." (105)

Harriet Ovard Lee—"Some were reading books." (114)

Harriet Salvina Beal Millet—"Led me into a . . . bed-room." Mother goes to kitchen. (58)

May Neville—"They . . . were preparing a beautiful home for his mother and her family." (92, 136)

Earl Stowell—"You will have ample time to study, learn, and socialize." (17)

William Wallace Raymond—"They eat and drink, and hold meetings like we do." (84)

The Restoration of the Gospel

Martha Jane Boice—"The Gospel is true. Joseph Smith is a prophet of the living God." (127)

Heroine Randall—When taught the gospel, Heroine recognized it from the spirit world. (127–128)

The Gospel Is Taught in the Spirit World

David Lynn Brooks—"She had been called by the priesthood to teach the gospel." (131)

Tom Gibson—"Seated in the auditorium were many men listening to instruction." (90)

Archie J. Graham—"He is very busy teaching . . . and preaching the Gospel." (116)

Mary Hales—"They were listening to a speech by a man." (93)

Peter E. Johnson—"I was informed that I would preach the Gospel to the spirits there." (63)

Harriet Ovard Lee—". . . and some preaching to crowds." (44)

John Peterson—"Two Apostles are coming to preach to these people." (132)

Henry Zollinger—Henry's brother-in-law was "Presiding over a large mission." (185)

Some Mortals Are Called to the Spirit World to Teach

May Neville—"His grandfather needed Merrill to help him with his missionary work." (136)

Agency and Repentance

Alpheus Cutler—Alpheus choose between receiving a crown or condemnation. (141)

Archie Graham—"Now they choose the thing they like most." (117)

Henry Zollinger—"I noticed that people had their free agency there like we do here." (140)

There Are Different Spheres in the Spirit World

Archie J. Graham—Archie saw various grades of cities—each had different levels. (147)

Jedediah Grant—"People . . . were organized in . . . perfect harmony." (152)

Harriet Ovard Lee—"That great black gulf . . . separate the righteous from the wicked." (41)

Harriet Salvina Beal Millet—"She said that was hell and was a long way off." (59)

John Peterson—"These are mostly your progenitors, and are now in the lowest sphere." (132)

Jennie Schnakenberg—Jennie saw two areas that were separated by a gulf. (80)

Thomas S. Thomas—"Many are from different spheres." (100)

Charles R. Woodbury—Charles saw two distinct kingdoms. (144)

Mary Hyde Woolf—She moved from sphere to sphere and saw her ancestors in prison. (72)

Lorenzo Dow Young—Saw people who were miserable, then went to a beautiful city. (27–28)

Children Are Saved in the Celestial Kingdom

Bertha Deusnup Elder—"There were many children." (148)

Mary Hales—"She was with other children in a little clearing in a pine forest." (93)

Archie J. Graham—"The atoning blood of Jesus Christ has paid for all children." (117)

Ella Jensen—"There were hundreds of small children." (169)

Harriet Ovard Lee—"Women were tending the children, some having babies in arms." (44)

William Wallace Raymond—"One sister . . . had charge of a number of children." (84)

The Spirit World Is Organized and Is Governed by the Priesthood

Ella Jensen—"They were all arranged in perfect order." (169)

Tom Gibson—"Everything seemed to be under control." (90)

Archie J. Graham—"Paved with different colors of cement to harmonize with." (118)

Jedediah M. Grant—"But O . . . the order and government that were there!" (153)

Peter E. Johnson—"They were perfectly organized for work they were doing." (66)

William Wallace Raymond—"They all live in perfect order, such as I have never seen." (84)

Herman Stulz [second experience]—"There exists a perfect organization with rules and laws." (75)

Requests Made to Priesthood Authorities

Martha Jane Boice—"I have . . . obtained permission to return." (127)

David Lynn Brooks—"Only tonight was I given permission by the priesthood." (154)

Joseph R. Murdock—"I sought for and obtained permission to return to life." (155)

Herman Stulz [2nd experience]—"He . . . obtained permission . . . to enter Paradise." (76)

J. R. Williams—"The prayers of your family . . . have come up to us . . . " (81)

Lorenzo Dow Young—"I begged of him the privilege of speaking . . . could not grant it." (27)

The Importance of Ordinance Work

Brother Cox—"She wants me to have my [ordinance] work done." (159)

Archie Graham—"Still held in prison . . . and they remain until . . . baptized." (118)

Harriet Salvina Beal Millet—"Preparing genealogy so that the work can be done on earth." (59)

John Peterson—"He spoke upon . . . temple building and the ordinances to be performed." (132)

Mary Hyde Woolf—She met people who were overjoyed that she had done their work. (72–73)

Henry Zollinger—"Asked me if I could do the work in the Temple . . . for his salvation." (178)

Ancestors Are Anxious to Have Ordinance Work Done

Peter E. Johnson—"It was their desire that I . . . do their work in the temple." (65)

Joseph Murdock—"Why have you not done the work for us? . . . We depended upon you." (155)

Lorena Wilson—Her ancestors ". . . were waiting with anxious hope for . . . baptism." (163)

Those in Spirit World Ask what People on Earth Are Doing

Tom Gibson—"People there are interested in the progress in ours [world]. (165)

Ella Jensen—"Some inquired about their friends and relatives on the earth." (169)

David Kimball—David's father, Heber C. Kimball, ". . . inquired about his children." (104)

Harriet Salvina Beal Millet—"Yes, I know and if you and Emily do not stop." (58)

William Wallace Raymond—"The people are acquainted with our doings on earth." (84)

Thomas S. Thomas—"They ask about the conditions of their kin." (100)

See Someone They Didn't Know Was Dead

David P. Kimball—"I saw Brother Pugmire and many others . . . I did not know were dead." (105)

Ella Jensen—"Yes, Ella, little Alphie is dead, too." (170)

W. W. Merrill—Elder Merrill sees a young woman he didn't know had died. (37)

No name, told by David O. McKay—"She knew he was gone." (176)

John Peterson—"The . . . man . . . was an apostle . . . who had lately been killed." (132)

Discovers that a Mortal Is Going to Die Soon

Martha Jane Boice—"You may keep two of them [her children] the other will go with me." (176)

James Marsh—"He was permitted to see . . . the departure of a young sister." (180)

Walter P. Monson—"Go back . . . I want Richard first. Then grandma . . . and then mama." (177)

Message Is Given

Martha Jane Boice—"I made a mistake in growing weary of the Gospel. The Gospel is true." (127)

Alpheus Cutler—"I was informed that I must . . . warn the people to repent." (141)

Bertha Deusnup Elder—"That is the purpose of this visit, to let you see them." (148)

Loisie Goates—"After this I could not greave [grieve] for my loved one was so happy." (49)

Richard H. Hamblin Jr.—"He brought messages back from some . . . to their families." (182)

Peter E. Johnson—"It was their desire that I should . . . hunt up my father's genealogies." (65)

David P. Kimball—"I received many reproofs for my wrong-doings." (105)

Charles John Lambert—"They told me that my death was caused by disobedience." (32)

Harriet Ovard Lee—"Go and finish your work . . . go my child, and be faithful." (43)

Harriet Salvina Beal Millet—"Mother was . . . telling me things . . . to tell Father." (58)

Joseph R. Murdock—"Activities . . . on earth seemed to be of little consequence." (155)

May Neville—"Attend to their prayers, and pay their tithing. . . . Give to the poor." (136)

No name, told by Frederick Babbel—"You shall yet accomplish many great things." (51)

Heroine Randall—"You shall have the opportunity to hear the gospel of Christ preached." (128)

Hannah Adeline Savage—Hannah was told she had to have struggles in life. (112–113)

Herman Stulz [2nd experience]—"Go back and finish the work that you promised." (182)

Thomas S. Thomas—"The essentials of earthly life are to know right from wrong." (101)

Lovisa Tuttle—"He told me that I must . . . warn the people to prepare for death." (181)

Lorena Wilson—Her father wanted Lorena "to take up the work and see that it was done." (182)

Phoebe Woodruff—She was told to "stand by her husband." (190)

Lorenzo Dow Young—He was told to "bear a faithful testimony . . . of . . . [the] Savior." (206)

Henry Zollinger—"She then warned me to . . . keep the faith . . . to warn my brothers." (185)

Tell Loved Ones to Stop Grieving

> Richard H. Hamblin Jr.—"Told him to tell his mother to quit grieving over him." (182)
>
> Ella Jensen—"She said it was not right for us to grieve and mourn so much for him." (184)
>
> May Neville—"Merrill wished the family not to mourn for him." (136)
>
> Henry Zollinger—"To tell his parents and his people not to mourn about him." (185)

Given Choice to Stay or Return to Mortality

> Archie Graham—"If that be the case, I prefer to remain upon the earth." (121)
>
> Peter E. Johnson—"If I chose, I might be granted the privilege of returning." (161)
>
> David P. Kimball—"He told me I could remain there if I chose to do so, but . . ." (105)
>
> Charles John Lambert—"I was then informed that I might return to it [body]." (32)
>
> Flora Mayer—"Nevertheless, she was free to decide . . . whether she would return." (30)
>
> Marriner Wood Merrill—"At his option he could re-enter his body or remain in spirit" (188)
>
> Joseph R. Murdock—"I sought for and obtained permission to return to life." (155, 161)
>
> Heroine Randall—Her guide said, "If you return to the earth, to your mortal body." (128)
>
> Earl Stowell—"One of relatively few who have been permitted to make a choice." (17)
>
> Thomas S. Thomas—"I had learned by this time that I was privileged to return if I desired." (101)
>
> Phoebe Woodruff—Phoebe was told she could return if she would stand by her husband. (189–191)

Told They Must Return

> Alpheus Cutler—"I begged to remain but was informed that I must return." (192)

Bertha Deusnup Elder—"Now we must return." (148)

Tom Gibson—"He said that I was to return." (91)

Loisie M. Goates—"I . . . had to return." (49)

Mary Hales—Her brother told her, "Don't you think it's time you went back?" (94)

Jacob Hamblin—"Your work is not yet done." (191)

Richard H. Hamblin Jr.—"He had some important work to do . . . and must come back." (191)

Ella Jensen—"I obeyed the call, [to return]." though it was very much against my desire." (169)

Iva Langford—"My life would be spared for a time." (37)

Harriet Ovard Lee—"You have a mighty work to do both for the living and for the dead." (43)

Walter P. Monson—"Go back, papa." (177)

No name, told by Frederick Babbel—"Your mission in life is not yet finished." (51)

Hannah Adeline Savage—"My guide told me . . . I must come back." (113)

Jennie Schnakenberg—"It is my will that you live." (80)

Herman Stulz [2nd experience]—"I was ordered to return to my lifeless body." (76)

Lovisa Tuttle—"He told me that I must return again." (181)

Eliza Ursenbach—"Heaven has granted that you return to your body." (20)

J. R. Williams—"We've decided to let you go back for a season." (81)

Lorenzo Dow Young—"I plead [sic] with my guide to let me remain." (29, 191)

Henry Zollinger—"I understood all the time . . . that I would return." (186)

Coming Back to Mortality

Return Occurs Because of Prayer or a Priesthood Blessing

George Brimhall—"I saw Thomas. . . and another man with their hands upon my head." (200)

Mitchell Dalton—"His father was still pleading and praying for him to live." (199)

Loisie Goates—"When my spirit return[ed] they were praying . . . all night." (49)

Ella Jensen—Lorenzo Snow commanded, "Sister Ella, you must come back." (169)

Peter E. Johnson—"I saw the apostle place his hands upon the head of my . . . body." (196)

Iva Langford—"The faith and prayers that had been exercised . . . had been so great." (37)

No name, told by Matthew Cowley—"An old man knelt and blessed the man." (196)

Hannah Adeline Savage—"My guide told me my family and friends were praying." (195)

Brigham Smoot—"How glorious, when you exercised your priesthood and anointed me." (198)

Eliza Ursenbach—"The Priesthood is so powerfully exercised . . . for your return." (20)

J. R. Williams—"Your prayers and the prayers of your family." (81)

Phoebe Woodruff—Her husband, Wilford Woodruff said, "I then . . . prayed." (189)

Physical Sensations upon Re-entering Physical Body

George W. Brimhall—"My spirit entering my body again, but not without much pain." (200)

Archie J. Graham—"I was cold and stiff and could not move." (122)

Ella Jensen—"[Pain] was nearly unbearable when coming back to earth." (170)

Peter E. Johnson—"I felt a warm life-giving spot on the crown of my head." (65)

Charles John Lambert—"My agony while recovering was fearful." (200)

Flora Mayer—"Returning to this life was very painful and difficult." (31)

Earl Stowell—"It was painful and took quite a bit of effort." (200)

Herman Stulz [2nd experience]—"I was ordered to return . . . which was very painful." (76)

Don't Want to Return—Body Appears Loathsome

Mr. Bertrand—"What a horrid thing is that body." (25)

Mitchell Dalton—"Why did you call me back?" (79)

Loisie Goates—"I wanted to stay but could not and had to return." (49)

Archie J. Graham—"I touched it [body] and shuddered. . . how can I[?]" (121)

Jedediah M. Grant—"He felt . . . sorrowful . . . looked upon his body with loathing." (154)

Jacob Hamblin—"It [body] was loathsome to me in appearance." (202)

Richard H. Hamblin Jr.—"He begged to be allowed to stay." (182, 191)

Ella Jensen—"I obeyed the call, [to return], though it was very much against my desire." (169)

Peter E. Johnson—"I . . . had no desire to return to the fever and misery." (63, 201)

Charles John Lambert—"It looked loathsome to me." (33)

Iva Langford—"I wanted to stay with them." (37)

Flora Ann Mayer—"She didn't want to leave." (30)

Herman Stulz [2nd experience]—"To my disappointment I was ordered to return." (76)

Lorenzo Dow Young—"I plead [sic] with my guide to let me remain." (29, 191)

Appendix Two

Alphabetical List of Names

B

Babbel, Frederick *50, 226, 231–32, 244, 246*
Ballard, Melvin J. *27, 34, 134, 138, 144, 148*
Benson, Ezra Taft *8, 9, 161, 164*
Bertrand, Mr. *25–26, 225, 228, 233, 247*
Boice, Martha Jane Herns *79, 85, 126, 128, 154, 156, 176, 180, 229, 234, 239, 242–43*
Boyce, Albert M. *12, 21, 225*
Brimhall, George W. *15, 85, 128, 156, 180, 200, 225–26, 229, 246–47*
Brooks, David Lynn *50, 131, 154, 227, 230, 232, 240, 242*

C

Cannon, George Q. *21, 73, 78, 111, 122, 203*
Clawson, Rudger J. *37–8, 111–12, 122, 130, 138, 152, 156, 158, 164, 167–68, 170–72*
Cowley, Matthew *xiv, 196, 202, 247*
Cutler, Alpheus *141, 191, 207, 240, 243, 245*

D

Dalton, Mitchell *79, 198, 234, 246, 247*

E

Elder, Bertha Deusnup *36, 147, 225–27, 230, 238, 241, 244, 246*
Eldridge, Joseph *11, 21, 108, 110, 225, 227, 229, 235, 237–38*

About the Author

*M*arlene Bateman Sullivan was born in Salt Lake City, Utah and grew up in Sandy, Utah. She graduated from the University of Utah with a Bachelor's degree in English. She is married to Kelly R. Sullivan and they are the parents of seven children. Her hobbies are gardening, camping, and reading. Marlene has been published extensively in magazines and newspapers and has written a number of non-fiction books, including *Latter-day Saint Heroes and Heroines,* vol.1; *Latter-day Saint Heroes and Heroines,* vol. 2; *And There Were Angels Among Them*; *Visits From Beyond the Veil*; *By the Ministering of Angels*; and *Brigham's Boys*. Marlene also wrote the best-selling novel *Light on Fire Island*.